Costa Del Sol Lifeline

by
Joanna Styles

SURVIVAL BOOKS • LONDON • ENGLAND

First published 2004

Survival Books Limited, 1st Floor,
60 St James's Street, London SW1A 1ZN, United Kingdom
☎ +44 (0)20-7493 4244, 🖥 +44 (0)20-7491 0605
✉ info@survivalbooks.net
🖳 www.survivalbooks.net
To order books, please refer to page 334.

British Library Cataloguing in Publication Data.
A CIP record for this book is available
from the British Library.
ISBN 1 901130 33 9

Printed and bound in Finland by WS Bookwell Ltd

ACKNOWLEDGEMENTS

I would like to thank those who contributed to the publication of this book, in particular family, friends and fellow members of the Costa Press Club for their encouragement and suggestions, numerous staff at tourist offices and local councils for help with queries, Kerry and Joe Laredo (editing, proof-reading and desktop publishing), Peter Read and Patronato de Turismo de la Costa del Sol for the photographs, and everyone else who provided information or contributed in any way. Also a special thank-you to Jim Watson for the illustrations, maps and cover design.

OTHER TITLES BY SURVIVAL BOOKS

The Alien's Guide To Britain;
The Alien's Guide To France;
The Best Places To Live
In France; The Best Places To
Live In Spain; Buying, Selling &
Letting Property;
Foreigners In France: Triumphs
& Disasters; Foreigners In Spain:
Triumphs & Disasters;
How To Avoid Holiday &
Travel Disasters;
Dordogne/Lot Lifeline;
Poitou-Charentes Lifeline;
Renovating & Maintaining Your
French Home; Retiring Abroad;
Rioja And Its Wines;
The Wines Of Spain

Living And Working Series

Abroad; America; Australia;
Britain; Canada; The Far East;
France; Germany; The Gulf
States & Saudi Arabia; Holland,
Belgium & Luxembourg;
Ireland; Italy; London; New
Zealand; Spain; Switzerland

Buying A Home Series

Abroad; Britain; Florida;
France; Greece & Cyprus;
Ireland; Italy;
Portugal; Spain

Order forms are on page 334.

WHAT READERS HAVE SAID ABOUT

Excellent book detailing everything you need to know before you go, as well as when you are there. If like me you are planning on a home in the sun, then this is the book for you before you go.

A revelation! This book tells it like it is – thank you Mr Hampshire, you obviously HAVE lived here, and your advice really hits the spot.

Mr Hampshire's book was invaluable. His research and data was excellent and very timely.

A must for all future ex-pats. Deals with every aspect of moving to Spain. I invested in several books but this is the only one you need. Every issue and concern is covered, every daft question you have on Spain but are frightened to ask is answered honestly without pulling any punches. Highly recommended.

I have been travelling to Spain for more than seven years and thought I knew everything – David has done his homework well. Excellent book and very informative! Buy it!

I am so glad that I chose this book from the others on offer. The author makes it simple to find information and it therefore becomes easier to remember, especially if your getting close to retirement!

We have been living in Marbella for nearly six months now but whenever we have a problem we turn to Living & Working Spain for the solution.

OTHER SURVIVAL BOOKS ON SPAIN

This book tells you the facts straight and simple. What I particularly liked was the way the author gave the advantages and disadvantages in most situations. All aspects are described in complete detail so that you won't miss anything. There is more information in this book than you could possibly hope for.

Everything from legal contracts to local climate. I would highly recommend this book as it gives very sound advice and a lot of facts.

This was a great help for me as I was preparing to move to Spain, and it was an enjoyable read.

The book is up to date and discusses all aspects of day to day life in Spain. I appreciate the book most because it is written in a way that will inform you no matter where you currently live. If you want to read just one book about living in Spain, this one is excellent.

Thank you David Hampshire for putting together such a marvellous book for everyone who wants to live in Sunny Spain! Have a question or concern – about housing, buying, leases, schools, money, even how to sort out your taxes – David gives you the answer.

A must for anyone wanting to travel in the Rioja region of Spain. I am planning a trip soon and this book will be my constant companion.

A very comprehensive guide to buying a place in Spain – presented in a very readable and humorous style – it has become my bible.

THE AUTHOR

Joanna Styles was born in London but has lived and worked for many years on the Costa del Sol, Spain. She is a freelance writer and the author of several books, including *The Best Places to Buy a Home in Spain*, *Buying a Home in Greece and Cyprus*, *Living & Working in the EU* and *Costa del Sol Lifeline*, all published by Survival Books. She also regularly contributes to and updates many other Survival Books publications. Joanna is married with two daughters.

CONTENTS

Appendices   315

Index   327

Order Forms   334

IMPORTANT NOTE

Every effort has been made to ensure that the information contained in this book is accurate and up-to-date. However, the transient nature of businesses and organisations on the Costa del Sol – where people and businesses come and go with surprising speed – means that information can quickly change or become outdated.

It's advisable to check with an official and reliable source before making major decisions or undertaking an irreversible course of action. If you're planning to travel long-distance to visit somewhere, always phone beforehand to check the opening times, availability of goods, prices, etc., and other relevant information.

Unless specifically stated, a reference to any company, organisation or product doesn't constitute an endorsement or recommendation.

Author's Notes

- In this book the Costa del Sol is also frequently referred to as 'the coast' or 'here'.

- Times are shown using am for before noon and pm for after noon. All times are local, therefore you should check the time difference when making international calls. The Costa del Sol is one hour ahead of GMT.

- Costs and prices are shown in euros (€) where appropriate. They should be taken as guides only, although they were accurate at the time of publication.

- Unless otherwise stated, all telephone numbers have been given as if dialling from Spain. To dial from abroad, use your local international access code (e.g. 00 from the UK) followed by 34 for Spain.

- His/he/him/man/men also means her/she/her/woman/women and is done to make life easier for the reader and isn't intended to be sexist.

- The A-7 main road along the Costa del Sol is also know as the Ctra de Cádiz (Carretera de Cádiz/Cadiz road), particularly in addresses. References are made in this book to the A-7 when referring to the road itself and the Ctra de Cádiz for address purposes.

- Frequent references are made to 'urbanisations' a 'Costa-speak' term translated from the Spanish 'urbanización' meaning a purpose-built development of dwellings.

- In some addresses s/n' (*sin número*) is used. This usually means that the location in question is the most important building on the street or at one end of it.

- All spelling is (or should be) British English not American English

- The Spanish translation of many key words is shown in brackets in *italics*.

- Warnings and important points are shown in **bold** type.

- The following symbols are used in this book: ☎ (telephone), 🗏 (fax), 🖥 (internet) and ✉ (email).

- Maps of the Costa del Sol are included: maps of the different areas can be found in **Chapter 4**, a map of airports in **Chapter 2** and a map showing the main roads in the area in **Chapter 3**.

- Lists of **Publications**, **Property Exhibitions** and **Useful Websites** are included in **Appendices A, B** and **C** respectively.

Estepona

INTRODUCTION

If you're thinking of living, working, buying a home or spending an extended holiday on the Costa del Sol, then this is **the book** for you. *Costa del Sol Lifeline* has been written to answer all those important questions about life on the Costa del Sol that aren't answered in other books. Whether you're planning to spend a few months or a lifetime on the coast, to work, retire or buy a holiday home, this book is essential reading.

An abundance of tourist guides and information is available about the Costa del Sol, but until now it has been difficult to find comprehensive information about local costs, facilities and services, particularly in one book. *Costa del Sol Lifeline* fills this gap and contains accurate, up-to-date practical information about the most important aspects of daily life on the Costa del Sol. Its contents include a comprehensive guide to the different areas; accommodation and property prices; employment prospects; health care; education; local transport and communications; getting there; leisure and sport options; plus much more.

Information is derived from a variety of sources, both official and unofficial, not least the experiences of the author, her friends, family and colleagues. *Costa del Sol Lifeline* is a comprehensive handbook and is designed to make your stay on the Costa del Sol – however long or short – easier and less stressful. **It will also help you save valuable time, trouble and money, and will repay your investment many times over!** (For comprehensive information about living and working in Spain in general and buying a home in Spain, this book's sister publications, *Living and Working in Spain* and *Buying a Home in Spain*, written by David Hampshire, are highly recommended reading.)

The Costa del Sol is one of the world's most popular holiday destinations and a wonderful place to live – few regions can compete with its mild, sunny winters and long, hot summers; the panoramic Mediterranean views with the Rif mountains (Morocco) shimmering in the background; the delicious local cuisine and wine; not to mention the captivating Spanish lifestyle, with its emphasis on living life to the full **and** enjoying every minute of it! I trust this book will help make your life easier and more enjoyable, and smooth the way to a happy and rewarding life on the Costa del Sol.

¡Bienvenidos a la Costa del Sol!   **Joanna Styles**
                                                                      April 2004

Golf apartments, Manilva

1

Introducing The Costa Del Sol

The Costa del Sol is one of the world's top tourist destinations (some 9 million tourists visited the area in 2003), was voted the world's best retirement location by International Living in 2001 and is currently one of Europe's fastest growing residential areas.

FAST FACTS

> **Capital:** Malaga
> **Largest Cities:** Fuengirola and Marbella
> **Population of the Costa del Sol:** Around 1.1 million (up to 2 million during the summer). Around 400,000 people live on the western side, more than 500,000 in the capital and around 100,000 on the eastern side.
> **Foreign Population:** Around 100,000, although unofficial figures are considerably higher. Most foreigners are British.
> **Crime Rate:** Low
> **GDP Growth in 2003:** 3.9 per cent
> **Inflation in 2003:** 2.8 per cent
> **Average Price of Property:** €1,800 per m^2
> **Unemployment Rate:** 9.8 per cent

The population currently stands at 1.1 million and experts predict that if the current growth rate continues, some 1 million new residents will make the Costa del Sol their home over the next six years. It's also estimated that by 2025 over 3 million foreigners will live there. Foreigners who relocate to the coast are mainly British, although the area is popular with Germans and Scandinavians too.

The Costa del Sol lies on the coast of southern Spain and stretches from Sotogrande in the west, to Nerja in the east, for some 160km (100mi). It's part of the region of Andalusia, Spain's most varied region and most of the Costa del Sol lies in the province of Malaga from Estepona to Nerja, where tourism is highly developed and the area's main industry.

Foreigners are attracted to the Costa del Sol for many different reasons, including the following:

- The area's pleasant climate for most of the year (see page 283);

- Very good communications by road and air (see **Chapter 2** and **Chapter 3**) and excellent telecommunications. It's now increasingly popular to 'telecommute' by internet and video conference;

- It's easy to get to and from Europe, particularly the UK, and many other parts of the world. Most European capitals are within three hours flying time of Malaga (see **Chapter 2**);

- Attractive surroundings. The Costa del Sol has very diverse natural and urban landscapes, and is within easy reach of stunning unspoilt scenery;

- Excellent leisure facilities – there's something for everyone (see **Chapter 10**);

- Excellent sports facilities (see **Chapter 11**);

- Good shopping (see **Chapter 12**);

- Friendly environment and cosmopolitan society. *Malagueños* are famed for their warm welcome to newcomers;

- Good expatriate network.

The Costa del Sol isn't, however, perfect and disadvantages include:

- Overcrowding during the summer when many resort areas are packed to bursting point;

- Rising property prices (see **Chapter 5**);

- Over-development in some areas of the coast – a high price to pay for the area's popularity;

- Poor infrastructure in some areas where demand hasn't kept up with investment in roads, hospitals and schools;

- The excess of foreigners can make it difficult to integrate with Spaniards and learn Spanish, although there are many areas that have preserved their Spanish identity in the face of tourism.

In spite of the disadvantages, most residents would agree that the Costa del Sol is a very pleasant place to live and judging by the rising population figures, it seems that many newcomers think so too!

FINDING OUT MORE

Essential Reading

- *Buying a Home in Spain 2003/4*, David Hampshire (Survival Books);

- *Living & Working in Spain*, David Hampshire (Survival Books).

Tourist guides to the Costa del Sol:

- *AA Essential Costa del Sol*, M.King (AA Publishing);

- *Costa del Sol*, S. Bryant (New Holland Publishers);

- *Costa del Sol Insight Pocket Guide* (Insight Guides).

Tourist guides including sections on the Costa del Sol:

- *Andalucía: the Rough Guide* (Rough Guides);

- *Excursions in Southern Spain*, David Baird (Santana);

- *Inside Andalucía*, David Baird (Santana);

- *Lazy Days Out in Andalucía*, Jeremy Wayne (Cadogan);

- *Lonely Planet Andalucía* (Lonely Planet).

For a list of English-language publications available on the Costa del Sol see **Appendix B**.

Websites

The following sites provide tourist and general information in English. For websites about living and working in Spain see **Appendix C**.

- *www.andalucia.com* (general information about the whole region of Andalusia including the Costa del Sol);

- *www.costadelsol.com* (a general guide to the area);

- *www.costaguide.com* (general information);

- *www.visitacostadelsol.com* (the official tourist website for the area);

- *www.webmalaga.com* (comprehensive information about Malaga province).

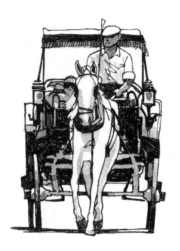

Antequera

2

Getting There

One of the Costa del Sol's main advantages is that it's easy and relatively quick to get to from most European countries, particularly the UK. Most visitors fly to Malaga airport, but many travel by car via ferry to northern Spain or through France. This chapter looks at the different options for getting to the Costa del Sol and includes information on Malaga airport, flights and car hire, train information and road routes.

AIR

Malaga Airport

Malaga's Pablo Picasso airport is the main entry point for visitors and residents on the Costa del Sol. The airport (8km/5mi to the west of Malaga city) is Spain's fourth busiest and handles an annual average of more than 10 million passengers, the vast majority from the European Union (EU) with London Gatwick and Heathrow, Manchester and Luton airports at the head. This figure is expected to rise to 20 million by 2007, when a new terminal will be finished. Experts predict that with the increased volume of passengers and air traffic the airport will also need a second runway, although as yet the government hasn't made any provisions for this in future budgets.

The main airport terminal for arrivals and departures was built in the early '90s and is large and spacious.

Information

The airport authorities publish *Aeropuerto de Málaga*, a useful guide to Malaga airport including timetables in Spanish and English which is available from the airport or tourist offices on the Costa del Sol. For more airport information contact ☎ 952-048 484/844 or visit 💻 *www.aena.es* (when you visit this website, go to *aeropuerto* and scroll down to Malaga).

Check-In

The check-in area is situated on the first floor with 65 check-in desks and plenty of seating areas. Numerous flight companies including Iberia and British Airways have their offices here where last-minute ticket purchases are possible. Facilities include a post box, a small coffee bar and suitcase wrapping. In the old terminal building (to the left of the main building) is a larger restaurant, a Burger King, a chemist, gift shop and a games arcade.

Departures

Once you go through security you reach the departure area which has a large main restaurant upstairs and several small snack-bars downstairs. Upstairs are also numerous shops including a newsagents, cosmetics and perfumes, leather goods, duty-free, sportswear and fashion, gifts and music. There are numerous seating areas and several play areas for children with small slides and other play items. The airport also has VIP lounges for some airlines.

Departure area B (for some flights to non-EU countries) has a small duty-free shop and small snack bar. Once you're passed through passport control into area B, you cannot return to the main shopping and restaurant area.

Arrivals

Arrivals are on the ground floor and are currently rather cramped, especially when there are several flights due in at the same time. There's a small information office, tourist information (often closed), banking facilities, a café and a small newsagents. If you have a long time to wait for a flight to arrive, your best bet is to go upstairs to the more spacious departure facilities.

Banking Facilities

Unicaja Bank: Open Mondays to Saturdays 9am to 1.30pm and 4 to 7.30pm. Sundays from 9am to 3.30pm.
ATMs: Servired, Red 6000 and 4B.
Bureau De Change: Three offices (☎ 952-048 277).

Flights

Domestic Flights

Daily flights from Malaga are available to the following destinations in Spain: Alicante, Asturias, Bilbao, Barcelona (several flights daily), Ceuta, Gran Canaria, León, Madrid (several flights daily), Melilla, Palma de Mallorca, Salamanca, Santiago de Compostela, Tenerife, Valencia and Zaragoza. Domestic flights are operated by:

- Air Europa (☎ 902-410 501, 🖥 *www.air-europa.com*);

- Binter Canarias (☎ 928-579 601, 🖥 *www.bintercanarias.es*);

- Iberia (☎ 902-400 500, 🖥 *www.iberia.com*);

- Spanair (☎ 902-131 415, 🖥 *www.spanair.com*).

One-way flights to most destinations cost from €65 (€95 to the Canaries).

International Flights

Numerous airlines (scheduled, charter and the so-called 'budget' or 'no-frills' companies) fly to Malaga from destinations all over Europe with the UK and Germany being particularly well-served. Budget airlines are an increasingly popular means of travelling to the Costa del Sol, particularly for those wishing to travel there from smaller airports in the UK and in 2003 some 1.5 million passengers chose to fly to Malaga with a budget airline.

Prices vary greatly and one-way tickets range from as low as €40 during off-peak season to €250 during the summer months. Shop around (easy to do on the internet) and don't forget to enquire at your local travel agent who may have some good deals, particularly for last-minute flights or those booked well in advance. There are also several specialist flight shops on the Costa del Sol, many of which advertise in the English-language press and offer a good choice of prices and destinations.

If you have to travel literally last-minute it may be worth going to Malaga airport, where numerous airlines have offices in the check-in area, to see if any tickets are available. This is really only an option outside high season, although British Airways and Iberia often have (expensive) spare seats at any time of year on their scheduled flights.

When comparing prices don't forget to add airport taxes (sometimes nearly as much or more than the ticket itself). **In addition, many airlines charge for payment by credit card (around €7) when you book over the phone or online.**

Bear in mind that budget airlines are exactly that and you get nothing on the flight apart from your seat unless you pay for it! Food and drink is expensive on budget flights and the choice is limited. You can save money by taking your own or buying it beforehand in the airport, especially if you are travelling in a group. Other airlines are also following this trend – Iberia no longer provide a newspaper on flights leaving after 10am and you now have to pay for food on its European flights. Note, however, that there are still airlines (e.g. British Airways and Monarch) where you get a paper, the chance to watch a video, and drinks and a meal are included in the flight price.

The following airlines fly from the UK and Ireland to Malaga.

Company	Flies From	Contact Details
Aer Lingus	Cork, Dublin	☎ Ireland 0813-365 000
		🖳 *www.aerlingus.com*
Air Scotland	Edinburgh	☎ 0141-848 4990
		🖳 *www.air-scotland.com*
BA	Gatwick, Heathrow	☎ UK 0845-773 3377
		☎ Spain 902-111 333
		🖳 *www.ba.com*)
BMi Baby	Cardiff, East Midlands, Manchester, Teeside	☎ UK 0870-264 229
		☎ Spain 902-100 737
		🖳 *www.bmibaby.com*
City Jet	Dublin	☎ Ireland 01-844 5566
		🖳 *www.cityjet.com*
Easy Jet	Bristol, East Midlands, Liverpool, Gatwick, Luton, Stansted, Newcastle	☎ UK 0870-600 0000
		☎ Spain 902-299 992
		🖳 *www.easyjet.com*
FlyBe	Exeter (Feb. to Oct. only), Southampton	☎ UK 0871-700 0535
		🖳 *www2.flybe.com*
Flyglobe Span	Edinburgh, Glasgow	☎ UK 08705-561522
		🖳 *www.flyglobespan.com*
GB Airways	Gatwick, Heathrow	☎ 0845-773 3377
		🖳 *www.gbairways.com*
Iberia	Heathrow	☎ UK 0845-601 2854
		☎ Spain 902-400 515
		🖳 *www-iberia.com*

Jet2	Leeds Bradford	☎ UK 0870-737 8282
		☎ Spain 902-020 264
		🖳 *www.jet2.com*
Monarch	Gatwick, Luton, Manchester	☎ UK 0870-040 5040
		🖳 *www.monarch-airlines.com*
My Travel Lite	Birmingham	☎ UK 0870-156 4564
		🖳 *www.mytravellite.com*
Ryanair	Dublin	☎ UK 0871-246 0000
		🖳 *www.ryanair.com*

The tour operator Britannia also offer flights from numerous destinations in the UK to Malaga, although many flights are seasonal (☎ UK 0800-000 747, 🖳 *www.britanniadirect.com*).

Getting To & From Malaga Airport

By Train

The Malaga to Fuengirola train line stops at the airport. The train service runs from 6am to around 11am. Trains for Torremolinos (11 minute journey), Arroyo de la Miel (18 minute journey) and Fuengirola (35 minute journey) leave at 13 and 43 minutes past every hour. The last train leaves at 10.43pm. One-way tickets cost €1, €1.60 and €2.15 respectively. Trains for Malaga centre and the mainline train station leave at 15 and 45 minutes past every hour. The last train leaves at 11.45pm and a one-way ticket costs €1.

Information can be obtained from ☎ 902-240 202 and 🖳 *www.renfe.es/cercanias/malaga*.

When the high-speed *Tren de Alta Velocidad Española* (*AVE*) line from Madrid to Malaga is completed in 2007, the service is expected to run to the airport.

By Bus

Airport To Malaga Bus Station: Buses leave from outside departures and arrivals every 30 minutes from 6.30am to midnight.
Cost: €1
Information: ☎ 952-210 295

Airport To Marbella Bus Station: Buses leave from outside departures and arrivals every 45 minutes from 5.30am to 11pm.
Cost: €4.18
Information: ☎ 952-764 401

By Taxi

There's a large taxi rank outside the arrivals terminal and taxis are provided by Radio Taxi (☎ 952-040 804) and Unitaxi (☎ 952-333 333) only.

Approximate prices to or from the airport are:

Destination	Price
Benalmadena Costa	€13
Estepona	€67
Fuengirola	€21
La Cala De Mijas	€29
Marbella	€43
Mijas	€25
Nerja	€61
Puerto Banus	€53
Torre Del Mar	€43
Torremolinos	€8
San Pedro	€56

By Car

Car Rental

There are numerous car rental companies based at the airport and most of those operating on the Costa del Sol offer an airport collection service. If you want to use the car from the airport it's advisable to book it before travel, although it isn't difficult to hire a car once you arrive. Reputable car hire companies belong to the Andalusian Car Hire Business Association – AESVA (Asociación Empresarial de Coches de Alquiler de Andalucía).

Local companies are cheaper than national companies, although car hire on the Costa del Sol is generally cheap, mainly due to the intense competition for clients so it's worth shopping around. When comparing companies make sure prices include insurance and taxes (VAT at 16 per cent), that insurance cover is adequate and there are no hidden costs.

> **Note that if you plan to drive anywhere other than the coastal strip it involves mountainous terrain and you need a car with at least a 1.6 litre engine. Air conditioning is a must from June to the end of September.**

Approximate starting prices in low season (from mid-November to late March) and in high season are as follows:

Category	Low-Season	High Season
Economy/Basic	€120	€150
Economy	€175	€225
Small Car	€240	€300

Standard Family Car	€330	€400
Large Family Car	€420	€500
People Carrier	€540	€630
Luxury Car	€1,200	€1,450

Most local and national companies operating on the coast offer the possibility of collecting the car in one location and dropping it off at another.

Main companies operating on the Costa del Sol are:

- **ATESA** – Offices at airport, Malaga and Marbella (☎ 902 100 101, 🖥 *www.atesa.es*);

- **Autos Lido** – Offices at airport (☎ 952 237 804, 🖥 *www.autoslido.es*);

- **Budget** – Offices at airport, Fuengirola, Marbella and Nerja (☎ 901 201 212, 🖥 *www.budget.es*);

- **Crown Car Hire** – Offices at airport, Marbella, Nerja and Sotogrande (☎ 952-176 486, 🖥 *www.crowncarhire.com*);

- **Europcar** – Offices at airport, Benalmadena Costa, Estepona, Malaga, Marbella, Mijas Costa, Nerja, San Pedro and Torremolinos (☎ 902 105 030, 🖥 *www.europcar.es*);

- **Helle Hollis** – Offices at airport, Fuengirola, Marbella and Nerja. Helle Hollis run a Holiday Home Owners rental club whose members and guests are entitled to discounts on car hire. For further details contact the Malaga airport office (☎ 952 245 544, 🖥 *www.hellehollis.com*);

- **Hertz** – Offices at airport, Fuengirola, Malaga, Marbella and Torremolinos (☎ 902 402 405, 🖥 *www.hertz.es*);

- **Holiday Car Hire** – Offices at airport, Calahonda and Riviera del Sol (☎ 952 932 443, 🖥 *www.holidaycarhire.com*);

- **Niza Cars** – Offices at airport (☎ 952 336 179, 🖥 *www.nizacars.es*);

- **Sixt** – Offices at airport, Mijas Costa, Marbella (☎ 902 287 600, 🖥 *www.sixt.es*);

- **Yellow Car** – Offices at La Cala and Marbella (☎ 952 831 492, 🖥 *www. yellowcar.com*).

Other companies can be found in the yellow pages under '*Automóviles y furgonetas (alquiler)*'.

There are also rental companies who specialise in the rental of luxury cars (including chauffeur-driven), vans, mini-buses and lorries.

Rental cars are popular targets for thieves and most rental cars are obvious so don't leave valuables on show or easily accessible when you leave your car. Also, don't leave valuables on the seat with the window open when driving in towns.

Private Cars

The airport is easily reached via the N-340/A-7 and access is well-signposted. The airport has parking for some 1,450 cars and out of season there are usually plenty of spaces. There's limited parking space for set-down only on the esplanade outside the departure terminal, **but it's best not to leave your car for long since tow-away trucks are often in action and no one really knows how long you're allowed to leave a car there!**

Airport parking costs €0.60 for the first 30 minutes, €1.16 for the first hour and €0.84 for any subsequent hours or part of up to a maximum of 24 hours. Long-term parking is available in the smaller car park outside the old terminal (Terminal 1) for a minimum of four days at €4.21 a day.

Several private companies offer secure long-term parking facilities, which are considerably cheaper than airport parking, e.g. €3 per day, including an airport collection and drop-off service. These companies are found opposite the main airport building over the railway line and several advertise in newspapers such as *Sur in English*. **Make sure the company you choose has adequate insurance including fire and flood.**

Gibraltar Airport

Gibraltar airport also serves the Costa del Sol, although there are few flights and they're almost exclusively to and from the UK. Queues to leave Gibraltar (particularly by car) are often long and customs checks are lengthy. There's no public transport from the Costa del Sol except taxis, which may drop you off at the border rather than queue to get into and out of Gibraltar. **Note that you may require a visa to enter Spain from Gibraltar, which is not part of the EU.**

Airport information is available from: ☎ 350-73026 from abroad or ☎ 956-773 026 from Spain.

The following airlines fly from the UK to Gibraltar.

Company	Flies From	Contact Details
GB Airways	Gatwick	☎ 0845-773 3377
		💻 *www.gbairways.com*
Monarch	Luton, Manchester	☎ UK 0870-040 5040
		💻 *www.monarch-airlines.com*

TRAINS

The only access by train to the Costa del Sol is to Malaga's mainline station served by trains from Madrid, Granada and Seville. The journey from Madrid takes just over four hours by high-speed '*TALGO*' (*Tren Articulado Ligero Goicoechea Oriol 200*) train and there are seven trains a day. One-way tickets cost €49 or €54 in tourist class (*clase turista*) and €73 or €81 in first class (*clase preferente*). Return tickets are cheaper. Information is available from ☎ 902-240 202 and 💻 *www.renfe.es* (look under '*Quiero Viajar*' and select Malaga and Madrid).

The high-speed *AVE* line from Madrid to Malaga via Cordoba is currently under construction and is due to be completed by 2007. The journey time will then be reduced to around two and a half hours.

DRIVING

Many residents prefer to drive to the Costa del Sol from their country of origin, a practical option if you have lots of luggage or wish to have the use of your car while you're on the coast.

> **Bear in mind, however, that the journey is long (the French border is nearly 1,000km/625mi away – at least ten hours from the coast) and you need to take into account the cost of motorway toll fees, the ferry and one overnight stay.**

Suggested Routes

Via France

The main route is generally along the Atlantic through France, via San Sebastian and Madrid.

● **In France** – A-63 (toll) via Bayonne to the Spanish border at Irún;

● **In Spain** – AP-8 (toll);

- A-1 via Tolosa and Ordizia to Alsasua (last 20 kms not dual carriageway), A-1 to Miranda del Ebro and Burgos;

- A-1 to Madrid;

- A-4 to Bailén;

- A-44 to Granada

- A-92 to Cuesta de la Palma;

- A-359 to Las Pedrizas;

- A-45 to Malaga.

Via Bilbao

The Costa del Sol is 880km (550mi) from Bilbao.

If you get the ferry from Portsmouth to Bilbao the following route is the best to the Costa del Sol:

- N-634 to the AP-8 toll motorway;

- A-1 via Tolosa and Ordizia to Alsasua (last 20 kms not dual carriageway), A-1 to Miranda del Ebro and Burgos;

- A-1 to Madrid;

- A-4 to Bailén;

- A-44 to Granada;

- A-92 to Cuesta de la Palma;

- A-359 to Las Pedrizas;

- A-45 to Malaga.

From Santander

The Costa del Sol is 880km (550mi) from Santander.

If you get the ferry from Plymouth to Santander the following route is the best to the Costa del Sol:

- N-623 to Burgos (this route is not dual-carriageway for most of the journey and is slow over the mountain pass between Cantabria and Castilla-León);

- A-1 to Madrid;

- A-4 to Bailén;

- A-44 to Granada;

- A-92 to Cuesta de la Palma;

- A-359 to Las Pedrizas;

- A-45 to Malaga.

Roads are generally good and are dual carriageway throughout most of Spain. Traffic information is available in France from 🖳 *www.bison-fute.equipment.gouv.fr* (in French only) and in Spain from 🖳 *www.dgt.es* (in Spanish only).

Aqueduct, Nerja

3

Getting Around

This chapter examines the public transport system, i.e. trains, buses and taxis, in different localities on the Costa del Sol as well as various aspects of getting around by car, including roads, the toll motorway, driving rules, car maintenance and road tax.

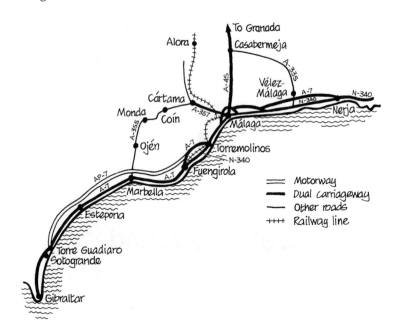

PUBLIC TRANSPORT

Public transport on the coast varies from excellent to poor. In some areas you can use public transport as an efficient means of commuting, whilst in others buses put in a sporadic appearance and are often full so they don't stop. However, public transport is improving and local and regional authorities are making a concerted effort to provide more efficient means of getting around other than by car. Several towns on the coast have recently reached an agreement to form a consortium of public transport, which should provide a more co-ordinated service and plans have now been approved for the Costa del Sol train line. **In general, however, and until the train line is finished, unless you live and work in the centre of a town or city, private transport is essential.**

This section deals with public transport for the whole of the Costa del Sol. For information about public transport within each locality see **Chapter 4**.

Trains

At present there are two train lines serving part of the coast: Malaga to Fuengirola and Malaga to Alora. Both lines are efficient and very popular – the Malaga to Fuengirola line is the most profitable line in Spain and used by some 8 million passengers a year. Information is available from ☎ 902-240 202 and 🖥 *www.renfe.es/cercanias/malaga*.

The trains are comfortable with air-conditioning and piped classical music. Tickets can be bought from machines at most stations or from ticket offices (found only at main stations). If there isn't a machine at a station you may be able to buy your ticket on the train from the inspector. **Note, however, that RENFE has reduced its staff numbers and many inspectors no longer sell tickets, although they're quite prepared to fine you for travelling without one! And fines are at least double the normal ticket price.**

Malaga To Fuengirola

This service runs two trains per hour with stops at:

- **Zone 0** – Malaga centre (two stops – at the mainline station and by the river, opposite the Corte Inglés);

- **Zone 1** – San Andrés, Guadalhorce and the airport;

- **Zone 2** – Plaza Mayor, Los Alamos, La Colina, Torremolinos, Montemar-Alto and El Pinillo;

- **Zone 3** – Benalmadena, Arroyo de la Miel, Torremuelle, Carvajal and Torreblanca;

- **Zone 4** – Los Boliches and Fuengirola.

The journey from Malaga to Fuengirola takes just under 45 minutes and the service is generally very efficient with a high degree of punctuality. The first train leaves Malaga centre at 5.45am. Subsequent trains leave on the hour and at half past the hour. The last train is at 10.30pm. The first train leaves Fuengirola at 6.33am. Subsequent trains leave at 15 and 45 minutes past the hour. The last train leaves at 11.15pm.

Journey times are as follows:

- Malaga to Arroyo de la Miel in Benalmadena (32 minutes);

- Malaga to Fuengirola (45 minutes);

- Malaga to Torremolinos (25 minutes).

Malaga To Alora

This line runs north from Malaga centre (mainline station) and stops at:

- **Zone 0** – Malaga mainline station;

- **Zone 1** – Los Prados;

- **Zone 2** – Campanillas and Cártama;

- **Zone 3** – Aljaima and Pizarra;

- **Zone 4** – Alora.

The first train leaves Alora at 6am and the last at 9.25pm. From Malaga, the first train is at 6.45am and the last at 10.30pm. There's one train per hour in the mornings and evenings, and one every two hours for the rest of the day.

Journey times are as follows:

- Malaga to Aljaima (30 minutes);

- Malaga to Alora (40 minutes);

- Malaga to Cártama (20 minutes);

- Malaga to Pizarra (35 minutes).

Ticket Prices

Tickets are priced depending on the number of zones you travel through (e.g. Malaga to Arroyo de la Miel is four zones and Malaga to Fuengirola takes you through five). On both train lines there are five travel zones and prices are as follows:

	1/2 Zones	3 Zones	4 Zones	5 Zones
Mondays To Fridays	€1.00	€1.15	€1.60	€2.15
Weekends/Bank Holidays	€1.10	€1.20	€1.75	€2.25
Return Any Day	€1.45	€1.65	€2.55	€3.30

Monthly season tickets are also available and cost €52.05 for travel over five zones.

Future Plans

Work started in December 2003 on the conversion of the Malaga to Fuengirola line to double-track to allow trains to run more frequently and there will probably be four trains an hour with some direct services. Work is expected to take two years.

Plans have been approved to continue the link from Fuengirola to Marbella and Estepona, and from Malaga to Nerja. The first stretches to be built will be Fuengirola to Marbella and Malaga to Rincón de la Victoria. The Fuengirola to Marbella line was originally planned to follow the line of the AP-7 motorway, but as this is a considerable distance from the main residential areas the authorities have opted for an underground line closely following the coastal road. The line, which will be very expensive to build (first estimates are more than €2.400 million) but highly profitable, is expected to be in operation by 2012. When complete it will take around 90 minutes to travel from Estepona to Nerja, and one hour from Estepona to Malaga.

Stations are expected to be as follows:

● **Fuengirola To Marbella Line** – La Cala, Calahonda, Elviria, Los Monteros, Marbella centre, Marbella west, Puerto Banús, San Pedro, Benamara, Estepona and Estepona west;

● **Malaga To Nerja Line** – La Cala del Moral, Rincón de la Victoria, Torre de Benagalbón, Benajarafe, Torre del Mar, Caleta de Vélez, Los Llanos (Torrox Costa) and Nerja.

Buses

Buses are the principal means of public transport and the main routes in the west are run by Portillo, a company who at present holds a monopoly, and by Portillo and Alsina Graells in the east. There are also some other local bus operators. Services range from reasonable to poor depending on the route (and the bus driver!) and few residents speak highly of the service. Things have improved somewhat in recent months, although buses still arrive infrequently and it's not uncommon to wait 45 minutes for a bus that supposed to come every 20 minutes! A local reporter recently made the journey by bus from Estepona to Nerja, an odyssey that took more than four hours to cover a distance of 135km (84mi)! **If you can, get a direct bus since the journey time will be considerably shorter.**

The following alphabetical listing provides information about bus stations on the Costa del Sol and the services provided.

Alhaurín El Grande

Several buses run daily to Coín and Malaga with a reduced service on Sundays and public holidays. There isn't a bus station and buses leave from the main square. For more information contact ☎ 952-490 196.

Coin

Several buses daily to Alhaurín el Grande (15 minutes), Fuengirola (70 minutes), Malaga, Marbella via Guaro and Monda, Mijas (30 minutes) and Tolox. A much reduced service on Sundays and public holidays. Buses currently leave from Plaza de la Villa and a bus station is currently under construction near the Parque San Agustín, which is expected to be finished in mid-2004. For more information contact ☎ 952-450 366.

Estepona

The bus station is situated near the sea front on C/ San Roque. There are several buses daily to Algeciras, Granada, La Línea and Seville. Buses to Madrid and Barcelona leave once a day. Local services to Fuengirola, Malaga (one hour journey) and Torremolinos leave frequently, and the main local bus route is from Estepona to Marbella via San Pedro. There's little parking for cars at the bus station. For more information contact ☎ 952-800 249.

Fuengirola

The bus station (badly in need of a facelift) is situated at the main crossroads between C/ Alfonso XII and Avda Sáenz de Tejada. There are frequent buses to Marbella (every 20 minutes), Malaga (every hour), Mijas (every 30 minutes) and Torremolinos (every 30 mins). There are also daily bus services to Alhaurín de la Torre and Coín. Several buses run daily to Granada, Cordoba, Madrid, Ronda, Seville and Algeciras. **Note that there is no parking space at the bus station and no indoor waiting room.** For more information contact ☎ 952-475 066.

Istán

Buses run to Marbella twice a day.

Malaga

The main centre for buses is in Malaga in a modern bus station situated in Los Tilos near the mainline train station and the Larios Centro shopping centre. The bus station has several small shops and cafés, a *bureau de change* and internet facilities. The Larios shopping centre is near by. There are several services daily to the main capitals in Andalusia and express coaches to Madrid and Barcelona. Coach services for Europe and Morocco are available. Buses also depart from here to the main centres on the coast (journey times follow in brackets). Benalmadena (20 minutes), Estepona (2 hours), Fuengirola (45 minutes), Marbella (75 minutes; 45 minutes direct service) and Nerja (90 minutes).

For long-distance journeys you can book a seat by phone (tickets must be collected at least 15 minutes before the bus departs), **but Portillo**

still hasn't got a website, let alone online booking! Alsina Graells has a telephone and website booking where you can book medium and long-distance journeys (☎ 902-330 400 – lines open from 7am to 10am and 🖳 *www.continental-auto.es*). For more information contact ☎ 952-350 061 or 🖳 *www.estabus.emtsam.es*.

Manilva

Three buses a day run from Manilva to Estepona from Mondays to Saturdays. The journey takes around 45 minutes. There's no service on Sundays.

Marbella

The bus station is on the A-7 to the north of the city on the km 184 exit and is modern and spacious with good facilities including shops, restaurants and a large waiting room. Parking for private cars is ample. Frequent buses run to Benalmadena Costa, Estepona, Fuengirola (every 20 minutes), Malaga (75 minutes; 45 minutes direct service), Ronda and San Pedro. There are also several buses daily to the main cities in Andalucía and Madrid. Buses also serve the villages in the vicinity (Coín, Istán, Monda and Ojén). For more information contact ☎ 952-764 400.

Mijas

Mijas doesn't have a bus station and buses leave from the main square opposite the town hall. There are buses every 30 minutes to Fuengirola and several buses daily to Coín.

Nerja

The bus station is on the N-340 at the junction with Calle San Miguel and frequent buses run to Malaga (a direct service leaves four times a day), Granada, Malaga airport and the hospital in Vélez-Málaga as well as local services to Maro, Frigiliana and Torre del Mar. For more information contact ☎ 952-521 504.

San Pedro

The bus terminal is situated on the N340 in the centre of the town. There are several daily buses to Ronda and San Roque, frequent services to Estepona, Fuengirola, Malaga (journey takes 1 hour 35 minutes), Marbella and Torremolinos. Buses for Benahavís run twice a day. For more information contact ☎ 952-781 396.

Sotogrande

Buses stop at Guadiaro. Bus services run several times a day from Estepona to La Línea (and back), although not all stop at Guadiaro for

Sotogrande. The Malaga to Algeciras bus service also has a stop at Sotogrande and buses run more or less hourly from 5am to 7pm (Malaga) and from 8am to 10pm (Algeciras). This bus service gets very crowded and it's best to book in advance. For more information contact Portillo in San Roque (☎ 956-172 396).

Torremolinos

The bus station is on Calle Hoyos and there are frequent bus services to Benalmadena and Fuengirola (buses leave every 30 minutes), Malaga and Marbella. There's no parking for cars at the station. For more information contact ☎ 952-382 419.

Vélez-Málaga

The bus station is on the main road into the town from Torre del Mar, the Avenida Vívar Téllez opposite the main park. Bus services are available to Malaga, Nerja and surrounding villages. For more information contact ☎ 952-503 162.

Taxis

Taxis (white vehicles) are plentiful on the Costa del Sol and aren't expensive, particularly if there are several of you to share the cost. Within urban areas rates are metered and for other journeys there are fixed fees. Taxis charge extra for luggage and after 10pm. You can either take a taxi from an authorised tax rank or telephone for one.

Telephone numbers for taxis in the main localities are listed below:

Alhaurín De La Torre	☎ 952-410 444
Alhaurín El Grande	☎ 952-490 066
Benalmadena	☎ 952-441 545
Cártama	☎ 952-422 324
Casares	☎ 952-894 044
Coín	☎ 952-453 587
Estepona	☎ 952-802 900
Fuengirola	☎ 952-471 000
Malaga	☎ 952-333 333
	☎ 952-040 804
Manilva	☎ 952-892 900
Marbella	☎ 952-774 488
Mijas	☎ 952-478 288
Mijas Costa	☎ 952-478 288
Nerja	☎ 952-520 537
Ojén	☎ 952-881 280

Rincón De La Victoria	☎ 952-401 773
San Pedro	☎ 952-781 396
Sotogrande	☎ 956-616 078
Torremolinos	☎ 952-380 600
Vélez Malaga	☎ 952-327 950

DRIVING

By Car

Unless you live in the centre of a town or near a local train station, private transport is essential on the Costa del Sol. Although road communications have improved enormously in recent years, they haven't kept up with demand. Since the mid-'90s, traffic density has doubled on the coast, yet the AP-7 toll motorway is the only new road in the area and experts now forecast the A-7 will reach saturation point within the next two or three years.

Malaga, in particular, is in desperate need of a second ring-road, a project that's been in the government infrastructure pipeline for several years, but has yet to materialise, although plans were approved in March 2004 – just before the general elections! Until public transport improves (the coastal train line is expected to relieve traffic considerably but not until 2012), **expect to spend many frustrating hours in slow traffic!**

Traffic Information

Traffic bulletins are broadcast every hour by SER Málaga and Estepona, M-80 Málaga and Onda Cero Málaga and Marbella in Spanish, and in English on most of the expatriate radio stations (see **Radio** on page 308). The national Traffic Department also provides information by phone (☎ 900-123 505 – phonelines are often overloaded) and on the internet (🖳 www. dgt.es). There are also illuminated information panels located at intervals over the A-7 warning of accidents and driving conditions – although the information often isn't much use as you're usually already stuck in the traffic jam when you read it!

Roads

The A-7 (Old N-340)

The A-7 or Autovía del Mediterráneo is the new name for the N-340, but although the signs on the road have changed, it's likely to be years before residents stop calling it the N-340! Some stretches of the old N-340 are now officially known as N-340 such as from Fuengirola to Torremolinos via the coast, Marbella to Puerto Banús and Rincón de la Victoria to Nerja (N-340a).

The A-7 (which runs the length of the Mediterranean from Cadiz to Barcelona) forms the backbone of road communications along the coast and in many areas provides the only means of getting from one place to another. The road is mostly dual carriageway – except for the stretch beyond Nerja to Motril where the road is still single lane and the Malaga and Marbella bypasses where the road has three lanes. In 2002 the dual carriageway from Estepona to Sotogrande was finished, but note that this section of the road has numerous roundabouts and progress can be slow.

There are numerous service stations along the A-7. Some are self-service and others are manned (*servicio atendido*), but not all are 24-hours. To prevent drivers filling up without paying some service stations have pumps that require pre-payment. At all 24-hour stations if you want to fill up after 11pm you have to pay at the cash desk beforehand.

The road has the reputation for being one of the most dangerous in Spain and accidents are frequent, usually caused by speeding. The speed limit is generally 100kph (62mph), although the density of traffic often means real speed is slower. **Note that on some stretches, e.g. from Torreguadiaro to Manilva the limit is 70kph or 80kph.** Driving along the A-7 can be very stressful as a lot of drivers insist of driving far over the speed limit and tail gating anyone in their way. Added to this are numerous cars turning on and off the road (in some stretches entries and exits to the road are about every 100m), turning a journey into an obstacle course. The A-7 is currently in a very bad state of repair with countless potholes and cracks, although the long overdue resurfacing work has recently started in the Fuengirola area.

Traffic congestion is chronic at certain times of the day in some areas. If you can, avoid the following peak times:

- Travelling west from Fuengirola to Marbella from 7 to 9.30am;

- The Malaga bypass in both directions from 7 to 10am and from 6 to 8pm (a recent study claimed the inside lane is gridlocked 12 hours a day and the outside 6);

- Travelling east from Marbella to Malaga from 6 to 8pm.

San Pedro: A main black spot at any time of day in the year is the section through Puerto Banús and San Pedro where the road passes through the town (it's the only town on the Costa del Sol without a bypass) with four sets of traffic lights and a roundabout. **Expect lengthy hold ups.**

Note that hold-ups occur anywhere at any time and the A-7 is expected to reach saturation point sometime in the near future.

The Old N-340: Some stretches of the coastal road such as the sections from Urb Torreblanca in Fuengirola to the airport and from Rincón de la Victoria to Nerja are no longer used by main traffic since bypasses have been built. As a result the dual carriageway has been converted into an urban boulevard with trees, roundabouts and much lower speed limits (usually 50kph (31mph)), providing a pleasant and relaxed alternative to the aggressive and fast main road, **but watch out for speed traps along these stretches.**

The AP-7 Motorway

The AP-7 toll motorway, known as the *Autopista del Sol*, along the western side of the Costa del Sol is almost complete and provides a good alternative to the A-7 if you're travelling long distances. The motorway has three stretches:

● Estepona to Sotogrande (one exit only for Manilva);

● Fuengirola to Marbella (one exit only for Calahonda);

● Marbella to Estepona (one exit only for San Pedro and Ronda).

Driving conditions on the AP-7 are excellent and the speed limit is 120kph (75mph), although beware of cars doing considerably more. The road's generally quiet and you can save time by using it instead of the A-7. Bear in mind, however, that there are few exits so it's only practical for long distances and that the motorway lies a considerable distance from the coast meaning it takes time to get to and from the motorway at Calahonda and San Pedro. The tolls are expensive (one of the reasons why the road is so quiet!), particularly from June to September and during Easter week. Low season is from 1st October to 31st May excluding Easter week. The following table shows high and low season tolls.

	Toll Cost For Cars	
Journey	**Low-Season**	**High-Season**
Calahonda To Marbella	€2.00	€3.20
Estepona To Guadiaro	€1.55	€2.55
Estepona To Manilva	€0.75	€1.25
Fuengirola To Calahonda	€2.00	€3.20
Fuengirola To Marbella	€3.20	€5.15
Manilva To Guadiaro	€0.75	€1.25
Marbella To Estepona	€2.15	€3.50
Marbella To San Pedro	€1.25	€2.00
San Pedro To Estepona	€1.25	€2.00

Season tickets for frequent users are available at discounted prices, although you must use the motorway at least 44 times in four months and you must always pay by the same credit card (see also **Automated Tolls** below). Discounts range from 5 per cent for between 11 and 15 uses a month to 50 per cent for more than 36 uses a month. Discounts are applied at the end of each month and are credited to your credit card. Frequent users pay low season tolls all year round.

Automated Tolls: At each toll point there's an automated toll lane for cars only, identified by an illuminated green 'T' (*Telepeaje*). In order to use this lane, cars must be fitted with a 'TAG' machine (about the size of a small camera), which is attached to the windscreen behind the rear view mirror. Cars don't have to stop, which makes the payment process quicker and easier. As you approach the barrier, your TAG is automatically detected, the transaction is recorded and the barrier lifts. Toll fees are automatically charged to your bank account or credit card at the end of the month. TAG machines can be obtained from Autopista del Sol offices or any branch of the Unicaja bank and cost around €7. A TAG can also be used on some other Spanish motorways.

AP-7 & A-7 Interchanges

At several points on the coast the road divides into the AP-7 toll stretches and the A-7 non-toll stretches, and it's easy to find yourself on the wrong one. The AP-7 motorway is signposted and has a red circle under it saying '*Peaje*' (toll) and the A-7 is usually signposted 'A-7 Costa'. **Once you're on a toll stretch you cannot get off until the next exit nor avoid paying the toll fee.** Apart from concentrating when approaching the division of the road, an easy rule is to always keep right for the A-7 or always keep left for the AP-7. **Beware of drivers changing lanes at the last minute on or near the interchanges.**

Further information (in English and Spanish) about the AP-7 along the Costa del Sol is available from 🖥 *www.autopistadelsol.com*.

Other Roads

East-West

If you're travelling east-west along the coast you cannot avoid the A-7 or the AP-7 and there are few alternative routes. Sometimes it's quicker to drive through the towns rather than use the congested by pass, but the chances are that if the bypass is busy, the town will be too. Numerous traffic lights and roundabouts also slow progress down. If you find yourself in a lengthy traffic jam, the following alternative routes may be helpful. **Note that roads are single lane and often winding and/or steep.**

La Cala Via Entrerríos To Fuengirola/Coín

Take the road to La Cala Golf and follow to Entrerríos. The road then joins the main Fuengirola to Coín route. Bear in mind that this road into Fuengirola centre is almost always gridlocked.

La Cala Via The Race Course To Fuengirola

Take the road in La Cala signposted to the race course (*hipódromo*), which then joins the A-7 at the Myramar complex next to the river. This road is a good alternative for those who live in the urbanisations between Fuengirola castle and La Cala.

South-North – Benalmadena To Mijas (MA-408)

A narrow winding mountain road, only recommended for those who live along it.

Fuengirola To Mijas (A-387)

A good road, although it's steep going up to Mijas and progress can be slow if you get behind a slow vehicle or a bus. The stretch from the motorway to Fuengirola is always busy and often gridlocked near the centre, although the section from the AP-7 motorway to the A-7 overpass will be dual carriageway in the near future.

Fuengirola To Coín (MA-426)

A long and winding road with numerous sharp bends, currently being resurfaced. **It is in poor condition in many sections particularly around Mijas Golf and the Entrerríos intersection.** The Fuengirola section is often gridlocked in both directions. Just before the local elections in May 2003 Mijas council produced plans to build a dual-carriageway by-pass round this section, but the plans as yet are still on the drawing board.

Malaga To Colmenar Via The Montes De Malaga (C-345)

This road used to be the main route to Granada (the journey took around four hours). The road is extremely winding and the ascent is steep. The surface in some sections is in poor condition and the first few kilometres out of Malaga are busy at the weekends as there are many popular restaurants situated here.

Malaga To Ronda Via Churriana (A-366)

Dual carriageway for the stretch until Churriana and then a good road through Alhaurín El Grande and Alhaurín De La Torre, which has been recently resurfaced and upgraded. **The section to Churriana is very busy and traffic can be heavy on other sections as well.**

Malaga To Campillos Via Cártama (A-357)

Dual carriageway until Cártama and then single-lane to Campillos. The road is in excellent condition and well sign-posted. **This road is very busy at peak times.**

Malaga To Antequera (A-45)

Apart from the A-7 this is the province's main road and the gateway to the rest of Andalusia via the A-92 and Madrid via the A-4. The road is dual-carriageway and is in the process of being resurfaced. A toll motorway (to be known as the AP-46) is planned from Malaga to Antequera as an alternative and is expected to be finished by 2007/8. This road will run from the west of Malaga via Almogía and Casabermeja to Antequera.

Marbella To Istán

Istán now has its own exit from the Marbella by-pass (previously you had to go to the old N-340 and then double back for Istán), which saves considerable time on the journey, **but the road is a mountain road and narrow and winding.** Views of the reservoir and the coast, however, are beautiful. The road beyond Istán is goes into the Sierra de las Nieves natural park and is only suitable for four-wheel drive vehicles.

Marbella/San Pedro To Ronda (A-376)

A good wide road, although it's mountain driving and some of the bends are very sharp, and it takes about 45 minutes to reach Ronda from the coast, although if you get behind a queue of slow traffic progress is much slower. **There are no lines on the road and no overtaking lanes. Fog is common at the top of the pass and snow occasionally falls in winter.** Spectacular views to Morocco to the south and the high mountains to the north do, however, compensate. This road is the main route from the western Costa del Sol to Seville.

Marbella To Vélez-Málaga Via Ojén, Monda & Coín (A-355)

An excellent and recently upgraded road, known as the Arc Road (*Carretera del Arco*) with an overtaking lane on much of the ascent to Ojén and dual carriageway for part of the way. Journey times from inland to the coast have been much reduced with this road.

A-7 To Casares (MA 546)

A reasonable road, although in a poor state of repair in some sections. Some parts have sharp bends.

Velez-Malaga To The Axarquía (C-335)

Conditions on this road vary, but most of the driving is along narrow and winding mountain roads.

Future Plans

The government has now finally approved the second ring-road for Malaga, which will run to the far west of the city crossing the A-366 at Churriana, the Guadalhorce Valley and rejoining the A-7 to the north of the city. The road will be 46km (29mi) long and is expected to be finished by 2007.

Basic Driving Rules

- Keep your driving licence, personal ID and car papers (including insurance) with you at all times when driving.

- Seat belts must be worn in the front and back, and children under 12 must sit in a proper child seat. **Note that children under 12 aren't permitted to sit in the front seat.**

- Cars must carry two red warning triangles, a spare set of bulbs and fuses, and a reflective waistcoat (to be worn if you get out of your car on the road or hard shoulder).

- There are various speed limits – 40kph or 50kph in built-up areas (*vías urbanas*); 90kph on main roads (*carreteras*); 100kph on dual carriageways (*autovías*); and 120kph on motorways (*autopistas*).

- **Don't drink and drive.** Maximum permitted alcohol levels are 0.5mg.

- **Don't leave valuables on show when you park your car and don't leave valuables on the seat with the window open when driving in towns.**

> **Something else to be beware of is that police are permitted to impose on-the-spot fines of up to €300 (even for minor infringements), which must be paid immediately unless you're a Spanish resident driving a Spanish-registered vehicle.**

Parking

Finding somewhere to park in towns and cities along the coast is a daily challenge and there's a chronic shortage of parking spaces in most localities. Free street parking is extremely difficult to find unless you're prepared to walk some distance to the centre or you can do as many Spanish drivers do, just park anywhere! **If you do, however, watch out for tow-away trucks**

who take illegally parked cars to the car pound (sometimes even if the driver's in it!) where it costs at least €60 to get your car back.

Most councils are investing heavily in car parks and in recent years many new underground car parks have been built. Expect to pay from €0.75 to €1.50 an hour in most municipal and private car parks. Street parking is also available in some areas in the blue zones and must be paid for from around 9am to 2pm and from 4 to 9pm. Parking in blue zones is free on Sundays and public holidays. Tickets cost from €0.70 to €1 an hour and you can usually park from 30 minutes up to a maximum of two hours.

Some towns and cities, e.g. Fuengirola and Malaga, have discount parking schemes for frequent users of public car parks and residents in many areas are entitled to reduced rates. Enquire at your local town hall for further information.

Maps

There are numerous good maps of the Costa del Sol, although most of them don't include maps of the towns or urbanisations apart from a map of Malaga. Guide books usually include a basic map, but if you want more detail it's better to buy a separate one. Maps, which can be bought on the Costa del Sol at bookshops and newsagents, priced from €3, include:

- **Decssa** – *Provincia de Malaga*. Good detail of the province and Fuengirola, Malaga and Marbella town plans;

- **Euro Tour** – Costa del Sol. Good detail.

- **Firestone** – Costa del Sol. Good detail;

- **Michelin** – *578 Andalucía*. Regional map with good detail of the coast and a Malaga city-plan;

- **RACE/Everest** – *Marbella* (good coast detail) and *Costas de Andalucía* (includes details of the Costa del Sol, Costa de Almería and Costa de la Luz).

Note that maps go out of date very quickly, particularly with regard to roads and that many urbanisations aren't marked on maps.

Tourist offices can provide detailed maps of a specific area and maps of towns and urbanisations are included in local telephone directories. **Note that most urbanisations are labyrinths and before trying to get somewhere within one you should make sure you've detailed instructions.** Many urbanisations have a map at the entrance.

Maps of the coast are also available on the internet (🖳 *www.maps costadelsol.com* is a particularly good site), but you need good printing quality if you want to use the maps other than on the screen.

Car Maintenance

Petrol & Service Stations

Service stations are easily found on the Costa del Sol and many also have small shops and a café or restaurant attached. Main service stations are 24-hour ones and those that aren't list the nearest 24-hour station. Petrol prices vary and if you do a lot of driving it may be worth shopping around to get a cheaper price. Prices per litre in February 2004 were as follows:

Type Of Fuel	Price Per Litre
Unleaded (*sin plomo*)	€0.89
Unleaded Premium (*sin plomo extra*)	€0.93
Diesel (*diésel*)	€0.70
Diesel Premium (*diésel extra*)	€0.73

Beware of thieves operating at service stations, particularly those on the main roads. Always lock your car while you pay for your petrol, especially at self-service stations and be wary of people asking for directions or drawing your attention to a burst tyre or similar – while you're distracted, their accomplice may be helping themselves to your luggage and belongings.

Garages & Repairs

Most places have several garages offering car servicing and repairs. The standard is generally good, although repair costs can be high (**ask for an estimate beforehand**). Many car dealers have garages attached to the showrooms where cars are serviced or repaired, and cars of any make can usually be serviced and repaired at any garages. However, for anything more than a minor repair it's advisable to take your car to the manufacturer's representative.

To find a reputable garage consult the dealer in your area (see below for contact information), ask around for a reliable garage or look in the yellow pages under *Talleres mecánicos para automóviles* or if you need body or paint work, *Talleres de chapa y pintura*.

For most services you need to book – note that garages are generally very busy and it's difficult to get an appointment at short notice. Some garages, e.g. Renault Minuto and Norauto, offer non-appointment services where you just arrive and wait your turn.

Car Dealers

Below is an alphabetical list of the main car dealers on the Costa del Sol. Addresses and telephone numbers can be found in the yellow pages under *Automóviles*: *concesionarios* or *Automóviles nuevos y de ocasión*.

Alfa Romeo

Malaga	Carmauto, Cno San Rafael 67-69 💻 *www.mundoalfa.com*	☎ 952-320 654

Audi

Fuengirola	Avda Santos Rein	☎ 952-660 696
Marbella	C/ Juan de la Cierva 7 💻 *www.audi.es*	☎ 952-771 097

BMW/Mini

Malaga	Guarnieri, Avda Velázquez 468	☎ 952-320 530
Marbella	Autos Sierra Blanca, Ctra de Cádiz km 175.3 💻 *www.bmw.es*	☎ 952-818 800

Chrysler

Fuengirola	Cobasa Autos, Avda Myramar	☎ 952-588 285
Malaga	Avda de Velázquez 204	☎ 952-243 869
Marbella	C/ Juan de la Cierva 5 💻 *www.chrysler-jeep.es*	☎ 952-865 775

Citroën

Alhaurín De La Torre	Autos Quiros, Pol Ind II Fase, nave 9	☎ 952-414 038
Estepona	Estebuna Motor SL, Pol Ind, C/ Alonso, Cano 43	☎ 952-805 594
Fuengirola	Emcasa, Avda Jacinto Benavente	☎ 952-460 550
Malaga	Goaz, Avda de Velázquez 198	☎ 952-247 272
Torre Del Mar	Caloga SA, Ctra de Cádiz km 275	☎ 952-540 375
Torremolinos	Autopai, Avda Palma de Mallorca 58 💻 *www.citroen.es*	☎ 952-387 122

Daewoo

Estepona	Guerrero Salado, C/ Tajo 32	☎ 952-802 349
Malaga	Motor Sport II, Avda de Velázquez 198	☎ 952-246 693
Marbella	Motor Sport II, Ctra de Cádiz km 182	☎ 952-866 806
Mijas Costa	Motor Sport II, Cno de Coín 59 🖥 *www.daewoomotor.es*	☎ 952-474 726,

Fiat/Lancia

Malaga	Fimalaga SA, Cno San Rafael 39	☎ 952-360 500
Vélez-Málaga	AutoColor, Ctra Vélez-Torre del Mar 🖥 *www.mundofiat.com*	☎ 952-558 303

Ford

Malaga	Jarauto SA, Avda Jacinto Benavente	☎ 952-264 066
Marbella	Auto-Marbella, Ctra de Cádiz km 183	☎ 952-776 450
Mijas Costa	Garaje Victoria, Ctra de Cádiz km 210	☎ 952-477 200
Vélez-Málaga	Talleres Bustillo, Avda Juan Carlos I 🖥 *www.ford.es*	☎ 952-501 450

Honda

Malaga	Cotri SL, Avda de Velázquez 319	☎ 952-241 717
Marbella	Ctra de Cádiz km 182.5 🖥 *www.honda.es*	☎ 952-821 553

Hyundai

Fuengirola	Autos Fuenmijas SL, C/ Verónica 13	☎ 952-585 353
Marbella	Carmar SL, C/ Juan de la Cierva 5	☎ 952-865 775
Torre Del Mar	Axarquía Motor, Ctra de Cádiz km 269.5	☎ 952-541 762
Vélez-Málaga	Axarquía Motor, Avda Juan Carlos I 🖥 *www.hyundai.es*	☎ 952-508 135

Isuzu

Malaga   Avda Velázquez 198   ☎ 952-246 693
💻 *www.isuzu.es*

Jaguar

Malaga   Parque Empresarial Sta Bárbara, C/
Tucibibes 4   ☎ 952-105 151
💻 *www.jaguar.com*

Kia

Fuengirola   Cobasa Autos, Avda Myramar   ☎ 952-588 285

Malaga   Avda Juan XXIII 29   ☎ 952-350 611
💻 *www.kia.es*

Land Rover

Fuengirola   Sertasa, Ctra de Mijas km 4.7   ☎ 952-477 999

Malaga   Sertasa, Avda Velázquez 321   ☎ 952-176 828
💻 *www.landrover.es*

Lexus

Malaga   Avda de los Guindos 4   ☎ 952-105 383
💻 *www.mundolexus.com*

Mazda

Malaga   Koni Motor, Avda Velázquez 309   ☎ 952-105 330
💻 *www.mazda.es*

Mercedes

Malaga   R. Benet, Pol Ind, C/ Esteban Salazar 6   ☎ 952-247 096

Marbella   R. Benet, C/ Juan de la Cierva 12   ☎ 952-764 020

Mijas Costa   Talleres Leal, Cno de Coín   ☎ 952-475 142
💻 *www.mercedes-benz.es*

Mitsubishi

Malaga   Mavesa, Parque Empresarial Sta Bárbara,
C/ Tucídides 68-70   ☎ 952-240 421

| Marbella | Magasa, Ctra de Cádiz km 183
💻 *www.mitsubishi-motors.es* | ☎ 952-924 520 |

Nissan

Fuengirola	Canales y Lumbreras SA, Avda Mijas 4	☎ 952-664 253
Malaga	Canales y Lumbreras SA, Avda Juan XXIII 4	☎ 952-316 800
Marbella	Turismar, C/ Juan de la Cierva 5 💻 *www2.nissan.es*	☎ 952-866 050

Opel

Fuengirola	Diseño Motor 4 SA, Ctra de Mijas km 3.5	☎ 952-464 118
Malaga	Automóviles Nieto, Plaza de Toros Vieja 9	☎ 952-321 231
	Gálvez Motor, Avda de Velázquez 116	☎ 952-233 455
Marbella	Marbecar SA, C/ Ingeniero de la Cierva 15	☎ 952-778 597
Vélez-Málaga	Velezauto, Avda Juan Carlos I 💻 *www.opel.es*	☎ 952-503 062

Peugeot

Estepona	Star Car Systems, Pol Ind, C/ Alonso Cano 42	☎ 952-804 050
Fuengirola	Bugar Motor, Ctra de Mijas km 5.5	☎ 952-667 466
Malaga	Avda Velázquez 83	☎ 952-230 753
Marbella	Nuevo Motor 2 SL, Ctra de Cádiz km 183	☎ 952-778 035
Vélez-Málaga	Comau, Avda Juan Carlos I 💻 *www.peugeot.es*	☎ 952-505 200

Renault

| Alhaurín El Grande | Colorado SA, C/ Blasco Ibáñez 2 | ☎ 952-595 239 |
| Benalmadena | Autorreparaciones Arroyo, Pol Ind. 10 | ☎ 952-445 728 |

Coín	Colorado SA, Avda Reina Sofía	☎ 952-451 050
Estepona	Talleres Martín, Avda Litoral	☎ 952-801 934
Fuengirola	Garaje Alfín, Ctra de Mijas	☎ 952-476 400
Malaga	Tahermo, Polígono Sta Bárbara	☎ 952-176 238
Marbella	Costa Marbella Motor, Ctra de Cádiz km 183	☎ 952-778 004
Torre Del Mar	Autotalleres La Vega, Avda de Andalucía 169B	☎ 952-541 580
Torremolinos	Garaje Alfín, Avda Carlotsa Alessandri 41	☎ 952-374 890
Vélez-Málaga	Autotalleres La Vega, Avda Juan Carlos I 6 🖳 *www.renault.es*	☎ 952-502 000

Rover

Fuengirola	Sertasa, Ctra de Mijas km 4.7	☎ 952-477 999
Malaga	Sertasa, Avda Velázquez 321 🖳 *www.landrover.es*	☎ 952-176 828

Saab

Malaga	De Los Ríos Motor, Pol Sta Bárbara, C/ Hnos Lumiere 8	☎ 952-174 440
Marbella	Bel-Air Motor, Ctra de Cádiz km 166 🖳 *www.saab.com*	☎ 952-886 750

Seat

Fuengirola	Autos Bellamar, Ctra de Mijas, km 3.6	☎ 952-473 111
Malaga	Cormosa, Avda Carlos Haya 93	☎ 952-610 844
Marbella	Motor 93, Ctra de Cádiz km 182	☎ 952-778 800
Vélez-Málaga	Vélez Motor, Avda Juan Carlos I 🖳 *www.seat.es*	☎ 952-558 255

Skoda

Malaga	Cotyauto, Avda Velázquez 73	☎ 952-243 837

| **Marbella** | Autos Safamar, C/ Juan de la Cierva 5 | ☎ 952-900 091 |

🖳 *www.skoda.es*

Suzuki

| **Malaga** | Autofusión SL, Avda Velázquez 70 | ☎ 952-239 583 |

🖳 *www.suzuki.es*

Toyota

| **Estepona** | Gallardo Motor, Avda Martín Méndez | ☎ 952-803 539 |

🖳 *www.toyota.es*

Volkswagen

| **Fuengirola** | Safa, Avda Las Gaviotas 1 | ☎ 952-667 044 |

| **Malaga** | Málaga Wagen, Avda Velázquez 62 | ☎ 952-040 259 |

| **Marbella** | Safa, C/ Juan de la Cierva 3 | ☎ 952-828 212 |

🖳 *www.vw-es.com*

Volvo

| **Malaga** | Eymauto, Avda de los Guindos 8 | ☎ 952-360 018 |

| **Marbella** | Fernández Ríos, Ctra de Cádiz km 182 | ☎ 952-861 177 |

🖳 *www.volvocars.es*

Technical Inspection

All cars over four years old must have a control test (*Inspección Téchnica de Vehículos/ITV*) similar to an MOT in the UK, carried out at an authorised test station. You may receive notification of this from the Junta de Andalucía but the onus is on you to remember to take the car for the test. **Note that there are heavy fines for not having a current test certificate.**

The test is valid for two years and is then carried out every two years until the car is ten years old, after which time the test is annual. When your car passes the test you receive a sticker (different colours depending on the year) with the month and year of test punched on it. You should display the sticker on the right-hand side of the windscreen and keep the *ITV* paperwork in your car. The *ITV* test costs around €55 for a car. **Note that ITV stations don't usually accept credit or debit cards and you have to pay in cash.** Note also that employees at the stations may not speak English and if you don't speak enough Spanish to understand their instructions, you should take someone with you who does. Some companies (e.g. garages) provide a service whereby someone takes the car to the *ITV* for you.

ITV stations are always busy and it's best to book an appointment beforehand or to go between 3pm and 4pm when it's usually quiet.

ITV stations on the Costa del Sol are situated at:

- **Axarquía** – Ctra de Algarrobo km1.9, Algarrobo (☎ 952-550 862);

- **Estepona** – Pol Ind Estepona, C/ Graham Bell 15 (☎ 902-221 222);

- **Malaga** – Pol Ind Guadalhorce (☎ 902-221 222);

- **Malaga East** – El Palo, Ronda Este, Salida 247 (☎ 902-221 222).

There are also stations in Antequera and Ronda.

Car Tax

All vehicles registered in Spain are liable for road tax, payable to the local council annually. Rates vary depending on the fiscal horsepower (*potencia fiscal*) of your car, as calculated for tax purposes. The more powerful your car is, the more road tax you pay. Examples of road tax in the main towns on the Costa del Sol are shown in the table below:

Town	Fiscal Horsepower			
	8 – 11.99	12 – 15.99	16 – 19.99	Over 20
Alhaurin (Grande)	€55,55	€102,88	€146,06	€182,56
Benalmadena	€58.61	€123.74	€154.13	€192.64
Coín	€56.91	€120.14	€149.65	€187.04
Estepona	€44.30	€93.52	€116.49	€145.60
Fuengirola	€42.60	€90.00	€112.00	-
Malaga	€54.30	€114.65	€142.85	€178.55
Marbella	€34.08	€71.94	€89.61	€112.00
Mijas	€40.90	€86.34	€107.52	€134.40
Nerja	€50.00	€105.00	€130.00	€163.00
Rincón De La Victoria	€51.12	€107.91	€134.42	€168.00
Torremolinos	€37.08	€79.93	€99.77	€124.32
Vélez-Malaga	€51.12	€107.91	€134.42	€167.98

Note that several councils offer discounts for prompt payment of vehicle taxes. Information on road tax in all areas in the province of Malaga can be found on the Patronato de Recaudación Provincial website (🖳 *www.* prpmalaga.es). Go to '*Tarifas IVTM*' and scroll down and click on the area you're looking for.

Casares

4

Areas

Where to live is a top priority to consider before you move to the Costa del Sol and a difficult question to answer, especially if you're not familiar with the area. Undoubtedly the best move is to rent a property for a few months when you arrive and take your time to explore the different areas and find out what each one has to offer.

The Costa del Sol from Sotogrande to Nerja offers a huge variety of diverse areas with very different characteristics. You can choose from quiet, tranquil urbanisations or busy town centres; from a quiet village to Spain's fifth largest city; from a country retreat to a high-rise penthouse apartment; from urbanisations with a wealth of services to urbanisations with none; from essentially Spanish areas to ones where English is mainly heard.

When deciding where to live you may wish to bear in mind the following considerations:

- **Distance & Time From Malaga Airport** – This is particularly important if you plan to travel to and from the area regularly. Distances from each locality to the airport are included in this chapter, but bear in mind that times vary depending on the traffic and time of year. **Journeys in July and August can take considerably longer than at other times.**

- **Transport Provisions** – In most places on the Costa del Sol private transport is essential unless you live in a town centre or near a train station. If you have children, particularly adolescents, you may wish to consider living near a town centre or near a regular bus route or train station to cut down on the ferrying around you have to do from one activity to another. Further information on **Getting Around** is provided in **Chapter 3**.

- **Price Of Property** – A major deciding factor for most people, some of whom find themselves priced out of many areas of the coast. This chapter includes a brief guide to property prices within each area and further information on different types of accommodation including rental prices can be found in **Chapter 5**.

- **Proximity Of Services & Amenities** – Although the Costa del Sol as a whole provides just about any service imaginable, availability varies depending on the locality. Some are very well-serviced with excellent amenities while others have practically none. Most towns have a good range, but many urbanisations have little more than the odd shop. The proximity of a health centre or clinic may be important if you're older or have young children, and you may wish to live near a school or at least a school bus route. This chapter describes services and amenities in each area. Comprehensive information about health centres is provided in **Chapter 7** and information on state and private schools (both Spanish and international) can be found in **Chapter 8.**

● **Spanish Or Expatriate?** – In some areas the influence of foreigners is so strong, you may be forgiven for thinking you weren't in Spain, while in others the essentially Spanish ambience has been preserved. There are advantages and disadvantages for both environments, and you should consider carefully which you'd prefer. **Bear in mind that the expatriate world is somewhat artificial and, contrary to popular expatriate myth, isn't problem-free.** Your decision may be based on your willingness to learn to speak Spanish and integrate into Spanish society. In many areas English is widely spoken, although you should never assume it will be, and inland and in Malaga English is less widely spoken. **Note, however, that wherever you live, you should make a concerted effort to speak Spanish because in an emergency you will need it.** Further information for different areas is found in this chapter.

● **Peace Or Otherwise?** – Bear in mind that the Costa del Sol is one of the world's top tourist destinations and at peak times (Easter, July and August) the whole coast is packed to bursting point with tourists. Roads are grid-locked, there's only space for one more towel on the beaches and parking is even more impossible than usual. Few places escape the hoards, although undoubtedly inland locations are quieter. Some areas, e.g. Fuengirola and Torremolinos are busy almost all year round, whereas Malaga is relatively quiet in summer. Bear in mind also that Spain is essentially a noisy country (Madrid is the second loudest city in the world after Tokyo) and town and village centres everywhere have more than their fair share of roaring motorbikes, sirens, tooting horns and shouting neighbours. Spaniards are also night owls and noise can continue far into the small hours. **If you want total peace and quiet on the coast, choose a small urbanisation or a remote country property.**

The only real way to decide where to live is to have a good look round before you commit yourself, particularly before buying a property, **and rent before you buy**.

The following chapter provides a detailed description of the towns in the Costa del Sol together with useful information about facilities and services. Towns are divided into different areas and are listed in from west to east. Note that the word to describe a development or purpose-built residential area in Spanish is '*urbanización*', a term that has been 'translated' by expatriates on the Costa del Sol as '*urbanisation*'. The term 'urbanisation' is also used in this book.

AREA ONE – THE WEST

This area stretches from Sotogrande to Marbella.

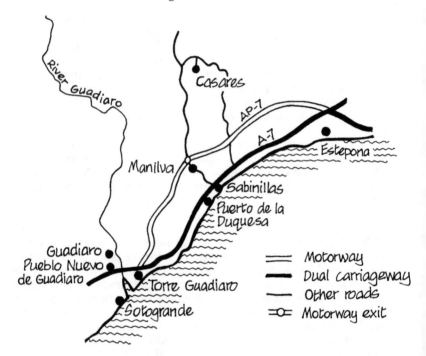

The main localities that can be found in the west of the Costa del Sol are as follows:

- **Estepona** – see page 72;

- **Manilva** –see page 70;

- **Marbella** –see page 77;

- **Sotogrande** –see page 67.

The far western side of the Costa del Sol is currently the least developed, although this is gradually changing as more foreign buyers are attracted to the area's relative tranquillity and in response to this, construction there is now intense, particularly on the Casares and Manilva coasts. The area is less mountainous to the west where there are rolling hills with green pastures and vast cork oak plantations, and several major rivers including the Guadiaro at Sotogrande. Estepona is backed by the dramatic Sierra Bermeja mountain range and Marbella lies at the foot of Sierra Blanca, the southern end of the high Sierra de las Nieves national park where the highest peaks are over 3,000m (nearly 10,000ft).

The western section from Sotogrande to Estepona has a slightly different climate to the rest of the Costa del Sol because of its proximity to the Strait of Gibraltar – it's considerably windier (often very windy hence the windsurfing at nearby Tarifa and the windmill combines in the hills) and wetter.

The section below provides information on the places found in this part of the coast from west to east (see **Map – Sotogrande to Estepona** on page 66).

Sotogrande

Sotogrande lies at the extreme west of the Costa del Sol in the province of Cadiz on the banks of the river Guadiaro and is a luxury purpose-built development of around 5,000 acres in size with its own marina. Much of the property is owned by Spaniards as holiday homes, although the area's also popular with wealthy Gibraltarians who commute daily. Note that although many foreigners own property in Sotogrande, the area has retained its essentially Spanish character. The urbanisation is well-maintained with very attractive tree-lined avenues and is one of the coast's most exclusive and expensive areas. Sotogrande is essentially a holiday destination and outside Easter week and July and August it is very quiet and many services are closed. The urbanisation has 24-hour security including manned security controls at all entrances.

Facts

Population: Resident population is estimated at around 4 to 5,000 (mainly Spanish and British), which swells to over 20,000 in the summer months.
Local Holidays: Sotogrande is administratively part of San Roque which has holidays on 25th May celebrating the foundation of the town and its main fair from 10th to 15th August in honour of San Roque.
Distance From Malaga Airport: 102km (64mi)
Town Hall: San Roque ☎ 956-780 106, Guadiaro ☎ 956-615 109, 🖳 *www. ayuntamientodesanroque.es.*
Local Police Station: ☎ 956-780 256
Medical Facilities: Two private medical centres, one chemist and a small (and inadequate) state health centre at the village of Guadiaro (see below).

Communications

The public transport service is poor and there is just one local service from San Roque to Torreguadiaro, which includes a stop at Sotogrande. There are four buses daily running every three hours or so from around 8.30am to 8pm. During July and August there's a free bus service around the development, but otherwise private transport is essential and distances within the urbanisation are huge.

Property

Sotogrande has some of the most expensive property in Spain and most villas cost in excess of €1 million. Properties are large (most plots are at least 2,000m^2) and built to luxury standards. Maintenance costs are also high, although community charges payable to the urbanisation as a whole are reasonable – €0.40 per m^2 of property a year. Property prices are as follows:

- Two bedroom apartment – from €300,000 (in the Marina from €400,000);

- Two bedroom apartment – from €400,000;

- Three bedroom townhouse – from €600,000;

- Three bedroom villa – from €800,000.

Sotogrande is divided into three main residential areas, these are detailed below.

Sotogrande Alto

Sotogrande Alto is to the north of the A-7 set in rolling hills and based around the Valderrama and Almenara golf courses, which are among the best in the world. Accommodation mainly consists of large villas and some new luxury apartment blocks. **This area has no services.**

Sotogrande Costa

Sotogrande Costa lies to the south of the A-7 and consists essentially of wide avenues with large villas, although some low-rise apartments have been built recently. Note that because the terrain is very flat, properties generally have few or no views. Services include the 'Galerías Paniagua' centre where there's a bank, a chemist, an English-video club, hairdressers, estate agents and property services as well as some bars and restaurants. There's also a recently opened SuperCor supermarket next to the A-7 and a Sotomarket shopping centre is currently under construction next door. The centre, due to be finished in 2005 will house numerous shops and services, and will do much to improve shopping facilities in the area. Sotogrande Costa is home to the Sotogrande Polo Club.

Puerto De Sotogrande

Sotogrande's marina lies to the east of the Guadiaro river and is one of the most attractive in Spain with multi-coloured well-designed apartment blocks. There are several restaurants, banks and shops at the marina, which is very quiet out of season (many businesses are closed during this time). Sotogrande's beaches are mainly grey sand and not particularly well-maintained out of season.

Guadiaro & Pueblo Nuevo De Guadiaro

These two villages lie to the north of the A-7 and are the main service centres for Sotogrande. Guadiaro is small and offers few services, although the post office, public health centre and state primary school are located there. Construction near the village is currently intense. Pueblo Nuevo is larger and offers a better choice of services including small supermarkets, banks, shops and other amenities.

Sotogrande To Manilva

Torreguadiaro lies to the east of Sotogrande marina, a small quiet place with several restaurants and ceramic stores. The coast in this part is quite rocky with little beach. After Torreguadiaro you rejoin the A-7 (**note that speed limit on this stretch is 70kph**) where several small urbanisations (Playa Paraíso, Altea Beach and El Castillo de la Duquesa) are found, consisting mainly of small villas and lowrise apartments, which out of season are very quiet and offer few services other than the odd restaurant and small general store.

Puerto De La Duquesa

This major development, now known as the Duquesa Golden Mile, includes Duquesa Golf, Coto Real Duquesa Golf and Duquesa Village (currently under construction) and Duquesa Marina. Property consists mainly of apartments, townhouses and some villas. Out of season the area is quiet, although it's becoming more popular with permanent residents. Foreign influence in this development is strong and English is widely spoken. Beaches are excellent and well-maintained. The marina is attractive and popular with both residents and tourists looking to get away from the busier resorts on the coast. The marina has a supermarket, several small shops, a bank and numerous restaurants. Property prices are as follows:

- Two bedroom apartment – from €160,000;

- Small villa – from €450,000.

Manilva & Sabinilla

Manilva, on the boundary of the province of Cadiz, has two centres: the main town and administrative centre, some 5km from the coast and Sabinillas, situated on the A-7 itself. Manilva is an attractive white town, famous for its desert grapes (claimed by some to be the best in Spain and ready at the end of August) and wine, and the surrounding countryside is covered in vines. Manilva offers several shops, banks, a health centre, primary and secondary schools, and sports facilities.

Sabinillas is a thriving services centre, divided by the busy A-7, with numerous shops including supermarkets, banks, a health centre and schools. Parking provision is very poor. The area is busy all year round and is essentially Spanish. Property mainly consists of apartment blocks, many of which are holiday homes.

Facts

Population: 7,800
Foreign Population: Approximately 1,100 (mainly British)
Local Holidays: 16th July celebrating the Virgen del Carmen (patron saint of fishermen) and 26th July celebrating Santa Ana, the patron saint.
Distance From Malaga Airport: 90km (56mi)
Town Hall: Manilva ☎ 952-890 065, 🖳 *www.manilva-costadelsol.com* and Sabinillas ☎ 952-890 029.
Local Police Station: ☎ 952-890 945

Property

Manilva and its surrounding area is currently one of the fastest growing on the Costa del Sol and construction in the area is intense – more than 5,000 new homes were built in 2003 and most land in the vicinity is now either under construction or about to be so. Property on offer is mainly apartment accommodation and there's a good choice of both new and resale properties, many of which are either front-line golf or beach. Price per m^2 = €1,767. Property prices are as follows:

● Two bedroom apartment – from €160,000;

● Three bedroom apartment – from €225,000;

● Three bedroom townhouse – from €330,000.

Manilva To Estepona

Once you leave Sabinillas you enter the district of Casares (see below) where the coastline is currently under rapid construction, particularly on the north side of the A-7 where numerous apartment blocks are nearly finished. On the beach side there are several attractive developments including Marina de Casares, Casares del Mar and La Perla de la Bahía. **These developments have no services and private transport is essential.**

Casares

The village of Casares, a popular destination for many foreign residents, lies in the mountains to the north of the coast, some 14km from the A-7, and is considered to be one of the most beautiful villages in the province of Malaga. Its steep streets set on a rocky outcrop crowned by the church and well-preserved Moorish castle have earned it the name of 'hanging village'. The surrounding countryside is stunning, particularly in spring and autumn. Casares is also famous as the birthplace of Blas Infante, the father of Andalusian nationalism. The village has several small shops, a bank, a chemist, a health centre and primary and secondary schools. Casares has higher rainfall than most of the Costa del Sol.

Facts

Population: 3,670
Foreign Population: Approximately 800 (over 20 per cent)
Local Holidays: The main fair takes place during the first two weeks of August; the *Feria de la Virgen del Rosario* at the beginning of September; and the *Feria del Cristo* in mid-September.
Distance From Malaga Airport: 96km (60mi). Exit the A-7 at km 146.
Town Hall: ☎ 952-894 056

Property

Casares is a highly sought after area and as a consequence property is expensive, particularly country houses, although there's a good choice of property on the market. Property on the Casares coast and village houses are cheaper, but note that parking within the village can be difficult. Price per m^2 = €2,003. Property prices are as follows:

● Two bedroom apartment – from €250,000;

● Three bedroom townhouse – from €325,000;

● Three bedroom villa – from €650,000.

Between Casares and Estepona there are several small urbanisations (Bahía Dorada, Arena Beach and Costa Galera), which lie on the coast and consist mainly of small villas with few services.

Estepona

The largest town and main services centre to the west of the Costa del Sol is Estepona, which lies in beautiful natural surroundings and at the foot of the stunning crimson Sierra Bermeja mountains, home to the rare *Pinsapo* pine tree. It's a medium sized town, although growth in the last few years has been spectacular and one that's increasingly popular with foreign residents. The town is attractive and centred around the main church with several pedestrian streets and squares. The promenade is also attractive and the town has tree-lined boulevards at its entrances. The town is less developed than other coastal towns and has retained much of its original character and is probably the most 'Spanish' of the tourism resorts. The 23km (14mi) of coastline has excellent and well-maintained beaches with life-saving staff during the summer months.

Facts

Population: 47,000
Foreign Population: Approximately 7,500 (mainly British)
Local Holidays: 15th May is the town's patron saint's day (*día de San Isidro Labrador*). The main fair takes places during the first week of July and Estepona also celebrates the Virgen del Carmen on 16th July.
Distance From Malaga Airport: 80km (50mi)
Town Hall: Estepona ☎ 952-801 100 and Cancelada ☎ 952-883 785
Local Police Station: ☎ 952-808 040
Foreign Residents Department: ☎ 952-802 002. The office is based at the tourist office.

Services

Estepona has excellent services and amenities. Shopping facilities are good and include a Carrefour hypermarket (open 9am to 10pm Mondays to Saturdays) on the outskirts in the east and a daily indoor market for fresh produce as well as numerous shops in the centre. The town has numerous leisure facilities including a sports centre, marina and many golf courses in the immediate vicinity. An indoor pool is due to open shortly.
Medical Services: There are two public health centres and advanced plans for a day hospital, which will include beds for emergency cases, due to be completed in the near future. There are also numerous private clinics and practices.

Communications

There is one local bus that runs from the *policía local* station in the west of the town to Carrefour in the east and back. The services run hourly from 7am to 9pm and costs €0.90. Parking is difficult in Estepona, particularly around the centre, although a large municipal car park in the Avda de Andalucía in the centre is currently under construction.

Property

The property market in Estepona, both in the town and district, is currently booming and there are a lot of new developments. There's a good choice of property available, both resale and new. Reflecting the current boom, prices in Estepona have risen even more sharply than the rest of the Costa del Sol and since September 2002 have gone up some 34 per cent! The average price per m^2 in the town is now €2,481. Property prices are as follows:

● Two bedroom apartment – from €220,000 (not front-line beach);

● Three bedroom apartment – from €250,000;

● Three bedroom townhouse – from €350,000;

● Three bedroom villa – from €600,000.

Estepona To Marbella

The Estepona coastline to the east of the town is growing fast and development is currently intense and there's now little land left to build on.

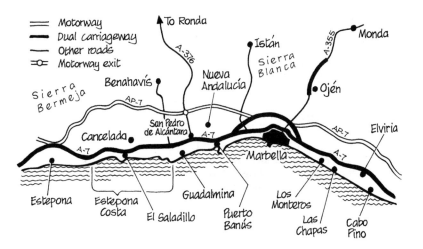

This area is home to numerous urbanisations on both sides of the A-7, some of which are luxury (e.g. Dominion Beach and Cabo Bermejo), others more modest (e.g. El Saladillo and Costalita), as well as several commercial centres and hotels, including the 5-star 'Great Luxury' Kempinsky and Las Dunas hotels. The area is very much influenced by foreigners and English is widely spoken. Property is mainly apartments and townhouses, although some small urbanisations also have villas. The beaches are grey sand and well-maintained all-year round.

From west to east the main urbanisations are: Alcazaba Beach; Dominion Beach; Hacienda Beach; Selwo Hills; Cabo Bermejo where Estepona's Golden Mile is situated (known as the New Golden Mile) and Costalita II development; Park Beach; Costalita; El Saladillo (one of the coast's first developments) on the beach side opposite Bel Air; Benamara and the large El Paraiso to the north of the A-7; and Atalaya on the west bank of the Guadalmina river.

Facts

Services

There are several small commercial centres (e.g. CC Diana, CC Bel Air) housing a variety of services, although estate agents, restaurants and furniture shops predominate. The area has chemists, two supermarkets (Mercadona and Supersol at km 166) and little else in the way of essential shops. There are also several large garden centres. **Private transport is essential in this area since you may need to go from one commercial centre to another to buy different things or go to Estepona or Marbella.**

The administrative area of Estepona ends at the Guadalmina river, where on the east side the district of Marbella starts. There's a short stretch of the A-7 before you reach San Pedro de Alcántara, where the exclusive urbanisation of Guadalmina is found. This is home to an attractive golf course and many luxury residences.

San Pedro De Alcantara

San Pedro de Alcántara (known simply as San Pedro) lies to the west of Marbella and although it belongs to Marbella it's really a town in its own right rather than an outlying district. The town is centred around the attractive church square, although there are many new developments to the south of the A-7 (Nueva Alcántara) and to the north of the town, known as San Pedro Norte. The town is popular with foreign residents and has all the services and amenities you'd expect including numerous shops, restaurants and bars, schools and sports facilities. English is widely spoken and in some parts of the town it is the only language you hear. San Pedro has an attractive sea-front walk with numerous beach bars. Beaches are generally good and well-maintained.

Nueva Alcántara

This new development to the south of the town centre includes a port, residential blocks (mainly apartments), Kings College, and shops and businesses. The shopping centre, Alcántara Plaza, due to open in 2005 will house a large supermarket and multi-screen cinema.

Facts

Local Holidays: San Bernabé on 11th June and the main fair during the third week of October (19th is a holiday) in honour of San Pedro, the patron saint.
Distance From Malaga Airport: 63km (39mi)
Town Hall: ☎ 952-782 800
Local Police Station: ☎   952-783 099

Communications

There is one bus route: Line 4 (San Pedro centre to La Campana-Puerto Banús). Buses run from 7am to 11pm. San Pedro's main disadvantage is the fact that the A-7 runs right through the centre and its almost continual gridlocks ruin the town's general tranquillity. The long-awaited bypass appears to have been approved at last and work should start it in the very near future. Most of the A-7 will be underground as it goes through San Pedro. Parking is difficult in the town centre.

Property

Property prices are as follows:

- Two bedroom apartment – from €250,000;

- Three bedroom apartment – from €275,000;

- Three bedroom townhouse – from €350,000;

- Three bedroom villa – from €650,000.

Across the Verde river bridge to the east of San Pedro lies Nueva Andalucía (to the north of the A-7) and Puerto Banús (to the south of the A-7). **This area is very 'foreign' and in many areas English is the main language you will hear.**

Nueva Andalucía

Nueva Andalucía is one of the Costa del Sol's largest urbanisations and is popular with foreign residents, particularly golfers (the northern end of Nueva Andalucía is home to several golf courses and is known as 'Golf

Valley' – see page 245) and has many attractive developments, with both apartment and villa accommodation. Many new developments are currently under construction, particularly to the north and east along the river. Services are concentrated mainly near the A-7 where there are schools (state and private), shops, a supermarket, banks, numerous restaurants and bars, and other services. The area's health centre is found on the west side **near** the church. Local buses run to and from Marbella.
Town Hall: ☎ 952-814 119

Puerto Banús

Puerto Banús (often referred to as just Banús) is Spain's jet-set haunt *par excellence*, set against the magnificent backdrop of Sierra Blanca and home to one of the world's finest luxury marinas. The marina has berths for over 900 boats and depth for the world's largest private yachts. It's surrounded by attractive apartment blocks, most of which are luxury, with a wealth of shops, mainly fashion (glitter and sequins line most of the shelves) including many top designer names, restaurants (from fastfood to *haute cuisine*) and bars. In the summer Banús is **the** place to be seen (and to see!) on the Costa del Sol and famous faces abound. It's also the place to go if you're rich and need to show it.

Note that the port gets very busy at night during high season when there are long queues to get in. Parking is available at several underground carparks (at a cost of around €1.50 an hour) and at the Corte Inglés during shopping hours (10am to 10pm). Parking in the port is for berth owners only.

Banús has good services including two shopping centres, a large Corte Inglés and multi-screen cinema. Buses run from Marbella and San Pedro. Banús has several small well-maintained beaches and is connected to Marbella by a attractive promenade. More information about Banús is available from the town hall (☎ 952-908 037).

Banus To Marbella Centre

From the east of Banús to Marbella city centre is the Costa del Sol's most exclusive area known as the Golden Mile (*Milla de Oro*). Residences include huge luxury mansions such as the vast palatial residence belonging to King Fahd of Saudi Arabia, complete with mosque. Some of Marbella's top hotels such as Marbella Club and Puente Romano are also found along this stretch where green areas predominate. Development has been intense over the last few years in this area and some feel some of its quintessential tranquillity and exclusiveness has been lost. Services in the area are mainly concentrated towards the east end. As you'd expect, property is very expensive and apartments start at €500,000 and villas at well over €1 million.

Marbella

Marbella is the Costa del Sol's most famous resort and was one of Spain's first tourist destinations in the early '60s. The city, once a humble fishing village, has a worldwide reputation for attracting *la crème de la crème* tourists and certainly many rich and famous visit throughout the year or have homes there. The original town is based around a Moorish castle fortress (some walls are still visible) and has many attractive and typically Andalusian small streets centred around the Plaza de los Naranjos (Orange Square). Since the '60s the city has grown in all directions and has had a major facelift in recent years, the main results of which are large tree and plant-lined boulevards, and a much improved sea-front. Development has been frenetic in the city over the last eight years and practically all available land has been built on.

Marbella's most exclusive areas are: the Golden Mile between the city and Puerto Banús, home to several top hotels and some of Europe's most expensive properties; Nagüeles and Urb Sierra Blanca to the north-west of the city; and Hacienda Las Chapas and Los Monteros to the east.
Marbella has excellent well-maintained beaches with some of the best beach bars on the coast.

Facts

Population: 115,871
Foreign Population: Approximately 16,000
Local Holidays: San Bernabé on 11th June (the main fair takes place during this week) and San Pedro on 19th October.
Distance From Malaga Airport: 55km (34mi)
Town Hall: ☎ 952-761 100, 🖥 *www.marbella.es*
Local Police Station: ☎ 952-899 900
Foreign Residents Department: ☎ 952-761 116

Services

Marbella has generally excellent services and amenities, although critics claim the rapid increase in population has outgrown the services, which are now over-stretched. Shopping is good, although many of the shops in the town centre are for those with fat wallets only. More modest prices can be found in the smaller shops in the less-exclusive districts to the north or east and in La Cañada shopping centre, north of the A-7. Sports facilities are excellent.
Medical Services: Marbella has two public health centres and numerous private clinics and practices (if you cannot get something done medically in Marbella, you cannot get it done anywhere!). The Western Costa del Sol's hospital lies to the east of the city and there's also a large private hospital in the centre.

Communications

Marbella has two local bus routes: Line 1 (West end to centre/centre to La Cañada) and Line 2 (Las Albarizas to centre/centre to Don Miguel). Buses run from 7am to 11pm. **Traffic congestion is chronic throughout most of Marbella, particularly round the old ring-road and at the main entrances to the centre.** Parking facilities are much improved and there are several underground car parks.

Property

Marbella has some of the most expensive property in Spain (and in Europe) and since September 2002 prices for apartments alone have risen some 25 per cent. There's a buoyant property market in the city for both resale and new developments, and a range of property is available from an apartment in a more-Spanish district to a luxury residence in huge grounds. In 2003 new construction finally slowed down after years of frantic building, although Marbella was still the area where most new building projects started (some 15,000!). Property rates in Marbella are the highest on the Costa del Sol and there's also a twice-yearly refuse collection tax, also extremely high. Rates are set to increase in the very near future as the council attempts to find ways to finance its legacy of huge municipal debt (see **Politics** below). Price per m^2 = €2,263. Property prices are as follows:

- Two bedroom apartment – from €275,000;

- Three bedroom apartment – from €325,000;

- Three bedroom townhouse – from €375,000;

- Three bedroom villa – from €700,000.

In recent years numerous developments have been built in the city with illegal building licences issued by the council with disregard to regional planning laws. As a result, certain developments currently have an uncertain legal status – some are subject to ongoing court cases. The situation is currently uncertain and it will take a while for the authorities to come to a compromise over the legal status. Meanwhile if you plan to buy an off-plan property or a new or recently finished property in Marbella, ask your lawyer to double-check its legal status.

Politics

It's difficult to talk about Marbella without mentioning its politics, which are infamous in Spain and the on-going 'soap opera' of scandals, corruption and political *coups* has filled many a news bulletin. Marbella was governed for eight years (1995 to 2003) by GIL, led by Jesús Gil a businessman whose main interests were property and football (he was the president of Atlético Madrid) and whose self-proclaimed aim was to transform the rather decadent city into an attractive vibrant one where people would flock to buy property (including his developments).

Whilst undoubtedly he did much to improve Marbella, he also allowed unrestrained development throughout the area including areas designated for green zones and services such as schools and municipal centres. Much of this development was illegal and led to numerous confrontations with provincial and regional authorities. Numerous scandals emerged and in 2002 Jesús Gil was banned from public office.

The current situation is somewhat delicate since the council has astronomical debts, several councillors are awaiting trial for embezzlement of public funds and corruption, and numerous new developments have been halted because they were given illegal building licences by the council. Recent events have led to talks between the council and regional authorities to try to solve the building licence problem, but the financial problems are likely to last well into the future.

Inland From Marbella

In the mountains north of Marbella are several small villages, many of which are popular with foreign residents and visitors seeking tranquillity and a more-Spanish environment, yet one that's still within easy reach of the services and amenities on the coast. The main villages are Benahavís, Istán, Monda and Ojén.

Benahavís

The small village of Benahavís lies to the west of San Pedro some 8km from the A-7 (exit at km 169) at the end of a beautiful verdant valley where the Guadalmina river runs. The Guadalmanza and Guadaiza rivers are also in the area. It's an attractive mountain village known for its numerous excellent restaurants (Benahavís claims to be the Costa del Sol's gastronomic capital) and art work (crafts and painting). There are several small shops, one bank, a small health centre and a primary school.

Facts

Population: 2,204
Foreign Population: Approximately 644 (around 475 are British)
Local Holidays: Main fair from 11th to 15th August and Virgin of the Rosary 6th and 7th October.

Distance From Malaga Airport: 72km (45mi)
Town Hall: ☎ 952-855 025
Local Police Station: ☎ 952-855 544

Property

The village has several urbanisations within and around the centre such as La Fuente de Benahavís, Las Lomas de Benahavís and La Pacheca where property is expensive. New construction is currently intense at the foot of the village and along the river valley. Several developments on the Ronda road (Los Arqueros, La Zagaleta and Urb Madroñal) lie within the village's administrative district. Property prices are as follows:

● Two bedroom apartment – from €170,000;

● Three bedroom townhouse – from €350,000;

● Villas – from €850,000.

Istan

Istán is situated some 16km to the west of Marbella at the foot of the Sierra de las Nieves natural park and at the north end of the *Concepción* reservoir, which provides the main water supply for most of the west of the coast. Access to the village is from the Golden Mile or the A-7 km 177 exit.

The small mountain village, set in stunning scenery, is famous for its pure spring water and has numerous fountains. The architecture mainly consists of cubic, flat-roofed houses reminiscent of Moroccan architecture. The village has several small shops, two banks, a small health centre and a primary school as well as restaurants and rural hotels. The village is popular with mountain bikers and walkers as there are several hiking routes in the vicinity.

Few foreigners live in the village itself which remains essentially Spanish, although the Cerros del Lago and Sierra Blanca Country Club developments on the way to Istán is very popular with foreign buyers.

Facts

Population: 1,340
Foreign Population: Approximately 120
Local Holidays: 25th April in honour of San Marcos and 29th September in honour of San Miguel (the festivities last three days).
Distance From Malaga Airport: 70km (44mi)
Town Hall: ☎ 952-869 603, 🖳 *www.istan.es*

Property

Little property is available in the village itself, but the urbanisations situated on the way to Istán are popular with foreign residents. Property starts at €350,000 for a 3-bedroom townhouse and from €900,000 for a villa.

Monda

The white village of Monda lies 20km north of Marbella on the A-355 road, set in small plots of agricultural land (mainly citrus plantations) and behind the high Sierra de las Nieves mountains. The village is famous for its Roman castle, which crowns the village and is now a popular hotel and restaurant. The Marbella Gun & Country Club is also nearby. Monda has several small shops, two banks, numerous restaurants and a school. The village remains essentially Spanish, although English is spoken in most places.

Facts

Population: 2,085
Foreign Population: Officially around 150, mainly British and German, although unofficial figures estimate the true population to be nearer 300.
Local Holidays: 16th August in honour of San Roque (festivities last for four days).
Distance From Malaga Airport: 71km (44mi)
Town Hall: ☎ 952-457 069

Property

Monda is increasingly popular with foreign buyers looking for cheaper property than that found on the coast. The type of property available is mainly village townhouses or country properties (*fincas*), most of which have large plots of land. Price per m^2 = €1,302. Property prices are as follows:

● Two bedroom townhouse – from €170,000;

● Three bedroom townhouse – from €230,000;

● Three bedroom *finca* – from €500,000.

Ojén

Ojén (8km north of Marbella) is a very attractive white village set in the Sierra de la Nieves Natural Park and is popular with foreign residents looking for peace and quiet in natural surroundings yet within easy reach of services and facilities on the coast. Views of the coast and Mediterranean from practically all properties in the village are stunning. Ojén has several small shops, two banks, restaurants, a school, health centre and a sports complex with outdoor pool. **Note that streets in the village are steep and many are unsuitable for car access.** The Ojén flamenco singing festival (Festival del Cante Jondo) in August in one of the most famous in Spain.

Ojén is also famous for other reasons. The village is a socialist stronghold and has its own television station, Ojén TV, which provides an opportunity for Marbella residents to rant and rave about criminal activities in the city and the mayor's alleged involvement in them ... and all with public money!

Facts

Population: 2,085
Foreign Population: Officially around 200, although the unofficial figure is higher.
Local Holidays: Ojén's main festivities take place from 9th to 13th October in honour of the village's (difficult to pronounce) patron saint, San Dionisio de Aeropaguita.
Distance From Malaga Airport: 65km (41mi)
Town Hall: ☎ 952-881 003, 🖳 *www.webojen.org*

Property

There's little property for sale in the village itself, but you may find country properties on the outskirts on the market. Price per m^2 = €1,302. Prices start at €300,000 for a small property needing renovation.

Marbella To Cabopino Marina

This stretch of the coast has some of the most prestigious urbanisations in Marbella and several are classed as luxury. Property on this side of the city also has the best and uninterrupted views, although the terrain on the north side of the A-7 can be steep. This area also has some of the best beaches on the Costa del Sol – the sand is golden and clean, and the sea is safe and doesn't slope quickly. **Note that to reach anywhere along this stretch of the coast you have to use the A-7 since the motorway exits are in Marbella and Calahonda only.** Urbanisations from west to east are detailed below.

Urb El Real, home to one of the coast's oldest golf courses, Río Real, and to the world-famous Incosol clinic where the rich go for de-stressing and slimming treatments.

Urb Los Monteros to the south of the A-7 is among the largest on the this side of Marbella and houses many luxury villas as well as numerous new developments including Bahía de Marbella and the luxury Monteros hotel.

On the opposite side is the new Santa Clara Golf development where property mainly consists of large semi-detached villas. A shopping centre, which will include a large supermarket is being built near the hospital and is expected to be finished in late 2004. Otherwise there are no services.

Urb Las Chapas is a small development with apartments at the north and south ends, and villas along most of its streets. On the other side is El Rosario, a luxury urbanisation consisting of large villas and popular with Germans and British particularly. El Rosario and Las Chapas have two supermarkets, a newsagents and limited property services.

Urb Playas Andaluzas and Urb Costabella are popular areas with tourists and foreign residents, as property is cheaper than in the rest of Marbella. New development has been intense in recent years and many apartment blocks have been built. Services include a supermarket, chemist and ironmongers.

Elviria

Elviria is the main services and administrative centre for the surrounding area known as Las Chapas. The urbanisation is well-designed and has a mixture of high-quality apartments (particularly to the north in the area known as Elviria Hills) and villas. The area is popular with foreign residents, particularly British and German. Elviria has a church, state primary school (up to the of age 14 – a secondary school for the area is long overdue), numerous shops and a sizeable shopping centre with many services including a large supermarket, restaurants and bars, and some of the best beaches on the Costa del Sol. Private health services are available. Property is expensive and you can expect to pay from €325,000 for a two-bedroom apartment and from €800,000 for a villa.

Up in the mountains is La Mairena, an exclusive development with some of the best views anywhere, although it's quite a drive to get up to see them and down again to any services and amenities!
Town Hall: ☎ 952-838 410

To the east of Elviria is one of Marbella's most exclusive urbanisations, Hacienda Las Chapas where there are many large attractive villas on large plots, although no services. Construction (mainly apartment blocks) is currently intense to the north of this urbanisation, which some claim is losing its exclusiveness. The urbanisations of Carib Playa and Artola follow, a mixture of apartment, townhouse and villa accommodation with some of the cheapest prices and some of the most expensive. Artola has a chemist and there's a small commercial centre opposite at Doña Pepa. Artola is home to one of the Costa del Sol's last dune areas (*las Dunas de Artola*), which have recently been declared a protected area. Cabopino is the eastern-most urbanisation in Marbella and is an attractive small marina with apartments, many restaurants and bars, and some small shops. A new commercial centre has recently opened housing several shops.

AREA TWO – CENTRAL COSTA DEL SOL

The main localities that can be found in central Costa del Sol are as follows:

● **Benalmadena** – see page 95;

● **Fuengirola** – see page 92;

● **Mijas Costa** – see page 85;

● **Torremolinos**– see page 97.

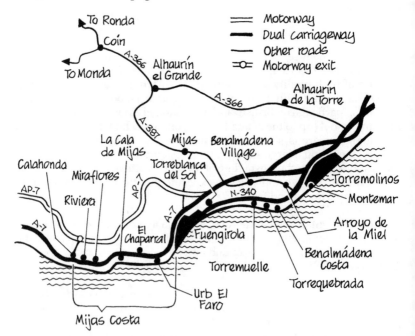

The Costa del Sol in the section from Calahonda to Torremolinos is, with the exception of the city of Malaga, the most densely populated and built-up. There's little unbuilt terrain left along the coast in this section and the urbanisations and towns merge into one long urban sprawl. Within the sprawl there are great contrasts: low-rise urbanisations with the emphasis on green zones and natural surroundings as well as stretches of high-rise tower blocks reflecting some of the worst urban planning in Spain (mostly a legacy from the '60s and '70s).

Many parts of this section of the coast are more accessible to the average wage earner and, although some areas can be classed as up-market, there's not the same degree of luxury as is found in Marbella and Sotogrande. This area is also probably the most influenced by foreigners and in many towns and villages you're more likely to hear a foreign language spoken in the street than Spanish.

The huge advantage of this part of the coast is that it offers the biggest choice of amenities and services within easy reach as well as lying within close proximity to Malaga. The following section provides a description of the localities along the coast from west to east: Mijas Costa, Mijas, Fuengirola, Benalmadena and Torremolinos as well as the inland towns of Alhaurín de la Torre, Alhaurín el Grande and Coín.

Mijas Costa

Calahonda To La Cala

Mijas Costa is the area that runs along the coast from Cabopino in the west to Fuengirola in the east. The area is residential with numerous urbanisations, popular with both holiday-makers and permanent foreign residents who are mainly British, German or Scandinavian. **Note that although the urbanisations start on the coast at the A-7, many continue several kilometres to the north on often steep roads.** Services and amenities are mainly concentrated near the A-7 and if you choose to live up at the north end of the urbanisations, you will need a car for practically everything. **Many of the urbanisations are labyrinths of streets and it's often impossible to find your way around.** Most have a map at the entrance or strategically placed around the maze, but it's best to make sure you have good instructions about how to find somewhere.

Property

A huge choice of property is on the market on the western side of Mijas Costa, particularly new constructions; some 12,000 new properties were started in and around Mijas in 2003, an increase of 43 per cent, and many of these are found in Calahonda and Riviera. Prices in Calahonda and Riviera del Sol are very similar, but you can expect to pay slightly more in Miraflores and less in Calypso and Torrenueva. Price per m^2 = €2,043. Property prices are as follows:

- Two bedroom apartment – from €175,000;

- Three bedroom apartment – from €220,000;

- Three bedroom townhouse – from €300,000;

- Three bedroom villa – from €500,000.

Below is a description of the main urbanisations to the west of La Cala in Mijas Costa (listed from west to east) together with a brief account of the services and amenities you can expect to find there.

Calahonda

Calahona (Urb Sitio de Calahonda) is an attractive residential area and Spain's largest urbanisation (estimated population around 10,000, mainly British and Scandinavian). The area is well-maintained with many green areas, including three parks. Housing is a mixture of villas and townhouses in the areas nearest the coast and apartment accommodation in the north.

Services

Calahonda has three shopping centres, all situated on the A-7 with supermarkets, banks and other small shops where you get most daily necessities; a petrol station at nearby Calypso; numerous restaurants and bars and several night clubs; several private health clinics and a garden centre. There's also a Catholic Church (services in English on Sunday) and Baptist Church.

Communications

Calahonda is the only place in the area with an exit from the A-7 motorway from Fuengirola to Marbella. Calahonda also has a local 'train' service from Mondays to Saturdays, running from east to west via the top of the urbanisation. The train runs every hour for most of the year and every half hour during the summer months.

Urb Calypso

Calypso is a small urbanisation, consisting mainly of small villas and some apartment blocks situated mostly near the A-7. Facilities include a petrol station, chemist, supermarket, banks and restaurants. Property in Calypso is among the cheapest in the area.

Riviera del Sol

Riviera de Sol (usually known simply as Riviera) is a built-up urbanisation with mainly apartment accommodation and several holiday complexes, and extensive development is currently taking place in the north. There are attractive wide avenues flanked by palm trees and services include a supermarket, restaurants and a chemist, which are all situated near the A-7. Riviera has a sports centre (Aztec) and a golf course. Other facilities can be found at nearby Calahonda.

Miraflores

This exclusive development lies to the east of Riviera and consists of the attractive Miraflores Golf Club and Course (one of the oldest and most prestigious in the area) and apartment and villa accommodation.

The beaches on this stretch of the coast are poor, mainly small coves with a mixture of sand and stones, and are rarely maintained out of season. **Beware of treading on sea urchins – the spikes are very painful and difficult to get out.**

Torrenueva

Torrenueva is currently under vast expansion, particularly to the north and east where the development joins La Cala. The older part of the urbanisation mainly consists of villas with apartment blocks near the A-7 and facilities include a supermarket and chemist. The new section, known as Jardín Botánico, has mainly apartment accommodation and restaurants. Torrenueva has recently been connected to Miraflores and Riviera by road, providing an alternative to the A-7. Torrenueva has excellent sandy and well-maintained beaches (a continuation of La Cala bay), **but beware that the sea shelves sharply and you can find yourself very quickly out of your depth.**

La Cala To Fuengirola

La Cala De Mijas

The small village of La Cala de Mijas (known simply as La Cala) lies in a long sandy bay and remains a quiet fishing village in spite of the development around it. Central to the village is a recently restored 10th century watchtower, now a museum, set in a small square surrounded by restaurants and bars. La Cala has retained its essentially Spanish character and is popular with young families. The prestigious Cala Golf Resort is situated in the valley a few miles north of the village. The golf resort forms part of Mijas Golf Valley, which stretches as far as Alhaurín el Grande and currently includes several top courses, with advanced plans for more (see page 247).

Facts

Local Holidays: The village fair is held around 25th July and on 15th October the patron of La Cala, Santa Teresa, is honoured.
Town Hall: ☎ 952-493 208
Local Police Station: ☎ 952-460 808
Foreign Residents Department: ☎ 952-493 208

Services

The village is the local services and administrative centre for the council where you can pay local taxes, present paperwork and register with the council. Amenities include a health centre, chemist, several private clinics and one dental clinic. All serve English-language speakers. La Cala has a large shopping centre with a supermarket, opticians, restaurants, banks and other services including a post office. There are also numerous small shops within the village where you can get just about anything. There are two state primary schools, CP El Chaparral and CP García del Olmo (3 to 12-year-olds) plus one secondary school (12 to 16-year-olds), which are designated for the Mijas Costa catchment areas. There's also a state nursery school (1 to 3-year-olds).

Property

There are advanced projects for major development in La Cala, particularly in the area to the north of the A-7 and several thousand homes are planned. Currently under extensive development is the huge Cala Nova golf resort consisting of some 2,000 homes (mainly apartments), a hotel and 18-hole golf course due to be finished in stages between now and 2008. Prices for a two-bedroom apartment start at €255,000. The emblematic regional Hotel School is also under construction and due to open in late 2004.

Other Urbanisations

Urb Los Claveles, Urb La Cortijera, Urb Alcántara and Urb Las Buganvillas are urbanisations which lie to the east and are within easy reach of La Cala and consist mainly of villas on large plots, although there is some apartment accommodation. Los Clavales is the main development and the other urbanisations are relatively small. The area is quiet and has plenty of green areas, including pine woods. There are few facilities except for a chemist and some restaurants situated near the A-7.

Urb El Chaparral is the largest urbanisation to the east of La Cala and is an exclusive development consisting mainly of large villas and plots. There are no services other than a couple of restaurants on the A-7. There are small coves (sand and stones) and a very popular beach bar. There are also two more urbanisations called Urb Oasis and Urb Las Farolas.

Urb Playa Marina and Urb El Faro are small urbanisations which lie just before the point where the coast turns northwards and the lighthouse is situated. Playa Marina is mainly apartment accommodation (some of which is time share) and has a chemist and some restaurants. El Faro, popular with German residents, is larger and has both apartment and villa accommodation. There are several restaurants in the area. The main beach is a small cove (sand and stones) with a beach bar.

The Fuengirola bus service has a route from Playa Marina to the town, which runs every hour.

El Faro de Calaburras is a small urbanisation with steep, winding streets, currently poorly maintained. Property is mainly villas. The other urbanisations, such as Urb Marina del Sol, Urb La Ponderosa & Urb El Castillo, offer apartment, townhouse and villa accommodation, and are popular because they're quiet but within close proximity to Fuengirola. The main beach is at Faro de Calaburras and is a narrow strip of sand, which in spite of its small size and being right next to the A-7, is packed to capacity during the summer. There's a local bus service to Fuengirola with stops on the A-7, which runs every hour.

Facts

Property

Expect to pay more for property in Los Claveles and El Chaparral, but less in Urb El Faro and El Castillo. Price per m² = €2,043. Property prices are as follows:

- Two bedroom apartment – from €210,000;

- Three bedroom apartment – from €250,000;

- Three bedroom townhouse – from €330,000;

- Three bedroom villa – from €750,000.

Mijas

Mijas is the administrative centre for Mijas Costa, Las Lagunas and numerous urbanisations to the north and west of Fuengirola, which together cover an area of 150km². Mijas is a typical Andalusian white village with attractive narrow streets situated in the mountain range above Fuengirola. Sites of interest in this much visited village are the church, bull ring and the typical Andalusian streets. Donkey taxis are another attraction. The large council building with all departments is situated in the centre of the village, which is usually busy in the mornings when coach loads of tourists visit, but quiet otherwise.

Mijas is one of the richest places in Spain and was, during the '90s, one of the few councils 'in the black'. Municipal finance has since moved into the red, but Mijas' income remains high, mainly thanks to rates paid by the numerous residential areas on the coast. **Note, however, that the council invests little in the urbanisations.**

Facts

Population: 55,413
Foreign Population: Mijas has a large foreign population, which accounts for nearly 40 per cent of the total and this population continues to grow, almost daily. Almost half the foreigners are British.
Local Holidays: On 2nd June the patron of the village, la Virgen de la Peña, is honoured and a week-long fair is also held in her name in the second week of September.
Distance From Malaga Airport: 24 km (15mi)
Town Hall: ☎ 952-485 900, 🖳 *www.mijas.es*
Local Police Station: ☎ 952-486 228
Foreign Residents Department: ☎ 952-485 900

Services

Services and amenities in the village are limited and there's little choice in the small shops unless you're a souvenir buyer in which case Mijas is your oyster! There's an adequate health centre and chemist. Mijas also has a post office, primary and secondary schools, and sports facilities situated mainly at Osunillas to the east of the village.

Property

Within the village itself property is expensive and some luxury apartments fetch among the highest prices on the coast. Outside the centre, however, you can find cheaper property unless you want to buy in one of the exclusive urbanisations such as Las Lomas where villas cost from €800,000. Price per m^2 = €2,043. Property prices are as follows:

- Two bedroom apartment – from €165,000 outside village, from €200,000 in village;

- Three bedroom apartment – from €225,000;

- Three bedroom townhouse – from €350,000;

- Three bedroom villa – from €600,000.

Mijas includes the densely populated area of Las Lagunas and numerous urbanisations to the north of Fuengirola, which aren't really part of Mijas Costa. The main localities are as follows:

Las Lagunas

This residential area, popular with Spaniards but less so with foreigners, is densely populated and currently under huge expansion. Housing is mainly apartments and townhouses. Services and facilities are good and include numerous shops, schools, a health centre, chemists, supermarkets and a large municipal sports centre with indoor pool. The Mijas Costa Corte Inglés shopping centre will be situated in Las Lagunas (due to open at Easter in 2005). A bus service runs from the area to Fuengirola. **Traffic congestion is chronic in the area, particularly during rush hour, mainly because there are only two access roads to the district, both of which are single-lane.** Property is among the cheapest on this side of the coast and prices for a two-bedroom apartment start at €130,000.

Facts

Local Holidays: The area's annual fair takes place during the first week of June and 15th October, Santa Teresa. Because of the area's close proximity to Fuengirola, residents in Las Lagunas quite often take Fuengirola local holidays as well.
Town Hall: Las Lagunas ☎ 952-473 125

Other Urbanisations

Urb El Coto, Urb Campo Mijas & Urb La Sierrezuela are urbanisations located directly north of Fuengirola and can be reached from the Avda de Mijas continuation or from the Mijas road at the BP roundabout. **Both access roads get very congested, particularly the Avda de Mijas.** Urb El Coto is the largest and consists mainly of villa accommodation. Services are good and include several small shops, a chemist, a school, restaurants and a bus service from Fuengirola. La Sierrezuela is an upmarket urbanisation with many exclusive villas and the most expensive property in the area.

Urb Cerros del Aguila is a small but rapidly expanding development situated to the west of Fuengirola and the river in attractive rolling hills. Access is via the Myramar complex opposite the castle. Housing is mainly villas and apartments, and there are few services on site. There's a bus service to and from Fuengirola starting at the cemetary on route to Cerros del Aguila.

Urb Mijas Golf

This urbanisation lies to the north of Fuengirola on the east side of the Fuengirola River and is centred around the attractive Mijas Golf course. Accommodation is mainly apartment and villas, and the area has several prestigious hotels including the luxury Hotel Byblos Andaluz. **There are few amenities on site and private transport is essential.** Access to the area is poor via the Coín road from Fuengirola, which is often gridlocked for the first few kilometres.

Property

There's usually a good selection of resale property and most apartments are front-line golf. Property prices are as follows:

● Two bedroom apartment – from €225,000;

● Three bedroom apartment – from €275,000;

● Three bedroom villa – from €700,000.

Fuengirola

Fuengirola has traditionally been a resort favoured by British and Spanish tourists, although recent years have seen an influx of other nationalities making it one of the most cosmopolitan places on the Costa del Sol. Fuengirola is very built-up and its long beaches and wide promenade stretching for over 8km (5mi) are flanked by high-rise apartment blocks and hotels, although there's a small town centre where traditional squares with white houses still survive.

The town's had an almost complete facelift in recent months and as a result has improved beyond recognition – many streets have wide pavements and are tree-lined, and parking is easier. The sea-front promenade is attractive. Beaches are excellent, sandy and well-maintained with access for the disabled and numerous beach bars. Sohail Castle, at the entrance to the town in the west, dates from the 10th century and is now used for cultural and social events.

Fuengirola is one of the coast's busiest towns – low season no longer exists and the streets are always very busy with both tourists and residents.

Los Boliches

The area to the east of the town and the dry river known as Los Boliches, is almost a town in its own right and is particularly popular with foreigners. Services and amenities are excellent, and it's generally quieter than the centre.

Los Pacos

The area of Los Pacos, situated to the east of the centre between the N-340 and the A-7, is currently Fuengirola's main expansion zone and construction is intense (apartments and townhouses mainly), principally because it's the only part of Fuengirola left to build on! Access is currently via the Avda de Finlandia, which is single-lane and congestion is chronic.

A further access road (north-west of the Avda de Finlandia) is currently under construction – it will link directly with the A-7. This area, popular with Finns in particular, has good services including state and private schools, small shops and a bus route (red line) from Fuengirola.

Facts

Population: 53,270
Foreign Population: Approximately 10,600 (mainly British and Finnish)
Local Holidays: 16th July (Virgen del Carmen) and 8th October celebrating the Virgen del Rosario, the patron saint of the town, when the main fair lasts a week.
Distance From Malaga Airport: 24 km (15mi)
Town Hall: ☎ 952-589 300, 🖥 *www.fuengirola.org* and Los Boliches ☎ 952-460 750.
Local Police Station: ☎ 952-589 324
Foreign Residents Department: ☎ 952-589 357

Services

Generally excellent and just about everything is available. Shopping is particularly good and the town centre has a huge variety of stores ranging from chain stores to exclusive boutiques. The large Parque Miramar shopping centre, opposite the castle, opened in March 2004 and provides further shopping services for the town. Restaurants and bars are everywhere. Most services are orientated towards the foreign market and the vast majority of people speak English. There's a lively cultural scene with frequent concerts and plays as well as the annual Festival of Musicals and prestigious Festival of Fuengirola, mainly music and dance, held in the castle. Sports facilities are good and the town has two sports centres and an indoor pool.

Medical Services: Fuengirola has two public health centres and a hospital is currently under construction next to the mosque, to the west of the centre. There's an excellent choice of private clinics and practices.

Communications

Fuengirola has several bus routes, most of which stop in the centre. Buses generally run from 7.30am to around 9 or 10pm. The main routes are:

● Boquetillo to Carvajal (green line) every hour;

● Boquetillo to Carvajal (blue line) every 30 minutes;

● Miramar to Carvajal (yellow line) every hour;

● Playa Marina (near the lighthouse) to Los Pacos (red line) every hour;

- Town Hall to Torreblanca every 15 minutes;

- Town Hall to Miramar (every 30 minutes).

Traffic congestion is chronic in Fuengirola where queues to get in and out are perpetual. Street parking is a challenge unless you're prepared to walk some distance to the centre. There are several car parks in the centre and some belong to a municipal discount scheme.

Property

The property market in Fuengirola is generally good, although top-quality front-line beach apartments are in short supply and there are few villas in the town. Apartment and townhouse accommodation is plentiful and prices are among the cheapest on the coast. Price per m^2 = €1,865. Property prices are as follows:

- Two bedroom apartment – from €150,000;

- Three bedroom apartment – from €175,000;

- Three bedroom townhouse – from €250,000;

- Three bedroom villa – from €300,000.

Fuengirola To Benalmadena

This area (see **Map – Mijas Costa to Torremolinos** on page 84), which runs along the N-340, now a pleasant tree-lined boulevard for much of the way, is currently under extensive construction and new developments are springing up all along the route. **Note that the N-340 has a maximum speed limit of 80kph, reduced to 50kph or 60kph in some stretches and that speed traps operate in the area.** There are also numerous roundabouts, some of which are quite tight, so you should drive with care along this stretch. The main urbanisations from west to east are as follows:

Urb Torreblanca Del Sol

This large urbanisation, situated to the east of Fuengirola, is a mixture of apartment blocks, hotel blocks (some of which are high), townhouse developments and villas. Its roads have recently been resurfaced and the urbanisation's infrastructures upgraded with the result that the general appearance has been much improved. The northern section is high and the access roads to it are winding and labyrinth-like (make sure you have good directions!). Communications are good: there's a local bus service into Fuengirola and the urbanisation has a train station on the Fuengirola to

Malaga line. Services (found mainly on the N-340) include supermarkets, small shops, restaurants and bars.

Urb Carvajal

Carvajal is at the very east of Fuengirola and crammed between the seafront and the high cliffs near the coast. It's a small development with mainly apartment accommodation and limited services, but there are local buses to Fuengirola and a train station.

Other Urbanisations

Urb Capellanía and Urb Torremar are the first urbanisations in the area known as Benalmadena Costa – Capellanía is one of the oldest in this part of the coast. Both urbanisations stretch from the coast right up to the A-7 and offer apartment and villa accommodation. The large new development, Reserva del Higuerón, lies at the top of the Capellanía. A couple of small supermarkets are the only shops in the area, although Reserva del Higuerón plans to build a large shopping centre near the A-7 exit.

Urb Torremuelle is a large urbanisation with mainly villa accommodation, although there are some apartment blocks near the beach. Torremuelle has several small shops and a supermarket, and is also on the train line.

Nueva Torrequebrada is a new urbanisation is currently under massive construction, mainly apartment blocks and at present there are few services, although this will undoubtedly change once building work is completed.

Urb Torrequebrada has one of the coast's most famous landmarks, the Torrequebrada Casino building, which can be seen from beaches for miles around. This urbanisation is also home to the Torrequebrada Golf course, one of the oldest in the area. There are several hotels along the coast and residences are mainly villas and apartments. Some shops are situated near the N-340.

Benalmadena

Benalmadena is one of the Costa del Sol's newest and fastest growing resorts (hence the skyline of cranes) and is now the area's second most popular tourist destination after Torremolinos. The area is centred around two main parts which are within a short distance of each other: the village and Arroyo de la Miel set up in the mountain and Benalmadena Costa on the coast. The village is the administrative centre for the area and has preserved its traditional quiet character, although there are many new developments (mostly townhouses and villas) around it. Services in Benalmadena are excellent and there are numerous amenities, including excellent sport facilities. An indoor pool and ice-skating rink are currently under construction.

Arroyo De La Miel

This busy popular district (known usually as simply Arroyo) to the east of the village has excellent services (there are numerous shops) and communications – Arroyo de la Miel has direct access from the A-7 and a train station. Local transport (bus and tourist train) links Arroyo with Benalmadena village and Costa. Accommodation is mainly apartment blocks in the centre of the development with townhouses on the outskirts. Arroyo is one of the most 'English' parts of the Costa del Sol.

Benalmadena Costa

The coastal part of Benalmadena has many hotels and apartment blocks, and is popular with tourists as well as residents. The prestigious and spectacular marina, Puerto Marina, that won the Best International Port in the World award when it was built in the early '90s, is in this part of Benalmadena. The marina includes a series of man-made islands each with its own exclusive apartments and moorings as well as numerous shops, restaurants and bars. Benalmadena's beaches are clean and well-maintained.

Facts

Population: 43,000 according to official figures, although the council estimates that around 80,000 people live in the area.
Foreign Population: Officially around 6,000, mainly British, but unofficial figures estimate the true population to be higher than 30,000.
Local Holidays: 24 June (San Juan) and 16 July, in honour of la Virgen del Carmen, patron of fishermen.
Distance From Malaga Airport: 12km (7.5mi)
Town Hall: ☎ 952-579 891, 🖳 *www.benalmadena.com*
Local Police Station: ☎ 952-562 142
Foreign Residents Department: ☎ 952-561 231

Property

Benalmadena has seen some of the most intense construction on the coast over the last few years, and judging by the number of cranes, there's no sign of this slowing down for the moment. New developments (mainly townhouses) are numerous, particularly in Arroyo de la Miel and on the outskirts of the village. Price per m² = €1,851. Property prices are as follows:

- Two bedroom apartment – from €150,000 (Puerto Marina from €400,000);

- Three bedroom apartment – from €190,000;

- Three bedroom townhouse – from €300,000;

- Three bedroom villa – from €475,000.

Property Rates: In an attempt to encourage resident homeowners to register with the council so that more funds can be received from the central government, Benalmadena is introducing an 'incentive' scheme, under which **non-registered** resident homeowners will pay a surcharge of 20 per cent on all rates bills. It's hoped that resident owners who haven't registered will do so in order to avoid the increase. For further information on registering with the local council see page 298.

Torremolinos

Torremolinos, one of Spain's top tourist resorts and the epitome of package tourism is a busy town to the west of Malaga. It was one of the first places in the country to open itself to tourism in the early '60s, and consists of rows of high-rise apartment and hotel blocks, although the area to the west has residential streets of townhouses and villas. The town has recently undergone a major facelift and improvements include the extension of the seafront to Los Alamos in the east.

The urbanisations of El Pinillo and Montemar are to the west of the centre; La Carihuela, Pueblo Blanco and El Bajondillo are in the centre and Playa Mar, El Pinar and Los Alamos are to the east. La Carihuela has retained much of its traditional fishing village character and has many narrow streets. The Costa del Sol's best fried fish is found in this area. The centre is attractive and well-maintained, and based around Calle San Miguel which runs from the centre to the steep cliff by the beach where El Bajondillo, the town's modern beach area, is situated.

Torremolinos is a major conference centre and has the most extensive range of hotels on the coast. The town's beaches are clean and well-maintained, and there's an almost infinite number of bars, restaurants and shops. The annual ballroom dancing contest is world-famous. **Note that Torremolinos is *very* busy in the summer months.**

Facts

Population: 46,683
Foreign Population: Approximately 11,000
Local Holidays: 16th July to celebrate the Virgen de Carmen and 29th September for San Miguel, the patron saint of the town.
Distance From Malaga Airport: 6km (3.5mi)
Town Hall: ☎ 952-379 400, 🖳 *www.ayto-torremolinos.org*

Local Police Station: ☎ 952-381 422
Foreign Residents Department: ☎ 952-374 231

Services

Excellent. Torremolinos has numerous shops, supermarkets, outstanding sports facilities (including an indoor pool, two sports stadiums and an athletics track), several health centres and numerous private clinics, and primary and secondary schools. There's an almost infinite number of bars, restaurants and shops, and the town has the best variety of nightlife and entertainment on the coast.

Communications

Torremolinos is very well connected both with the capital and rest of the coast. There are three train stations and good bus services. There are two local bus services: PlayaMar to La Carihuela; and El Bajondillo to Montemar, running approximately every 30 minutes from 8am to 10pm. **Traffic congestion is common in the centre and access roads and parking is difficult**, although some underground parking is available.

Property

Some of the cheapest property on the Costa del Sol can be found in Torremolinos, although beach-front apartments and penthouses fetch premium prices. Bargains can occasionally be found in older apartment blocks, in the centre, that were built in the '60s and '70s, although modernisation is usually required and the quality of construction may be poor. Extensive new construction is currently taking place in the east of the town. Price per m² = €2,123. Property prices are as follows:

- Two bedroom apartment – from €160,000;

- Three bedroom apartment – from €180,000;

- Three bedroom townhouse – from €220,000;

- Three bedroom villa – from €400,000.

Inland

Several small towns lie behind the central area of the Costa del Sol, mostly behind the Mijas Sierra, which are increasingly popular with foreign residents, mainly looking for cheaper property and a more 'Spanish' lifestyle. Amenities are generally good in most areas, although if you want more choice you will have to travel to the coast or Malaga. **Note that the** expatriate scene is somewhat restricted inland and leisure options are limited if you don't speak good Spanish. Bear in mind also that inland the climate is more extreme than on the coast – winters are colder and summers are hotter. The towns discussed in this section are Alhaurín de la Torre, Alhaurín el Grande and Coín (see **Map – Mijas Costa to Torremolinos** on page 84). For information on all areas in the Guadalhorce Valley see page 107.

Facts

Communications

Communications in the area have improved greatly in recent years, although some roads are still in poor condition and progress can be slow if you get behind a lorry. **Local roads are narrow and winding, often with sharper bends than you expect and are often in a bad state of repair.** Added to this are poor driving standards, ranging from a local chugging along in his ancient van down the middle of the road to the executive in a hurry to reach the coast and adamant on doing at least 100kph.

The main access roads are:

● **From Malaga Airport** – The A-366 Malaga to Ronda road runs from the N-340 to Churriana (dual-carriageway along this stretch) and passes through Alhaurín de la Torre, Alhaurín el Grande and Coín. This road is generally very good.

● **From Marbella** – The A-355, known as the 'arc road' (*carretera de arco*) from Marbella to Vélez-Málaga has been recently upgraded and communications to Coín have been much improved.

● **From Fuengirola And Mijas/Benalmadena** – The MA-246 from Fuengirola is currently being resurfaced (some stretches are currently in poor condition). The road is generally good, but winding. The MA-485 from Mijas is a good road, but very winding and narrow in parts.

Alhaurin De La Torre

Alhaurín de la Torre is situated south-west of Malaga and at the east end of the Mijas Sierra (which acts as a backdrop to the town) and is one of the nearest towns to the capital, making it popular for commuter homes. The surrounding countryside is attractive, mainly mountains and farmland (there are some citrus fruit plantations). The town is linear with the focal point being the town hall in the centre, where there are several attractive traditional village streets.

The town relies heavily on the nearby quarry industry, which, although provides a vital source of direct and indirect income, provokes substantial noise and dust pollution in the area. Most residents are in favour of closing the quarries and in the last municipal elections all political parties pledged to carry out the closure. In January 2004, however, after a prolonged quarry strike, an agreement was reached under which the quarries are allowed to continue their activity for several more decades.

Facts

Population: 23,774
Foreign Population: Approximately 1,520 (mainly British)
Local Holidays: 20th January when the town's patron saint, San Sebastián, is honoured and festivities last three days, and 2nd February, the Virgen de la Candelaria.
Distance From Malaga Airport: 8km (5mi)
Town Hall: ☎ 952-418 150, 🖳 *www.aytoalhaurindelatorre.es*
Local Police Station: ☎ 952-417 152

Services

A good range are available including a health centre, several chemists, schools (primary and secondary), a municipal sports centre (an indoor pool is currently under construction), and shops where you can buy most things and several supermarkets. Alhaurín de la Torre has an active cultural scene.

Property

Alhaurín de la Torre is one of the cheaper places to buy property on the Costa del Sol at the moment, although prices are rising in response to demand from commuters looking for property in this town, which serves as a dormitory town for the capital. New construction in urbanisations outside the town is intense at the moment, particularly in the area to the south of the town (on the road to Churriana) in the urbanisations of Retamar and Lagar. Price per m^2 = €1,570. Property prices are as follows:

- Two bedroom apartment – from €100,000;

- Three bedroom apartment – from €110,000;

- Three bedroom townhouse – from €150,000;

- Three bedroom villa – from €300,000.

Alhaurin El Grande

Alhaurín el Grande lies almost directly behind Mijas Sierra and is a busy country town in a stunning setting – much of the town looks out to the Guadalhorce Valley and the mountains beyond. The surrounding countryside is mostly agricultural under citrus cultivation. The central streets are well-maintained with several attractive squares and the imposing San Sebastian church. **Note that many streets are steep and not very pedestrian friendly and the pavements are narrow. Parking is also difficult.**

Alhaurín el Grande is famous for being the residence of nationally famous poet and author, Antonio Gala and was once the home of Gerald Brenan.

Facts

Population: 17,941
Foreign Population: Approximately 720 (mainly British)
Local Holidays: 3 May (festival de las Cruces de Mayo) and 25 May when the local fair takes place.
Distance From Malaga Airport: 20km (12.5mi)
Town Hall: ☎ 952-490 000, 🖳 *www.alhaurinelgrande.net*
Local Police Station: ☎ 952-491 074

Services

Alhaurín provides a good range of services including a well-functioning health centre, several chemists, a sports complex, primary and secondary schools, and numerous shops including supermarkets and other stores. Most shops and services are found at the 'bottom' of the town on the Guadalhorce side.

Property

The property market is buoyant, particularly for country properties in high demand from foreign buyers. Prices have risen significantly in recent months, but properties are still generally cheaper than on the coast. Price per m^2 = €1,998. Property prices are as follows:

● Two bedroom apartment – from €100,000;

● Three bedroom apartment – from €110,000;

● Three bedroom townhouse – from €150,000;

● Three bedroom villa – from €300,000.

Coin

Coín (pronounced 'co-een') is situated to the north of Mijas and Alhaurín el Grande in the valley of the Pereilas river and the abundance of spring water in the area has earned the town the nickname of 'Town of the Fountains'. The water supply for the town and neighbouring districts comes from a spring, known as the Nacimiento, currently being converted into a recreational area with an artificial lake. The surrounding scenery is very attractive, particularly the valley around the source of the Alaminos river.

Coín is a busy sprawling town dominated by the main church and square. The town has recently converted its central area to one-way only improving traffic congestion, but meaning you have to make long detours to get in and out. Access roads are often very congested, but work has recently finished on the A-366 access road to the town, removing an almost permanent bottleneck. **Parking is very difficult in the centre.**

The town has an important agricultural sector, particularly citrus fruit, and in addition construction is also a vital source of income and employment. Coín is famous for its Cinema City where the unsuccessful BBC soap, El Dorado, was filmed.

Facts

Population: 18,255
Foreign Population: Approximately 1,169 (mainly British)
Local Holidays 3rd May, festival de las Cruces de Mayo and the August fair from 10th to 14th.
Distance From Malaga Airport: 38km (24mi)
Town Hall: ☎ 952-453 018, 🖥 www.ayto-coin.es
Local Police Station: ☎ 952-453 267

Services

Generally good, although there's limited choice for shopping in the centre. Coín has a health centre, chemists, primary and secondary schools, and sports facilities. There's also a good choice of restaurants and bars in the town and surrounding area. The Trocha shopping centre (situated around 2km from the centre on the A-355 from Cártama) opens in late 2004 offering a Supercor hypermarket as well as around 50 other shops (fashion, homeware and accessories). Parking is free. The centre also has a seven-screen cinema.

Property

Coín is currently experiencing a property boom, mainly from foreigners and in 2003 newly built properties accounted for nearly 12 per cent of the total homes. Construction is intense both around the outskirts of the town and further out towards both Cártama (Urb Sierra Gorda and Sierra Chica) and Mijas (Urb Las Delicias). Prices have risen sharply and the current price per m² is €1,787. Property prices are as follows:

- Two bedroom apartment – from €125,000;

- Three bedroom apartment – from €140,000;

- Three bedroom townhouse – from €165,000;

- Three bedroom villa – from €350,000.

AREA THREE – MALAGA

The main localities that can be found in area three of the Costa del Sol are as follows:

- **Malaga Capital** – see below;

- **Alora** –see page 108;

- **Cártama** –see page 109;

- **Pizarra** –see page 110.

The city of Malaga is the capital of the Costa del Sol, but is, in many respects, a world apart from the thriving tourist resorts on the rest of the coast. Malaga has few foreign residents, although this may change in the near future as the centre of the city is now proving popular with foreign buyers looking for an authentic Spanish environment with services and amenities on their doorstep. The Guadalhorce Valley, north of the city, is already a popular destination for foreign buyers, mainly residents, attracted to the area's impressive natural beauty and relative tranquillity. This part of the Costa del Sol remains very Spanish and there isn't a large expatriate environment. **If you choose to settle in Malaga the ability to speak Spanish is essential.**

Malaga

Malaga is Spain's fifth largest city and the capital of the Costa del Sol as well as a major Mediterranean port. It's one of the most cosmopolitan cities in Spain and for centuries has been a popular destination for foreigners, as the names of many of the city's districts and streets testify. During the 19th century, Malaga was a thriving winter resort for wealthy Europeans.

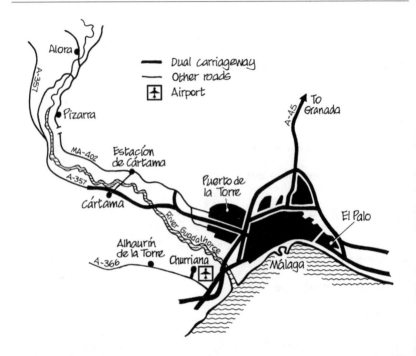

The city has a rich and colourful history, yet remains largely untouched by mass tourism and is a genuine Andalusian city. Its Phoenician and Roman ancestors left their mark all over the centre – the Roman amphitheatre has just been restored to its former glory –and Malaga's Moorish past can be clearly seen in the Alcazaba fortress and Gibralfaro castle (now a luxury Parador hotel). Pablo Picasso was born here and in 2003 a magnificent museum housing a selection of his works was opened. In conjunction with the new museum, the old quarters of the city are currently being restored and many parts pedestrianised.

At long last, Malaga is making a concerted effort (and successful one) to appeal to the millions of tourists visiting the area. New buildings include the emblematic (and controversially expensive) Conference and Exhibition Palace, and the Palace of Justice which is currently under construction in Teatinos.

Malaga is essentially a Spanish city and many people don't speak English, except for those dealing directly with tourists.

Facts

Population: 535,686
Foreign Population: Approximately 24,100

Local Holidays: 16th August when Malaga celebrates the union of the city with Castille in 1487 and 8th September for the Virgen de la Victoria (patron of the city).
Distance From Malaga Airport: 8km (5mi)
City Hall: ☎ 952-135 000, 🖳 *www.ayto-malaga.es*
Local Police Main Station: ☎ 952-126 500

Services

Malaga has excellent facilities and amenities, as you'd expect in the city of its size, and offers the best on the coast. There are numerous hospitals (private and public) and health centres. There's a vibrant cultural scene including international theatre, jazz and cinema festivals, and Malaga philharmonic orchestra is one of the most prestigious in Spain and offers a season of concerts from October to June. Malaga is making a bid for the European Capital of Culture in 2016.

Sports facilities are excellent: the Martín Carpena stadium in the west is home to the city's top basketball team, the Rosaleda football stadium is currently being upgraded and work has started on the athletics stadium in preparation for the European Athletics Championships in 2007.

Shopping is very good, both in the centre around the pedestrian C/ Larios and in the many centres around the periphery. Prices for many items in Malaga are cheaper than on the coast, particularly if you go to large stores or hypermarkets.

Communications

Communications in Malaga are generally very good. See below for more information on public transport and roads.

Buses: Malaga has an extensive network of bus services run by EMT, which connect most parts of the city with the centre. There are some 40 routes running from around 6.30am to midnight, seven days a week, although there are fewer services on Sundays and public holidays. The bus service is currently undergoing extensive modernisation, including the fitting of all buses with GPS navigation systems.

Tickets cost €0.85 per journey, although discounts are available, e.g. a *Tarjeta-Bus*, valid for 10 journeys, costs €5.70 and a monthly bus pass (*Tarjeta Mensual*) with unlimited travel costs €28.80 (€19.95 for students). **Pensioners travel free.** EMT has also just introduced an innovative bus card, similar to a credit card, which can be recharged for any amount and used on all buses as payment. Bus passes and cards can be bought at news kiosks, certain shops and bus stations around the city.

Further information about buses in Malaga can be found on the EMT website (🖳 *www.emtsam.es*) in Spanish and English or by phoning ☎ 902-527 200. EMT runs a customer service department at Alameda Principal 15 in the city centre.

Trains: Malaga main line train station has services to Córdoba, Granada, Madrid and Seville. The station has a waiting room, café and bar, and several small shops. In the near future the station will be rebuilt (most of it will be underground) in preparation for the new high-speed train line (*AVE*) due to be completed by 2007. The current station will become a shopping centre. The current underground station for local trains (Fuengirola and Alora) will be part of the new Malaga underground (metro) system (see below).

Malaga Metro: The underground train service is one of Malaga's most exciting new projects and contracts are currently being awarded for its construction. The metro will initially have two lines: Line 1 will run from Teatinos to the Malagueta every 6 minutes (journey time 15 minutes) and Line 2 will run from the Martín Carpena stadium to the Malagueta every 6 minutes (journey time 13 minutes). There will be a total of 21 stations, 16 of which will be underground. Work is expected to be finished by 2007. Further information is available from the Malaga Metro website (🖳 *www. metrodemalaga.info*).

Roads: Traffic congestion is chronic, particularly at peak times, although the new '*Red Rápida*' system in the centre (where police patrol to ensure there's no stopping or parking from Mondays to Saturdays) has helped to relieve the situation slightly. Parking is difficult, although there are now numerous underground car parks in the city. **Parking is expensive, but there's a discount scheme for residents and frequent users.**

Property

Property in Malaga is generally cheaper than in many other places on the Costa del Sol, although some parts of the city have very high prices and prices have risen dramatically everywhere in recent months. Nevertheless, Malaga is now the most expensive city in Andalusia and prices in various parts are detailed below.

Malaga Centre: The once decaying centre of Malaga is now under extensive restoration and there are numerous regional and local government grants available. As a result, the area is growing in popularity and prices are rising, although they're still lower than in other parts of the city. **If you buy a property that needs restoration, bear in mind that there are strict regulations regarding the restoration process and it can be costly.** Price per m^2 = €1,767. Property prices are as follows:

- Two bedroom apartment – from €120,000;

- Three bedroom apartment – from €150,000.

Malaga East: Some of Malaga's most expensive and desirable properties are found there, where it's less built-up and there are numerous green areas.

Price per m^2 = €1,936 to €3,143 on the seafront. Property prices are as follows:

- Two bedroom apartment – from €240,000;

- Three bedroom apartment – from €250,000;

- Three bedroom townhouse – from €420,000

- Three bedroom villa – from €600,000.

Malaga North & Teatinos: One of Malaga's fastest growing areas is Teatinos, situated near the university. Price per m^2 = €1,581 to €1,800. Property prices are as follows:

- Two bedroom apartment – from €105,000;

- Three bedroom apartment – from €130,000.

Malaga West: This fast expanding area includes the area known as the Nuevo Paseo Marítimo (New Seafront) where many luxury apartment blocks are under construction.

Price per m^2 = €1,930 to €2,470 on the seafront. Property prices are as follows:

- Two bedroom apartment – from €200,000;

- Three bedroom apartment – from €250,000.

Guadalhorce Valley

The Guadalhorce Valley (see map on page 104) is home to the Guadalhorce river, the province's largest, which runs from north of Antequera to the huge reservoir, known as El Chorro (a popular recreation and leisure park), before passing through the spectacular deep gorge, the Desfiladero de los Gaitanes, and into a wide valley where it reaches the sea to the west of Malaga. The Guadalhorce Valley (also known as the Sun Valley), with mountains on both sides, is spectacularly beautiful, particularly in the spring and autumn. The valley is extremely fertile and has vast plantations of fruit trees, mainly citrus which are laden with fruit during the winter and early spring. Olive groves lie on the lower reaches of the mountains and there are also small sections under plastic greenhouses.

The valley is one of the province's fastest growing and its vastly improved communications have made it attractive as a dormitory area for the coast. Properties in the country in the Guadalhorce Valley are also currently very popular with foreign buyers. As a consequence, prices have risen greatly and new construction is intense.

Facts

Communications

Roads have been vastly improved in the area, and the main route is the A-357 from Malaga to Campillos, which is now dual-carriageway to just beyond Cártama. Other roads in the area are currently being upgraded (resurfaced and widened in many cases) under the regional road plan, known as 'Plan Cerca'. As a result, the towns are quick and easy to reach from Malaga. The Cercanías train line runs from Malaga to Alora via Estación de Cártama and Pizarra, although there are few trains a day. Stations are situated outside the main towns and parking is available at the stations themselves. Bus services run between the main towns and Malaga, but services can be slow and not many buses run a day. **Private transport is a must if you choose to live in this area.**

The following section describes the most popular areas with foreign buyers and residents, namely Alora, Cártama and Pizarra.

Alora

Alora is a very attractive town perched on the Hacho peak (590m) above the Guadalhorce river, which flows round the base of the town. It's a typical white village and its main attractions are the Moorish castle, now mostly in ruins but still dominating the surroundings, the imposing church of Nuestra Señora de la Encarnación and the typically Andalusian architecture found in the streets. Views from much of the town are spectacular and you can see for miles.

Parking is difficult in the town, which has many narrow streets and it's difficult to find your way out again!

Facts

Population: 12,363
Foreign Population: Approximately 300

Local Holidays: Corpus Christi (June) and San Paulino (July). The town's main fair is during the first week of August.
Distance From Malaga Airport: 40km (25mi)
Town Hall: ☎ 952-496 100, 🖳 *www.ayto-alora.org*
Local Police Station: ☎ 952-496 468

Services

There's a good range of services including schools, a health centre, sports facilities, supermarkets and other smaller specialist shops. Alora is the main services centre for the area and it's also the starting point for the nearby Chorro national park.

Property

Property in the area has risen sharply in price in recent months, but as yet there's little construction in the immediate area of the town. Property prices are as follows:

- Two/three bedroom townhouse – from €95,000;

- Country property in need of restoration – from €100,000;

- Small country property – from €120,000.

Cartama

Cártama is the main town in the Guadalhorce Valley and currently one of the fastest growing in the province of Malaga. It is an attractive traditional town lying on the south side of the Mijas Sierra and to the west of the river. It's small with some shops and other services. The main attractions are the old quarter and the Remedios shrine. Parking is difficult in the town.
In addition to Cártama there is Estación de Cártama as well as numerous other smaller towns.

Estación de Cártama lies on the east side of the river, some 3km from Cártama itself and is a busy and modern town, based around Cártama train station. Services are good and you can buy just about everything. There's a large health centre and sports facilities. Sunland International School is just outside Estación de Cártama (see page 187).

Facts

Population: 16,040 (around 4,700 in the main town and 6,300 in Estación de Cártama)
Foreign Population: Approximately 400 (mainly British)

Local Holidays: Cártama – 23rd April (main fair lasting for five days) and 24th June (San Juan). Estación de Cártama – 23rd April (main fair lasting for five days) and 15th May (San Isidro).
Distance From Malaga Airport: 23km (14mi)
Town Hall: ☎ 952-422 126, 🖳 *www.cartama.ws*
Local Police Station: ☎ 952-422 126

Property

Cártama is currently experiencing a property boom, mainly spurred on by the new dual-carriageway to Malaga, which has made the area very attractive to commuters from Malaga. Property prices have risen by as much as 50 per cent over the last year. New construction, mainly townhouses, is intense around Cártama town and Estación de Cártama, although foreign buyers tend to prefer country properties. Price per m^2 = €1,622. Property prices are as follows:

- Three bedroom townhouse – from €180,000;

- Three bedroom country property – from €200,000;

- Plot of 2,500m^2 (urban) – from €120,000.

> **There has been a spate of illegal building on plots in the area and the council in Cártama now has an active policy of fining property owners and demolishing illegal construction. Before you buy a plot or start building on one, check with the council whether construction is allowed and what the latest regulations are. The town has just revised its urban planning regulations and so it's especially important to check. Be particularly wary of 'friendly' sellers or go-betweens trying to sell you a plot – many people have spent thousands of euros on plots that legally don't exist or that they cannot build on.**

Pizarra

Pizarra is a small town on the west side of the Guadalhorce with a limited range of services including small shops, a chemist, schools and sports facilities. The town has several interesting monuments including the Hollander Museum, with a collection of Spanish antiques.

Facts

Population: 7,330
Foreign Population: Approximately 300 (mainly British)
Local Holidays: The main fair is from 14th to 18th August when the town's patron, the Virgen de Fuensanta, is honoured.

Distance From Malaga Airport: 34km (21mi)
Town Hall: ☎ 952-483 015, 🖥 *www.pizarra.es*
Local Police Station: ☎ 952-483 636

Property

Prices in the town have risen in recent months, reflecting the interest in the area from both foreign buyers and commuters from Malaga. Townhouse and villa construction is currently taking place to the east of the town centre. Property prices are as follows:

● Two/three bedroom townhouse – from €100,000;

● Country property in need of restoration – from €110,000;

● Small country property – from €130,000.

AREA FOUR – THE EAST

The main towns that can be found in the east of the Costa del Sol are as follows:

● **Nerja** – see page 116;

● **Rincón De La Victoria** – see page 112;

● **Torre Del Mar** – see page 114;

● **Vélez-Málaga** – see page 115.

The Eastern side of the Costa del Sol has traditionally been less developed than the west and as a consequence not so built-up and less influenced by tourism. The area remains very agricultural and there are now many stretches under plastic greenhouses (which aren't particularly attractive). Most areas on this side of the coast, both resorts and inland villages, have retained their essentially Spanish character. This is changing, however, as communications improve and foreigners look for a more-Spanish environment as well as cheaper property.

The area around Torre del Mar is currently among the fastest expanding on the coast. Services and amenities on this side of the coast aren't as good or as plentiful as those on the west, although the city of Malaga is within easy reach of most towns and the situation has improved greatly over the last few years. **There's a poor choice of international schools (see page 184)** and there are currently only two golf courses on this side of the coast.

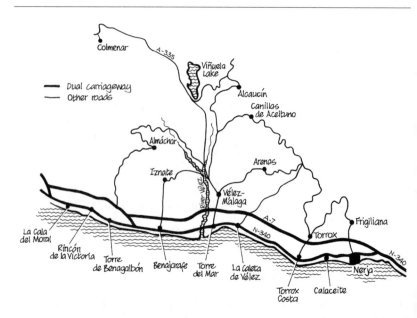

Communications are reasonably good, although the A-7 around Malaga and often as far as Rincón de la Victoria, is always busy and gridlocked at peak times. The N-340 coast road runs directly parallel to the beach from Rincón de la Victoria to Nerja and makes pleasant driving, although it's single-lane and the speed limit is 80kph outside urban areas where it's 50kph. This road gets very busy at weekends and during the summer months when people flock to the beaches. Local buses connect Malaga with all towns and there are also other bus services linking other towns and villages (see below for further details). **The ability to speak Spanish is essential in most parts of this area**, with perhaps the exception of Nerja where there's a large foreign population.

This section looks at towns west to east, from Rincón de la Victoria to Nerja including the Axarquía.

Rincon De La Victoria

Rincón de la Victoria is situated to the east of Malaga and includes four localities: Benagalbón, la Cala del Moral, Rincón de la Victoria and Torre de Benagalbón. Rincón de la Victoria (often known as just 'El Rincón') is the largest and was until very recently a traditional fishing village, but over the last fifteen years or so, its proximity to Malaga and good communications have made the town very attractive to commuters, with the result that population growth has been spectacular. The town's traditional architecture (small fishing houses) has been conserved in spite of intense new construction. The centre is attractive and includes several important monuments and the interesting Cueva del Tesoro (Treasure Cave) lies to the north of the town. Rincón de la Victoria is connected to La Cala del Moral by a seven kilometre sea front walk.

One of the area's most important festivals are the *Jábega* regattas, when boats modelled on those used for fishing in the Middle Ages race against each other. The Vitorian anchovy (*boquerón vitoriano*), smaller than usual, is very famous and is one of the local delicacies.

Rincón de la Victoria is an essentially Spanish town and there's not a large expatriate scene.

Facts

Population: 25,682
Foreign Population: Approximately 1,500
Local Holidays: 2nd February (Virgen de la Candelaria) and 16th July (Virgen del Carmen – patron saint of fishermen).
Distance From Malaga Airport: 20km (12.5mi)
Town Hall: ☎ 952-402 300, 💻 *www.rincondelavictoria.com*
Local Police Station: ☎ 952-402 300

Services

Rincón de la Victoria has excellent services and facilities with numerous shops, supermarkets, sports facilities, health centres and primary and secondary schools. Its proximity to the capital also means that a full-range of services are within easy reach.

Property

Property in this area is among the cheapest on the coast, although prices are rising in response to demand from new buyers. Construction is currently intense, particularly to the north of the town and in 2003 some 4,000 new homes were built, an increase of nearly 50 per cent. Price per m^2 = €1,808. Property prices are as follows:

● Two bedroom apartment – from €140,000;

● Three bedroom apartment – from €150,000;

● Three bedroom townhouse – from €200,000;

● Three bedroom villa – from €400,000.

Rincon De La Victoria To Vélez-Málaga

This section of the coast is relatively underdeveloped and agricultural land predominates – many crops are front-line beach! Development has started, however, and apartments and townhouses are planned for a large complex at Niza Beach and Almayate Costa. Beaches are small and narrow. Chilches is an attractive small resort with mainly villa accommodation.

Vélez-Málaga District

Vélez-Málaga (often called just 'Vélez) is one of the largest districts on this side of the coast and consists of three main areas: Torre del Mar on the coast (Vélez's beach resort); the main town Vélez-Málaga itself, situated strategically inland to escape tidal waves caused by earthquakes centuries ago and Vélez Costa consisting of several smaller resorts east of Torre del Mar, namely Caleta de Vélez, Benajarafe and Mezquitilla.

Communications between the towns are good. There are two local bus services: one connecting Torre del Mar with Vélez-Málaga every 30 minutes and the other connects the resorts within Vélez along the coast. **The Avda Juan Carlos I road links Torre del Mar with Vélez-Málaga, although traffic congestion is a problem.** An innovative tram service with nine stops between Torre del Mar and Vélez-Málaga is currently under construction and due to be finished in late 2004.

Torre Del Mar

Torre del Mar is the main town between Rincón de la Victoria and Nerja, and is essentially a modern beach resort with little character and few old buildings. It has, however, a pleasant seafront promenade and offers good services and amenities including the Axarquía hospital. It's a busy town with a mainly Spanish feel to it, although foreigners live there too. The beaches are coarse grey sand and not well-maintained out of season.

Facts

Population: 15,800
Distance From Malaga Airport: 36km (22.5mi)
Town Hall: ☎ 952-540 404

Property

Torre del Mar has, up until now, been relatively neglected by foreign buyers, but over the last few months interest in the area has risen sharply, particularly from those looking for cheaper property but within a more

Spanish environment. Development is currently intense to the north and east of the town, particularly low-rise apartments and townhouses. Price per m² = €1,461. Property prices are as follows:

- Two bedroom apartment – from €130,000;

- Three bedroom apartment – from €170,000;

- Three bedroom townhouse – from €255,000;

- Three bedroom villa – from €310,000.

Vélez-Málaga

Vélez-Málaga (5km from the coast) is the capital of the Axarquía, its largest town and main services centre for the east side of Malaga. The town is an attractive white town set in the foot hills of the Maroma mountain, one of the highest in the area and it is often snow-capped in the winter. The Moorish castle and church dominate the town and there are several other important monuments. The town is busy and essentially Spanish. Vélez-Málaga was the birthplace of María Zambrano, a nationally famous writer and philosopher, and the town is home to the Zambrano Foundation where many archives and original documents are kept.

Facts

Population: 60,200 of which some 32,000 live in the town itself.
Foreign Population: Around 1,700 (mainly British)
Local Holidays: 25th July (Santiago is the local patron saint) and 5th October when the town celebrates its main fair.
Distance From Malaga Airport: 36km (22.5mi)
Town Hall: ☎ 952-500 100, 🖳 *www.ayto-velezmalaga.es*
Local Police Station: ☎ 952-549 238

Services

Vélez offers a wide range of services and amenities, including two health centres, primary and secondary schools, sports facilities and numerous shops (including the El Ingenio shopping centre). The Teatro del Carmen has a good choice of cultural events throughout the year, although most are in Spanish.

Property

Property in Vélez is among the cheapest in the province, although prices have risen over the last few months and numerous new developments are currently under construction, particularly townhouses, to the south of the town near the A-7. Price per m² = €1,461. Property prices are as follows:

- Two bedroom apartment – from €130,000;

- Three bedroom apartment – from €150,000.

Vélez-Málaga Costa

East of Torre del Mar are several resort developments which make up Vélez-Málaga Costa. Caleta de Vélez is a small resort, centred around an attractive marina and offering limited services. New developments are currently under construction to the north of the N-340. Benajarafe is a very small resort and Mezquitilla is a long sprawl of apartment blocks with limited services. Algarrobo Costa (not part of Vélez-Málaga administrative district) has reasonably good services including banks and supermarkets and other small shops, and offers mainly apartment accommodation.

Torrox Costa

Torrox Costa, some 44km (27.5mi) from Malaga airport advertises itself as having the finest climate in Europe and aims to put itself on the tourist map. There's currently little development in the area, which consists of: El Morche which offers limited services and mainly apartment accommodation. There are several new developments currently under construction. Torrox Costa, the resort itself, a quiet (out of season) and pleasant place with shops and services and low-rise apartment accommodation. Calaceite where new development is now concentrated, including a major residential project with some 4,000 homes, an 18-hole golf course and a shopping centre. A golf course is also planned for Barranco del Puerto. At the moment Calaceite is little more than a few villas and townhouses. There's a local bus service connecting El Morche, Torrox Costa resort and Torrox village.

Beaches in Torrox Costa are generally small and narrow, except for the longer beach at Torrox Costa resort, and consist of coarse grey sand.

Nerja

Nerja lies at the eastern most point of the Costa del Sol and is probably the town that has best retained its traditional character in the face of tourism and much of the old town remains unchanged in spite of construction on the outskirts. The town has several famous beaches, including Burriana beach and is home to the world-famous Nerja caves (see page 229). The Balcón de Europa overlooking the Mediterranean is the town's central point around which there are numerous attractive and typically Andalusian streets with souvenir and gift shops, and boutiques. Although Nerja remains very much a traditional Spanish town, the influence of foreign residents and tourists is huge, and there's a thriving expatriate scene in the area.

Facts

Population: 19,000
Foreign Population: Officially 4,000, although the council believes some 10,000 actually live in the town. British are the most numerous (around 1,600).
Local Holidays: 15th May (San Isidro, patron saint of the town) and 10 October, the main fair in honour of the Virgen de las Angustias.
Distance From Malaga Airport: 60km (37.5mi)
Town Hall: ☎ 952-548 410, 💻 *www.nerja.org*
Local Police Station: ☎ 952-521 545
Foreign Residents Department: ☎ 952-548 401, ✉ *residentes@nerja.org*.
Nerja council has recently edited a book, *Living in Nerja*, with vital information for foreign residents and available in several languages from the town hall priced €1.

Services

Nerja is the main services centre for this side of the coast and a wide range of services are available including numerous shops, restaurants and bars, a health centre, private clinics, and primary and secondary schools. A new health centre is currently under construction and expected to be finished by 2006. There's an excellent cultural scene throughout the year and the local cultural centre offers opera, music and theatre.

Communications

There are two local bus services linking the east and west sides of Nerja with the centre. Line 1 runs from 9am to 9pm and Line 2 operates in the morning only in winter. The frequency of services is increased in the summer. Tickets cost €0.90. Buses run to Malaga every hour (the journey takes around an hour and there are several direct services) and there are also buses to Frigiliana, Maro, Torre del Mar, Torrox and Motril. **Traffic congestion is common on the access roads into the town,** although these are currently being improved in order to ease congestion **Parking in the centre is difficult,** although there's an underground car park next to the town hall with limited spaces.

Property

Prices in Nerja are the highest on the east side of Malaga with front-line apartments and villas fetching a premium. Construction is intense in Nerja at the moment, particularly to the north and west of the town. A recent report by the town council claimed that some 60 per cent of new construction is for the holiday home market with the result that nearly half Nerja's residences are now temporary holiday homes. Price per m^2 = €2,081. Property prices are as follows:

- Two bedroom apartment – from €200,000;

- Three bedroom apartment – from €250,000;

- Three bedroom townhouse – from €300,000;

- Three bedroom villa – from €500,000.

Frigiliana

The stunningly beautiful village of Frigiliana lies to the north of Nerja (2km) in the Tejeda Sierra and its narrow white streets crowned with flower-laden balconies include the best-preserved Mudejar quarter in the region. Frigiliana is famous for the battle of the Peñón de Frigiliana in 1568 when thousands of Moriscos (Moors forced to convert to Catholicism) were killed or expelled from the village where generations upon generations had lived before them. Monuments of note in the village include the Moorish castle and the San Antonio church, as well as just about every street.

The village has few services apart from some small shops, numerous restaurants and cafés, and limited sports facilities. The village is connected to nearby Nerja by a bus service (eight a day), which runs from Mondays to Saturdays.

Facts

Population: 2,213
Foreign Population: Approximately 270
Local Holidays: 20th January (San Sebastián) and 3rd May (fiesta de la cruz).
Distance From Malaga Airport: 64km (40mi)
Town Hall: ☎952-533 002, 🖳 *www.frigiliana.org*

Property

Property prices are as follows:

- Two bedroom apartment – from €150,000;

- Three bedroom apartment – from €200,000;

- Three bedroom townhouse – from €250,000;

- Three bedroom villa – from €500,000.

The Axarquia

The area directly behind the eastern Costa del Sol is known as the Axarquía (pronounced *axe-arc-key-a*) and is one of Malaga's most attractive rural areas. The Axarquía is high and verdant, and famous for its sweet wine (Malaga wine comes from here), quiet and attractive white villages, and its long tradition of *verdiales* music and dance, among the oldest in Spain. The area is essentially agricultural – crops include olives, almonds, grapes and tropical fruits nearer the coast – and it maintains a traditionally rural way of life so **you need to speak Spanish if you decide to live in this area.**

It's increasingly popular with foreign buyers, looking for both cheaper property and a quiet way of life. **Bear in mind that the Axarquía has a harsher climate than the coastal strip** – the mountains in Sierra Almijara in the north-east are often snow-capped in winter, when temperatures at night can be below zero and frosts are common. Temperatures are also higher in the summer than on the coast, although they fall at night. The Axarquía is also a dry area.

Facts

Main Population Areas: Vélez-Málaga (see page 115) is the capital of the Axarquía where there are numerous villages, some of which are tiny and remote, and the best known of which are Colmenar and Riogordo in the west. Both these villages are popular with foreigners; Alfarnate, Periana and Viñuela in the north. Viñuela is particularly popular due to its proximity to the reservoir, known as Lake Viñuela. A golf course is planned for the area; Almachar, Alcaucín, Arenas, Canillas de Aceituno and Cómpeta in the centre; and Torrox and Frigiliana in the east.

Further information about individual villages can be found on the Axarquía's official tourist website (🖳 *www.axarquiacostadelsol.org*).

Services

Services in the area vary, although in the smaller villages there's little more than a bar and a shop, and possibly a bank. The area's main service centre is Vélez-Málaga and you may have to travel to the coast for many transactions and purchases.

Communications

These vary from good to very poor. Communications are good in the villages of Colmenar, Riogordo, Viñuela and Vélez-Málaga, all on the A-355 (Ctra del Arco), which runs in an arch from Marbella to Torre del Mar, and villages on the western side that are in within easy reach of the A-45 Malaga to Antequera road. Communications are generally poor in central and eastern parts, where roads are narrow and mountainous. Bus services connect many villages with each other and Vélez-Málaga, but journeys are slow. Services are also infrequent and don't usually run on Sundays. **Private transport is essential in the Axarquía.**

Property

One of the main attractions for foreign buyers is lower property prices than on the coast, although just like everywhere else prices are rising. **The nearer a property is to the coast, the more expensive it is and properties in Viñuela and Frigiliana attract premium prices.** For property prices in Frigiliana see page 118. There's a good choice of property available for sale, which ranges from typical village houses to large country *fincas* with extensive land. Many properties need extensive restoration, although newly built properties are also for sale. **Bear in mind that restoration is expensive, particularly if the property is in a remote area and workers need to travel long distances to get there.** Note that parking is limited in village centres and may be some distance from a house. Property prices are as follows:

- Two/three bedroom village house needing restoration work – from €50,000;

- Two/three bedroom village house – from €100,000;

- Three bedroom villa – from €150,000 (up to €800,000 in the Viñuela area);

- Modernised country property (*finca*) – from €250,000 (up to €500,000 in Colmenar);

- Plots from €30,000.

In recent years there has been a spate of uncontrolled new construction in some parts of the Axarquía, particularly in the Viñuela area, some of which has since been declared illegal. If you plan to buy a newly built property, ask your lawyer to check it has been correctly registered and is totally legal. If you plan to buy a plot, check that construction is permitted on it (see Legislation Affecting Rural Plots in Andalusia on page 139).

Castillo de Gibralfaro, Málaga

5

Accommodation

A major concern for anyone relocating to a new area is somewhere to stay and if possible you should arrange some sort of accommodation before you arrive on the Costa del Sol This chapter looks at the accommodation options on the Costa del Sol, including temporary accommodation, rental accommodation, property purchase and retirement and nursing homes.

HOTELS & HOSTELS

There's a huge choice of hotels and hostels on the coast to suit all budgets from basic bedrooms with shared bathroom facilities to luxury top of the range suite accommodation. There are also numerous new hotels currently under construction. Hotel accommodation is officially classified with one to five stars, depending on the facilities they offer, rather than their price. **Note that hotels within the same category can vary considerably in quality and comfort.** A rough guide to room rates is shown below:

Star Rating	Price Range	Class
*****GL	€350++	Great Luxury/*Gran Lujo* (currently 7 hotels on the coast)
*****	€150 – 450++	Luxury/*Lujo* (currently 7 hotels on the coast)
****	€60 – 225+	Top Class (most hotels are in this category)
***	€30 – 150+	Very Comfortable
**	€20 – 80	Comfortable
*	€15 – 50	Basic

Prices above are for a double room with bathroom for one night. **Prices in hotels are usually quoted per room and not per person, and 7 per cent VAT (*IVA*) is added to all bills.** You pay your bill at the end of your stay and all but the smaller establishments accept credit cards.

There are also Hotel-Apartments (*Aparthotel*) in many locations on the coast, which offer better rates than standard hotels (although services may be fewer) and usually include cooking facilities, so you can save money on eating out. Some hotels (usually only three-star and below) offer special rates for long stay guests, particularly during the quieter winter months.

Finding A Hotel

If you arrive on the Costa del Sol during low season (e.g. November to the end of February), you will probably be able to find hotel accommodation with little difficulty. For most of the year, however, and particularly during July, August and Christmas, finding a hotel room on spec is virtually impossible. It's advisable to book ahead whenever you plan to come, not least so you don't waste valuable time tramping round hotels looking for a room. **When you book, you may be asked for your credit card number, particularly if it's a three-star or over hotel.** Booked accommodation is usually held until 6pm on the day of arrival unless you've advised the hotel of a later arrival time. Check-out is usually by noon. Methods of finding a hotel include the following:

- **Costa Del Sol Tourism Association** – The Costa del Sol Tourism Association (Patronato de Turismo de la Costa del Sol) publishes a *Directory of Hotels* on the Costa del Sol in English, which is downloadable in pdf format from their website (🖳 *www.visitacostadelsol.com*).

- **Guide Books** – Most guide books on Spain contain some information about hotel accommodation on the Costa del Sol and there are numerous Spanish hotel guides, including the *Michelin Red Guide España* and *Hoteles y Restaurantes* (El País Aguilar), available from bookshops.

- **Internet** – There's a wealth of information about hotels on the Costa del Sol on the internet (just type in 'hotels Costa del Sol' in any good search engine) and there may be links to the hotels themselves where you can book online or telephone to book a room. Most local council websites also provide information about hotels in the area or links to this information. Council websites can be found in **Chapter 4**.

- **Tourist Offices** – Local tourist offices can provide information about hotels in the area and many also offer information about accommodation on their website. For a full list of tourist offices on the Costa del Sol see **Chapter 10. Tourist offices don't usually provide a booking service.**

- **Travel Agents** – When you book your flight to the Costa del Sol you may be offered hotel accommodation as part of the deal or the travel agent may also be able to book your room for you.

- **Yellow Pages** – Look under '*hoteles*'. The Spanish yellow pages are also available on the internet (🖳 *www.paginasamarillas.es*). You need to type in the category of business you're looking for (i.e. hotel) and the area.

CAMPSITES

This is definitely a cheaper accommodation option, especially if you travel to the coast with a caravan or campervan. Campsites are divided into four categories: luxury (*lujo*), first class (*primera/1ª categoría*), second class (*segunda/2ª categoría*) and third class (*tercera/3ª categoría*), but there are no luxury or third class campsites on the coast. Camping costs from €2.50 to €3 per person, per day plus €3 for a car and around the same for a caravan or camping space. Most campsites are open all year round, and there may be special rates for long-term stays.

The following is a listing of campsites on the Costa del Sol:

Area One – The West

Estepona	Camping Parque Tropical (2ª cat), N-340 km 162	☎ 952-793 618
Manilva	Chullera II (2ª cat), N-340 km 142	☎ 952-890 196
	Chullera III (2ª cat), N-340 km 142.8	☎ 952-890 320
Marbella	Camping Cabopino (2ª cat), N-340 km 194.7, Cabopino 💻 *www.campingcabopino.com*	☎ 952-834 373
	Camping La Buganvilla (2ª cat), N-340 km 188.8 ✉ *info@campingbuganvilla.com*	☎ 952-831 973
	Camping Marbella Playa (1ª cat), N-340 km 192.8	☎ 952-833 998.

Area Two – Central Costa Del Sol

Alhaurín De La Torre	Camping Morales (2ª cat), C/ Arroyo Hondo 15	☎ 952-410 283
Fuengirola	Camping Fuengirola (2ª cat), N-340 km 207	☎ 952-474 108
	Camping La Rosaleda (2ª cat), N-340 km 211.5	☎ 952-460 191
Mijas Costa	Camping Calazul (2ª cat), N-340 km 200, La Cala de Mijas ✉ *calaazul@turinet.net*	☎ 952-493 219
	Camping Los Jarales (2ª cat), N-340 km 197, Calahonda.	☎ 952-830 003

Torremolinos	Camping Torremolinos (2ª cat), N-340 km 228	☎ 952-382 602.

Area Four – The East

Nerja	Camping Maro (2ª cat), N-340 km 297, Maro	☎ 952-529 714
Torre Del Mar	Camping Laguna Playa (1ª cat), Paseo Marítimo 💻 *www.lagunaplaya.com*	☎ 952-540 631
	Camping Torre del Mar (2ª cat), Paseo Marítimo	☎ 952-540 224
Torrox Costa	Camping El Pino (2ª cat), N-340 km 285, Urb El Peñoncillo	☎ 952-532 578
Vélez-Málaga	Camping Almanat (2ª cat), N-340 km 269, Almayate ✉ *info@almanat.de*	☎ 952-556 271

Note that camping is not permitted anywhere outside official campsites on the Costa del Sol or indeed anywhere in Andalusia unless you have permission from the owner of the land.

RURAL ACCOMMODATION

Rural accommodation is currently big business in Spain and there are options near the Costa del Sol, although some of the accommodation may be rather off the beaten track. You can either rent a room in a house (in which case meals are usually provided) or rent the whole house with self-catering facilities. Several books are published annually on rural tourism, e.g. *Guía de Alojamientos en Casas Rurales* (El País Aguilar) or *Guía de Alojamientos de Turismo Rural* (Anaya Touring), which both include sections on the province of Malaga. There are also numerous websites, the best of which are 💻 *www.azrural.com* and 💻 *www.toprural.com*. You can usually book accommodation online. Expect to pay from €60 a day for a house for two to four people and from €50 for a room for two people for one night.

RENTAL ACCOMMODATION

In common with the rest of Spain there's a shortage of long-term rental accommodation on the Costa del Sol where it's relatively easy to find somewhere to rent for up to two months, but difficult to find somewhere for longer. Many property owners rent their property for six month periods during the winter and spring, and then for short periods (usually weekly) in the summer in order to maximise their rental return. Short-term rentals are very expensive, particularly in the summer when a two-bedroom apartment can cost from €500 a week and a villa from €1,000. If you want to rent long-term, then make sure the rental period includes the summer period as well and that you're not required to vacate the property by July.

Finding Rental Accommodation

There are many ways of finding rental accommodation on the Costa del Sol, including the following:

- **Estate Agents** – Many estate agents act as agents for rental property and it may be worth asking to see what they have on their books. **Note, however, that you will have to pay the agent's commission, so the price could be higher.**

- **Local Press** – All the local newspapers carry advertisements for rental accommodation (*Alquileres* in Spanish) in the small advertisements section. *Sur* has a large section on Sunday and *Sur In English* has a large section on Friday. **If you're interested in a property, it's a good idea to telephone as soon as possible since demand is high, particularly for cheaper properties or those in good locations.**

- **Notice Boards** – Some property owners advertise their property on local notice boards or by sticking notices to lamp posts and telephone boxes.

- **Private Advertising** – Many property owners put signs outside the property (*Se Alquila*) with a telephone contact number.

- **Word Of Mouth** – Ask around (particularly in small towns or rural areas) in shops and bars if anyone knows of any rental accommodation.

Rental Costs

The cheapest rental accommodation is found inland and in the north of Malaga city, but prices vary depending on the quality of the accommodation and its location. The following table gives an idea of the minimum monthly rental rate you can expect to pay for a long-term contract in some localities on the Costa del Sol:

Locality	Rental Monthly Rates			
	2-Bed. Flat	3-Bed. Flat	3-Bed. T'house	Villa/Finca
Benalmadena	€600	€650	€850	€1,000
Estepona	€650	€750	€900	€1,200
Fuengirola	€650	€750	€850	€1,000
Inland	€350	€500	€600	€800
Malaga East	€600	€750	€850	€1,000
Malaga Centre	€400	€500	-	-
Malaga North	€350	€400	-	-
Malaga West	€500	€600	-	-
Marbella	€750	€900	€1,200	€1,500+
Mijas Costa	€600	€650	€850	€1,000
Nerja	€400	€500	€750	€1,000
Rincón De La Victoria	€500	€600	€700	€800
Torremolinos	€500	€600	€750	€1,000

BUYING PROPERTY

Property prices have risen spectacularly on the Costa del Sol over the last few years (28 per cent in Malaga province in 2003 alone) and as yet show no sign of stopping, although experts predict slower growth in 2004.

In February 2004 the average price per metre in the province had risen to €1,752, although in many areas on the west side of the coast this is much higher. On the coastal stretch bargains are now few and far between, and there isn't much available on the west side for under €150,000. Properties with a front-line beach or golf position attract a premium (sometimes as much as 100 per cent). Property inland is generally cheaper, although prices have risen sharply in response to demand from foreigners looking for alternatives to expensive property on the coast. Prices are rising fast in villages and small towns as far inland as Alora north of Malaga and Yunquera in the Sierra de las Nieves, and to find cheap property you now need to look beyond Antequera and Ronda.

Bear in mind that many sellers have jumped on the property bandwagon and prices in general are very high. Before you commit yourself to a purchase, consider whether the property is worth the asking price. More importantly, ask yourself if you could resell the property later at the same or higher price. It may be worth making an offer or paying slightly more for a superior property. Cheaper (or less expensive) property on the Costa del Sol can be found in the locations listed below.

Area One – The West

Estepona   Property in the north of the town.

Marbella   In areas popular with Spanish residents such as Las Ibarizas in the city, El Angel in Nueva Andalucía and areas north of San Pedro.

Area Two – Central Costa Del Sol

Benalmadena   Arroyo de la Miel.

Fuengirola   In areas away from the centre and beach, particularly in Los Pacos and Myramar.

Mijas Costa   Urb El Castillo, Urb El Faro de Calaburras and the area north of Fuengirola known as Las Lagunas.

Torremolinos   In the town centre and El Pinillo.

Area Three – Malaga

Malaga   Some of the Costa del Sol's cheapest property can be found in Malaga, although cheap flats tend to be in poor condition and situated in undesirable areas.

Area Four – The East

The East   Property situated to the east of Malaga is generally
considerably cheaper than that on the west side, although
properties in Nerja fetch a premium. The popular Spanish
resorts of Rincón de la Victoria and Torre de Mar have
cheaper apartments than Benalmadena and Fuengirola.

Property Prices

The following listing gives you an approximate idea of what you can buy
within a particular price range. The listing is by no means definitive and
prices are correct as of February 2004. A further guide to property prices in
each specific area is including in **Chapter 4**.

Property Under €150,000

On the coast west of Malaga there's little property for sale in this price
range except for studios and one-bedroom apartments (usually no bigger
than 50m^2). Larger properties are available in Fuengirola. Possibilities are
greater inland, particularly if you're prepared to travel as far as villages
such as Yunquera in the Sierra de las Nieves or the area north of Antequera.

Area One – The West

Estepona	One bedroom apartment
Manilva	One bedroom apartment
Marbella	One bedroom apartment (in a poor location)

Area Two – Central Costa Del Sol

Alhaurín	Small townhouse
Benalmadena	One bedroom apartment
Coín	Small two-bedroom flat
Fuengirola	Two bedroom apartment (from €110,000) in a poor location
Mijas Costa	One bedroom apartment in urbanisations on the coast Two bedroom apartment in Las Lagunas
Torremolinos	One bedroom apartment

Area Three – Malaga

Malaga	New one or two-bedroom apartment in central location New three-bedroom apartment outside centre One or two-bedroom apartment in the centre (but not around the old quarter) In some areas three-bedroom flats are available from under €150,000

Area Four – The East

Nerja	New two-bedroom apartment
Rincón De La Victoria	Two bedroom apartment (not front-line beach)
Torre Del Mar	Two bedroom apartment
Torrox Costa	Two bedroom apartment (not front-line beach)

From €150,000 To €250,000

Area One – The West

Alcaidesa	Two bedroom apartment, front-line beach

Estepona	Two bedroom apartment, front-line golf Three bedroom apartment in town
Manilva	Two bedroom apartment, front-line beach
Marbella	One bedroom apartment, front-line beach
Sotogrande	Two bedroom apartment New one-bedroom apartment

Area Two – Central Costa Del Sol

Alhaurín	Large townhouse (no garden)
Benalmadena	Two bedroom apartment, sea views Two or three-bedroom townhouse Small villa with no pool
Coín	Three bedroom apartment
Fuengirola	Two bedroom apartment, front-line beach Three bedroom apartment within walking distance of the beach
Mijas Costa	Two bedroom apartment, good location Two bedroom townhouse Small two-bedroom villa
Torremolinos	Two or three-bedroom apartment Three bedroom townhouse

Area Three – Malaga

Malaga	Three bedroom apartment in central location Two bedroom apartment on Malagueta seafront or on the east side of the city New three-bedroom apartment on the new seafront on the west side (Nuevo Paseo Marítimo)

Area Four – The East

Nerja	Two bedroom apartment
Rincón De La Victoria	Three bedroom apartment front-line golf or beach Three bedroom townhouse
Torre Del Mar	Three bedroom apartment
Torrox Costa	Three bedroom townhouse

From €250,000 To €400,000

Area One – The West

Estepona   Two bedroom apartment, front-line beach
Three bedroom townhouse

Manilva   Two or three-bedroom apartment

Marbella   Two or three-bedroom apartment, close to golf or beach
Three bedroom townhouse
Two bedroom apartment in Puerto Banús

Sotogrande   New two-bedroom apartment
For €400,000 you can just buy a two-bedroom apartment
on the marina

Area Two – Central Costa Del Sol

Alhaurín   Two bedroom apartment front-line golf
Three bedroom villa with pool

Benalmadena   Three bedroom penthouse
Three or four-bedroom townhouse
One or two-bedroom apartment front-line beach

Coín   Three bedroom villa with pool

Fuengirola   Three bedroom apartment front-line beach
Four bedroom townhouse
Small villa with pool

Mijas Costa   Three bedroom penthouse

Torremolinos   Small villa with pool

Area Three – Malaga

Malaga   Three bedroom apartment on the seafront or on the east
side of the city

Area Four – The East

Nerja   Two or three-bedroom apartment
Small two-bedroom townhouse
Townhouse in central Frigiliana
Semi-detached villa in Frigiliana

Rincón De La Victoria	New three-bedroom townhouse Villa with pool

Torre Del Mar Three bedroom townhouse in prime position
Villa with pool

From €400,000 To €600,000

Area One – The West

Estepona Four bedroom townhouse
Small villa without pool

Manilva Three bedroom townhouse

Marbella Three bedroom apartment front-line golf
Three bedroom townhouse
Two bedroom villa without pool
Three bedroom villa without pool on small plot

Sotogrande Two or three-bedroom apartment
Luxury two-bedroom apartment overlooking the marina

Area Two – Central Costa Del Sol

Alhaurín Large four-bedroom villa with pool
Large country property with pool

Benalmadena Three bedroom villa with pool
Four bedroom townhouse front-line golf

Coín Large villa with pool
Large country property with pool

Fuengirola Three bedroom villa with pool
Four bedroom penthouse front-line beach

Mijas Costa Three bedroom luxury apartment
Small villa with pool
Penthouse apartment

Torremolinos Villa with pool

Area Three – Malaga

Malaga Large luxury apartment on the east side
Small townhouse on the east side

Area Four – The East

Nerja	Luxury three-bedroom apartment Three bedroom villa with pool
Rincón De La Victoria	Large villa with pool
Torre Del Mar	Large villa with pool

From €600,000 To €800,000

Area One – The West

Estepona	Two or three-bedroom luxury apartment front-line beach Four bedroom villa with pool
Marbella	Two bedroom apartment front-line harbour in Puerto Banús Three or four-bedroom townhouse
Sotogrande	Three or four-bedroom villa on small plot, possibly with pool

Area Two – Central Costa Del Sol

Alhaurín	Very large house with pool
Benalmadena	Large townhouse Three or four-bedroom villa with pool
Fuengirola	Large three-bedroom apartment front-line beach
Mijas Costa	Large townhouse (around 200m^2) Three, four or five-bedroom villa with pool
Torremolinos	Three, four or five-bedroom villa with pool

Area Three – Malaga

Malaga	A large flat in a prime position (e.g. on the seafront or in El Limonar) Small villa in Cerrado del Calderón

Area Four – The East

Nerja	Large villa with pool Country property with large plot of land

From €800,000 To €1 million

Area One – The West

Estepona   Large villa with pool

Marbella   Two bedroom penthouse on the Golden Mile
Three bedroom luxury apartment
Three bedroom penthouse in La Mairena
Three or four-bedroom villa with pool on plot of under 1,000m²

Sotogrande   Three bedroom villa on medium plot with pool

Area Two – Central Costa Del Sol

Benalmadena   Luxury two-bedroom apartment in Puerto Marina

Coín   Large country property with large villa and pool

Mijas Costa   Large three or four-bedroom villa with pool and good size plot (at least 2,000m²) with views

Torremolinos Large villa on substantial plot with pool

Area Three – Malaga

Malaga   Villa on east side of the city

Area Four – The East

Nerja   Large villa in favourable position with sea views

From €1 Million

Several years ago, only the largest and most luxurious properties would have fetched prices over €1 million but nowadays it's common to find properties with this price tag – and they're not all luxury villas! Most properties in this price range are situated in Marbella in the areas of the Golden Mile, Las Chapas, La Zagaleta and Nagüeles, Mijas and Sotogrande.

You can expect to buy a two-bedroom apartment, a luxury four-bedroom townhouse front-line beach or a four-bedroom villa with pool in good location. Larger villas with larger plots in good locations are considerably more expensive and some are on sale for over €5 million.

New Property Or Off-Plan

Construction is a boom industry at the moment on the Costa del Sol as the endless skyline of cranes testifies – some 10 per cent of Spain's housing construction is currently taking place in the province of Malaga and in 2003 nearly 92,000 new building projects were started. In some areas, new construction increased by around 50 per cent (e.g. Manilva, Mijas and Rincón de la Victoria) with the extreme case of Nerja where there was an increase of 80 per cent. There are no signs that this tendency is starting to slow down and experts calculate that 2005 will see similar levels of new projects, until there simply isn't any more land to build on.

You can find off-plan properties by calling in at developments themselves (most have onsite offices open from 10am to 2pm and from 4 to 7pm); from estate agents – most of which have off-plan properties on their books and from the bi-monthly magazine, *De Primera Mano*, available in Spanish and English, priced €0.50 – it contains all off-plan developments on the Costa del Sol.

There's currently a huge choice of new property for purchase and experts generally agree that new property is a good investment – prices usually rise as soon as the building is finished. The down side to buying off-plan is the waiting, as building work rarely finishes when it's supposed to – **some take a year longer than originally planned** – and some promoters don't have the correct paperwork. If you're thinking of buying off-plan, it's especially important you use the services of a lawyer to check the paperwork including whether the promoter owns the land he's building on and if he has a bank guarantee to return payments if the company goes bankrupt.

In early 2004 there were press reports concerning promoters on the coast involved in scandals such as not starting building work on new developments several years after taking deposits from clients; not having a building licence for the development; or promoters 'disappearing'. Before handing over any money for the new or off-plan property, consult a lawyer and if a promoter cannot produce the correct paperwork within a reasonable period of time, look elsewhere!

Plots

There's now very little building land left on the Costa del Sol and in some areas there are no plots at all available for purchase. Possibilities are greater inland, although you need to make sure the plot is classed as urban (*urbana*) and not rural (*rústica* or *no urbanizable*) since under new regional laws, it's now very difficult to get planning permission to build on rural land unless you fulfil strict conditions (see **New Legislation** below).

Plot Prices

On The Coast: Plots on the coast are expensive and prices start at around €110 per m² for a plot in a poor position and can be as high as €600 or more for land in a prime position. A plot on the coast is usually from 500m² to 1,000m². When inspecting a plot, check the terrain – much of the land on the coast is sloping and it's expensive to dig out terraces and build retaining walls for construction. **Check the plot has water and electricity supplies nearby.**

Inland: Plots inland are considerably cheaper (from €10 per m²), although a plot near a town such as Coín can cost from €150 to €250 per m². Plots tend to be large (usually with a minimum of 2,000m², but often with several thousand more) and often have numerous fruit or olive trees. Such plots need extensive maintenance and before buying a large piece of land make sure you have both the time and inclination to maintain it. **Check there are water and electricity supplies in the vicinity** – it's very expensive to connect supplies over a distance – and check also if a telephone line is feasible. Investigate the access road – if it's little more than a track, bear in mind that when it pours with rain in the winter, the track may turn into an impassable quagmire suitable for four-wheel drive vehicles only.

New Legislation

In December 2002 Andalusia's regional authorities (the Junta de Andalucía) passed new legislation affecting building work in most of the region's rural areas in an attempt to preserve Andalusia's unique countryside and to prevent it being spoilt by uncontrolled construction such as that seen along much of the coastline. Under the new law it's now extremely difficult to build on a rural plot (known as a *parcela rústica* or *parcela no urbanizable*) unless the land already has a ruin or a building on it or you intend to make your living from agriculture.

Rural Andalusia is very popular at the moment mainly because foreign buyers find the property prices too high on the coast or are looking for a quieter area. However, many foreigners buying plots inland have been caught out by this new legislation and there are numerous stories of foreigners who have found they can do nothing with the rural plot they bought – except enjoy the views. In some cases foreigners who bought land several years ago have now discovered that their applications for a building licence will be refused. Some agents and owners will try to tell you that local authorities aren't imposing the regulations, but it would seem they're taking the legislation seriously – in January 2004 several building projects on rural land were stopped by Mijas town council. These projects will have to be abandoned (at huge costs to the owners) since it's no longer possible to pay a fine and continue building.

There are exceptions to the ruling, although these are somewhat difficult to fulfil since you can currently only build on a rural plot if you intend to live there and make your living from farming the land. Even if you buy a plot with an existing building or ruin permission to extend the building or restore the ruin may not necessarily be forthcoming.

The legislation is currently in its infancy and as a result the situation is unclear and chaotic with different authorities giving conflicting information and advice. Until things become clearer it's probably best to steer clear of rural plots unless you can obtain official confirmation in writing (preferably from the regional authorities themselves) that you can build on the land. Don't be taken in by promises made by owners (anxious to sell their land for a high profit to foreigners) or estate agents (anxious to get their commission) that a building licence can be obtained. Check yourself, or better still, employ a lawyer in the area to check for you. If there's any doubt about whether you can build then it's advisable to look at other properties.

Note that this law only affects rural plots and doesn't affect land classed as 'urbana'.

House Hunting

There are many ways of finding homes for sale on the Costa del Sol including the following:

- **Estate Agents** – Most property owners sell through an estate agent (see page 140).

- **Internet** – There are hundreds of sites dedicated to property on the Costa del Sol. These can be found by typing in 'Costa del Sol property' in a search engine such as Google (🖳 *www.google.com*). **Note that most sites belong to or are linked to an estate agent.**

- **Private Sales** – Many property owners sell privately to avoid paying the agent's commission and put up 'For Sale/ *Se vende*' signs outside the property.

- **Property Exhibitions** – See **Appendix A** for further details.

- **Publications** – Newspapers and magazines such as *Sur in English* (large property section), *Costa del Sol News*, *The Property Advertiser*, *Property News*, *Llave en Mano* (fortnightly in Spanish) and *De Primera Mano* (monthly). For a full listing of publications see **Appendix B**. Large estate agents also publish in-house property listings.

Estate Agents

There are literally hundreds of estate agents on the Costa del Sol, many of which are large companies with branches at different locations in the area.

The quality of service varies greatly, although the best offer a personalised approach without rushing the client into a purchase and may also provide after-sales services such as finding a school and buying a car. Properties for sale are usually with several agents (sometimes with different prices!) and there are few exclusive sales. Ask around for recommendations for a good estate agent. Reputable estate agents should be registered as a member of a professional association such as Agente de Propiedad Inmobiliaria (API) or Gestor Intermediario en Promociones de Edificios (GIPE). **Ask to see an agent's registration number and beware of unlicensed, amateur 'cowboy' agents, of which there are many**.

Purchase Procedure

The purchase procedure in Spain isn't especially complicated, but it's different from other countries and there are numerous pitfalls for the unwary. **Don't be tempted to buy a property without the conveyancing services of a registered lawyer.** Numerous lawyers specialise in conveyancing on the Costa del Sol and many speak good English –ask around for recommendations. You may wish to check with the Malaga Lawyers' Association that the lawyer is registered and has professional insurance cover (Colegio de Abogados de Málaga, Paseo de la Farola , Malaga, ☎ 952-219 910, 🖳 *www.icamalaga.es*). You can telephone the association and ask, or check on the website (go to *Directorio* and then to *Abogados*). **Lawyers charge between 1 and 2 per cent of the property price plus 16 per cent VAT for conveyancing.**

Other fees and taxes associated with property purchase are transfer tax of 7 per cent, notary and land registry fees and possibly plus *valia* tax (a sort of capital gains tax, usually paid by the seller, but often passed to the buyer particularly in the case of new properties). **In general you can expect to add around 10 per cent to the price for fees and taxes.**

For comprehensive information on the purchase procedure see this book's sister publication *Buying a Home in Spain* by David Hampshire (Survival Books).

PROPERTY TAXES

Property taxes, known as the *Impuesto sobre Bienes Inmuebles* (*IBI*), are payable annually and are calculated as a percentage of the cadastral value of the property, which is based on its fiscal value. There are different taxes for urban and rural properties, and many areas are currently revising the cadastral values so you can expect taxes to rise in the near future. Both Marbella and Mijas councils increased taxes by 10 per cent in 2004. Taxes are usually payable before the end of the October and some councils, e.g.

Fuengirola and Mijas, give discount for prompt payment. **Some areas also charge for refuse collection and disposal (***impuesto sobre residuos urbanos***, known as ***basura***) separately.** The following table gives examples of *IBI* and refuse tax rates in different locations on the Costa del Sol:

Town	Urban IBI (%)	Rural IBI (%)	Refuse Tax
Alhaurin (Grande)	0.43	0.7	No
Alhaurín (Torre)	0.6	0.8	No
Benahavís	0.6	0.4	No
Benalmadena	1.0	0.80	Yes
Coín	0.66	0.82	No
Estepona	0.85	0.30	Yes
Fuengirola	0.70	N/A	Yes
Malaga	0.68	0.63	Yes
Marbella	0.93	0.50	Yes
Mijas	0.67	0.63	Yes
Nerja	0.70	0.70	No
Rincón De la Victoria	0.75	0.80	Yes
Sotogrande	0.55	0.55	No
Torremolinos	0.66	0.80	Yes
Vélez-Malaga	0.85	0.60	Yes

Information on tax percentages in all areas in Malaga can be found on the National Cadastral website (🖥 *www.catastro.minhac.es*).

RETIREMENT & NURSING HOMES

State and private nursing homes are available on the Costa del Sol where demand has risen spectacularly in recent years. There are still few state nursing homes and places are in very short supply. Available places are usually given to pensioners with very low income. Facilities and services in private nursing homes vary, although all homes must fulfil strict minimum criteria and standards. Prices also vary, the average cost being around €1,200 a month, for someone sharing a room. Some homes also provide facilities for day care only. **Before committing yourself, look around carefully and compare criteria such as facilities, privacy, level of care, staff qualifications and extra services.** Social services departments in local councils can provide information on nursing homes in specific areas. You should also check that the home is registered with the local and regional authorities.

Private Nursing Homes

Area One – The West

Marbella   C/ Austria, Urb La Cantera, El Carmen ☎ 952-774 555

Quavitae Azul, Urb Azalea Beach,
Ctra de Cádiz km 172.8, Nueva
Andalucía   ☎ 952-906 217

Cortijo Park Nursing Home, Urb Cortijo
Blanco, San Pedro   ☎ 952-780 181

Urb Alicate Playa, Seniors   ☎ 952-838 806

Area Two – Central Costa Del Sol

Alhaurín De La Torre	C/ Chopo 1, Urb Altos de Viñagrande	☎ 952-410 273
Arroyo De La Miel	C/ Contreras s/n, Buenaventura	☎ 952-447 411
	Río Holanda, C/ Montilla 18, Tomillar Alto	☎ 952-562 068
Benalmadena	Centro, Prisal, Avda Mar y Sol 19	☎ 952-964 948
	Urb Myramar, Seniors	☎ 952-576 425
Mijas Costa	Residencia Villa Alhamar, C/ La Higuera 3, Urb El Lagarejo	☎ 952-666 114
Torremolinos	Las Gaviotas, Avda de la Riviera 54, Los Alamos	☎ 952-388 791
	Los Olivos, C/ Pinocho 6, El Pinillo	☎ 952-376 351
	Avda Sorolla 23, Miratorre	☎ 952-383 716
	Virgen De La Victoria, C/ Obispo Juan Martínez 9	☎ 952-389 879

Area Three – Malaga

Malaga	La Biznaga, C/ Fernández Shaw 59, Pedregalejo	☎ 952-200 200
	Octavio Picón, C/ Mariano de Cavia 55, Pedregalejo	☎ 952-292 030
	Residencia Guadalmar, C/ Castellón de la Plana 11, Urb Guadalmar	☎ 952-234 531

C/ Francisco Guillón 13, San Antonio	☎ 952-291 143
San Antonio de Padua, C/ Casanueva, Pto de la Torre	☎ 952-432 665
Virgen de Belén	☎ 952-339 195

There are homes at various locations in Malaga.

Villa de Aranjuez, Cártama	☎ 952-421 152

Area Four – The East

Rincón De La Victoria	Residencia Los Abuelos, Avda de la Torre de Benagalbón 58	☎ 952-404 420
Torre Del Mar	Residencia El Mirador, Avda del Sol s/n	☎ 952-547 551

Retirement Complexes

A few years ago, the Costa del Sol offered nothing specific for retirees other than state or private nursing homes. Over the last two years, however, retirement complexes have been springing up at locations around the coast and there's now a good choice both in facilities and price range. **Note, however, that demand is high and new properties are sold very quickly.** The following listing provides information about retirement complexes on the Costa del Sol:

Area One – The West

Marbella	Azul Marbella	☎ 952-906 217

💻 *www.azulmarbella.com*
This residence situated to the east of Puerto Banús in Urb Azalea Beach offers private room or apartment-type accommodation with numerous onsite facilities such as 24-hour on call medical assistance and a transport service to nearby areas.

Sanyres	☎ 952-908 900

💻 *www.sanyres.es*
This new complex (August 2003) set in Puerto Banús offers one and two-bedroom apartments with numerous onsite facilities such as 24-hour on call medical assistance, professionals such as physiotherapists and a fully equipped gymnasium. Further medical assistance and care is also provided for those residents who request it. Accommodation is offered on a rental basis and includes full-board, cleaning and laundry services. Prices start at €1,800 a month for one person sharing a one-bedroom apartment. **For people over 65 only.**

▲ *Rincón de la Victoria*

▲ *Mijas*

▼ *La Cala Golf Sur*

▲ *Burro taxi, Mijas*

▲ *Cable car, Benalmadena*

▲ *Malaga port and Alcazaba*

▼ *Benalmadena Pueblo*

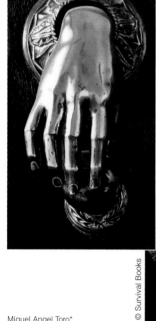

◄

Capobino Dunes, Malaga

▲ *Villas, Mijas*

Miguel Angel Toro*

▲ *Frigiliana*

Miguel Angel Toro*

▶

Pedragalejo Beach, Malaga

José Hidalgo*

▲ *Castello de Gibralfaro, Malaga*

▲ *Fuengirola*

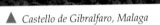

José Hidalgo

▲ *Puerto Marina,
Benalmadena*

Miguel Angel Toro*

▲ *Ronda house and countryside*

◄

Panoramic view of Istán

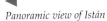

Sotogrande   Senior Community
Currently under construction in Avda Almenara in Sotogrande Alto, this luxury complex will include some 112 apartments (mostly one-bedroom), sports facilities, a spa and medical services. Medical assistance and care will provided for residents who require it. Further information available onsite.

Area Two – Central Costa Del Sol

Alhaurín De   Sol Andalusi   ☎ 952-640 642
La Torre   💻 *www.solandalusi.com*
A new complex currently under construction providing 1,000 homes (detached bungalows, townhouses and apartments) within a self-contained centre including restaurants, shops, fitness and health centre, 24-hour on call medical service plus several other extra. Services include catering, cleaning, shopping and laundry. Accommodation may be bought freehold or rented for between €1,300 to €2,500 a month depending on services provided. **The first phase should be finished by mid 2004.**

Arroyo De   Sanyres
La Miel   💻 *www.sanyres.es*
Sanyres plan to open a new complex in 2005. For more information visit their website.

Sensara   ☎ 952-569 111
💻 *www.sensara.com*
Luxury one and two-bedroom apartments currently under construction due to finish in 2005. Prices start at €150,000 for a one-bedroom apartment and at €180,000 for a two-bedroom apartment. Service charges are around €300 a month. **Occupants must be over 55.**

Mijas   Vitania Resort, Golf Valley
💻 *www.vitania.net*
A new complex due to be finished by the end of 2006 including 338 dwellings, around 60 of these will have maximum level of services, with a social and commercial centre, and a medical centre with 24-hour medical assistance. For more information visit their website.

Area Three – Malaga

Malaga   Interpares, C/ Olmos 19, Urb Cerrado
de Calderón   ☎ 952-290 229
💻 *www.interpares.eu.com*
The coast's oldest retirement complex set in the hills on the east side of the city. Private accommodation is available in one

and two-bedroom apartments costing from €150,000 to €500,000 depending on size and location. A monthly service charge is also payable. Facilities include home care service, restaurant and mini-market.

Sanyres
🖥 *www.sanyres.es*
A new complex is planned for El Limonar in 2004. For more information visit their website.

Area Four – The East

Rincón De La Victoria

Vitalis Park   ☎ 952-970 207
🖥 *www.vitalispark.com*
A new complex currently under construction providing 1 and two-bedroom apartments and numerous facilities such as club house with restaurant, coffee shop, bar, gymnasium, indoor pool and 24-hour medical assistance. Prices start at €181,000 for a one-bedroom apartment. Service charges (€150 a month) and community fees are payable monthly.

6

Employment

If you're relocating to the Costa Del Sol and need to work, one of your first priorities when you arrive will be to find a job. This chapter looks at the employment market, job opportunities, how to find a job and information about setting up a business.

EMPLOYMENT FIGURES

Unemployment on the Costa Del Sol is currently around 9.8 per cent, slightly higher than the national average (8.8 per cent), and in late 2003 some 57,700 people were officially unemployed in the area. The figure is considerably lower among men (6.5 per cent). Tourism and services provide nearly two thirds of employment opportunities in the area and there are comparatively few jobs in industry and agriculture.

WORKING ILLEGALLY

Many businesses on the coast offer casual employment paid in cash, a highly illegal practice, which leaves the employee with no rights whatsoever. Illegal workers employed without a contract and not registered with the social security system have no legal rights (holiday, compensation, unemployment benefit etc.), no right to health treatment (except emergency) and are open to fines from the tax authorities if caught.

If you're offered a job without a contract, as countless people are on the coast, remember it's illegal for both you and the employer, and you should seriously consider whether it's worth working for an employer under those conditions.

JOB OPPORTUNITIES

Most employment on the Costa Del Sol is found within the services sector and in particular jobs related to the tourist industry, the main engine behind the area's economy. **Bear in mind that many jobs, particularly those in the restaurant and bar businesses, are seasonal, i.e. from May to November.**

If you speak fluent Spanish you have a better chance of getting a well-paid job and there may be more opportunities, especially in larger towns or cities where large companies are often based. Many jobs require fluency in several languages (Spanish, English, German and possibly one or more Scandinavian languages).

Jobs are mainly available in the following sectors (listed alphabetically):

- **Administration/Secretarial Work** – Ability in several languages and good working knowledge of computer programmes are generally the requirements. Salary levels depend on experience and responsibility.

- **Construction** – The current building boom on the coast means there are plenty of vacancies for anyone with experience, from 'brickies' to site foremen. Jobs can be found by enquiring at building sites directly or at company offices.

- **Domestic Work** – Wealthy families in the area often require live-in staff to maintain properties, do housework, cooking and gardening, or work as a nanny. A driving licence may be a necessity. **Wages are often low and hours long, and if you're looking after a remote property while the owner's away, the work can be lonely.** Non live-in staff are also in demand, particularly as a nanny or a gardener.

- **Education** – Vacancies often arise for qualified teachers at international schools on the coast (many post vacancies on their website) and TEFL qualified teachers are also in demand for both language schools and private classes. **Note that salaries are generally lower than the equivalent in the UK.**

- **Holiday Companies** – Foreign holiday companies usually employ staff in their home country to work as holiday representatives on the coast, but vacancies for on-site representatives are sometimes advertised in the local press. Staff for hotel entertainment, children's representatives and nursery nurses are also required during the summer months. **Pay is generally low and hours are long, although you usually get free board and lodging.**

- **Hotel & Catering** – Work is mainly seasonal, although increasing numbers of hotels now open all-year round and require permanent staff. Hotels tend to recruit top posts via advertisements in national newspapers or a recruitment company, but other posts are advertised locally. **Shift work is common.**

- **Information Technology** – IT experts are always in demand, particularly those with knowledge of web design and programming.

- **Property Sales** – Probably the greatest number of vacancies are available in the property sector. Estate agencies need marketing staff, property finders, administrative personnel and property vendors. **Knowledge of English, Spanish and at least one other language plus computer literacy is generally required.** Basic salary plus commission is usually offered.

- **Restaurants & Bars** – Work is mainly seasonal, although many restaurants and bars now open all-year round to cater for the resident population. **A knowledge of Spanish is usually necessary and bear in mind that waiting is a respected profession in Spain and you may require previous experience if you wish to be taken on in a Spanish restaurant.** Casual waiting is more for beach bars.

  Working at a beach bar is strictly seasonal employment, although there's a high demand for staff in the summer months. Work is hard (and often physical, especially if you're in charge of the loungers!) and the hours are long – many beach bars open from noon to the small hours of the morning. **Wages are low, but tips can be good.**

- **Sales** – This is probably the area with the most opportunities for foreigners on the coast at the moment, particularly selling advertising space in the expatriate press or in-house magazines or selling products (often household or health and beauty-related). It's a very competitive area and you need to be good to succeed. You usually need your own transport and must be prepared to cover great distances. Pay is usually based on commission.

  There are several companies based on the coast whose advertising claims their sellers make thousands of euros from part-time work from home. These companies usually market health products (e.g. diet aids and beauty products) and their vendors make their commission by finding other people to sell the products, the classic pyramid structure, which is illegal in some countries. **Remember that usually the only people making thousands are those at the top!**

- **Services** – There's a seemingly unlimited demand for household services on the coast, such as cleaners, gardeners, 'odd-job' experts, swimming pool cleaners, and childminders. Work is often piecemeal (intermittent) and poorly paid.

- **Timeshare/Holiday Schemes** – Vacancies are often available for street vendors of timeshare or as on-site vendors. Basic salary plus commission is usually offered.

- **Telephone Sales** – Jobs selling holidays or property by telephone are available, usually based in so-called 'telecentres'. Work is often in shifts, including during the night when calls are made to countries in different time zones. Basic salary plus commission is usually offered.

FINDING A JOB

Your first step in finding a job should be to register as unemployed with the regionally-run Andalusian Employment Service (Servicio Andaluz de Empleo/SAE), which has offices in main towns (see below). Offices are open from 9am to 2pm Mondays to Fridays. **Note that staff may not speak English.** Once you've registered with the SAE you have six months in which to find a job, although there are no strict controls on this for EU nationals.

Servicio Andaluz De Empleo Offices

Area One – The West

Estepona	Avda Andalucía	☎ 952-801 396
Marbella	Avda Arias de Velasco 33	☎ 952-820 462
San Pedro	C/ Pepe Osorio 9	☎ 952-781 325

Area Two – Central Costa Del Sol

Arroyo De La Miel	C/ Las Flores	☎ 952-442 535
Benalmadena	C/ Las Flores	☎ 952-442 535
Coín	C/ Pozo Solís	☎ 952-451 041
Fuengirola	Avda Miramar 33	☎ 952-473 308
Torremolinos	C/ Montemar 46	☎ 952-382 321

Area Three – Malaga

Malaga	Avda Andalucía 27	☎ 952-320 050
	C/ Duque de Rivas 25, Capuchinos	☎ 952-253 404
	C/ Venezuela 1, El Pal	☎ 952-290 166
	C/ Carril de los Guindos 13, La Paz	☎ 952-232 104
	Avda Arrias de Velasco, blq 2, Las Palomas	☎ 952-820 462
	C/ Eguiluz 36, La Unión	☎ 952-325 650
	C/ Negrillos 8, Cártama	☎ 952-496 374

Area Four – The East

Nerja   C/ Jaén   ☎ 952-521 777

Vélez-Málaga   C/ Hnos Pinzón 13   ☎ 952-502 954

The SAE also has a website, but the only language option is Spanish (🖳 *www.juntadeandalucia.es/servicioandaluzdeempleo*). Local vacancies are advertised at SAE offices. **Don't expect staff to notify you of vacancies – the onus is on you to find yourself a job.**

Other Employment Agencies

Spanish Agencies

Spanish employment agencies tend to operate only as temporary employment bureaux (*empresas de trabajo temporal*) and work offered is usually for Spanish-speakers only. Look in the yellow pages under *Trabajo Temporal: Empresas*. **Bear in mind that contract conditions and wages are usually poor in temporary employment posts.**

Foreign Agencies

In recent months several companies specialising in the recruitment of English-speakers have been set up on the coast. Jobs on offer are numerous and range from waiters to top management posts. You can register online and apply for job vacancies from anywhere, although you're expected to be in the area for a personal interview with prospective employers. According to the companies, successful candidates must be able to speak both Spanish and English. Companies offering recruitment services are:

- **Empresolutions** – Offers job vacancies from Marbella to Gibraltar in both English-speaking and Spanish-speaking work places. Candidates should register online and email their CV. Further information is available from ☎ 952-891 328 and 🖳 *www.empresolutions.com*.

- **Recruit Spain** – Job vacancies from Malaga to Gibraltar as well as inland in both English-speaking and Spanish-speaking work places. Candidates are invited to send their CV by email. Further information is available from ☎ 952-898 136 or 952-491 842 and 🖳 *www.recruitspain.com*.

- **Wemploy** – Job vacancies from Malaga to Gibraltar in both English-speaking and Spanish-speaking work places. The company offers the chance to register your CV online and provides a job search facility. Further information is available from ☎ 902-021 200 and 🖳 *www. wemploy.com*.

Newspapers

Jobs are posted in the Spanish local newspapers, *Sur*, *La Opinión* and *El Correo de Málaga* everyday under '*Empleo*' and in national newspapers on Sundays, usually in the financial supplement. The English-language newspapers also advertise job vacancies –*Sur in English* has the most posted under '*Section 22: Situations Vacant*' in their small advertisements section. **This section is probably the one most used by expatriate job hunters on the coast.** Advertisements are also posted online (⌸ *www.surinenglish.com*).

You can also post an advertisement yourself under the '*Situations Wanted*' section, outlining the sort of employment you're looking for and your contact details.

Internet

There are hundreds of sites for job hunters on the internet, an increasingly popular method of finding employment. Most job vacancy websites also offer advice on finding a job and the opportunity to post your CV online. Below is a listing of the most popular sites. The sites are for Spain as a whole, although most list vacancies by province (Malaga), but there are as-yet no Costa Del Sol specific sites.

⌸ *http://jobs.escapeartist.com/openings/spain* (general website with numerous vacancies for the Costa Del Sol);

⌸ *www.laboris.net* (general website with a good selection for the Costa Del Sol);

⌸ *www.monster.es* (general website with a good selection of vacancies);

⌸ *www.tecnoempleo.com* (job vacancies in IT and telecommunications);

⌸ *www.trabajos.com* (general website with a good selection of vacancies).

Notice Boards

Job vacancies are often posted on notice boards outside supermarkets, churches and local businesses. It may be a good idea to post your contact details together with the sort of job you're looking for on the board. Many people include their telephone number in a tear-off section at the bottom to make it easier for the interested party.

Shops

Shops and businesses on the coast requiring staff often don't usually advertise vacancies but simply post a notice in the window stating what they're looking for. Notes usually start '*se busca*' or '*se necesita*' followed by the job. A contact number or the words '*información dentro*' or '*razón dentro*' (enquire within) usually follow.

SELF-EMPLOYMENT & STARTING A BUSINESS

A popular option with foreigners on the Costa Del Sol is to become self-employed or start their own business. **This isn't an option to be taken lightly and you should carefully consider all aspects of such a venture before you commit yourself.** Stories of failed businesses and bankruptcy are common on the Costa Del Sol and many people fail to realise that behind most self-employed and successful businesses there's a lot of very hard work. There are, however, numerous success stories and there are some 9,700 self-employed foreigners in the province of Malaga.

If you're seriously considering this option, the best place to start is at a reputable *gestoría* (an agency providing help and advice with form-filling and other paperwork) – ask friends or other professionals (banks, lawyers) to recommend one. For a reasonable fee, a gestoría will give you comprehensive information on the process involved, guide you through it and take charge of most of the paperwork for you. You can do it yourself, but your knowledge of Spanish needs to be good as well as your stamina and patience for standing in queues!

The Junta de Andalucía runs a useful service for people hoping to set up a business: the Andalusian Centre for Entrepreneurs (Centro Andaluz de Empresarios/CADE), who can provide useful help and advice. The CADE also runs a multi-cultural entrepreneurs service specifically for foreigners who need help in starting a business and advice on grants and subsidies available in the area. The CADE is based in Campanillas, Malaga, C/ Marie Curie 8, Edif B (☎ 951-231 730, 🖳 *www.juntadeandalucia.es/servicio andaluzdeempleo/cade*).

Self-Employment

Income Tax & VAT

The self-employed (*autónomos*) in Spain must register with the tax office both for income tax and for VAT. Income tax is levied at 20 per cent (levied on whatever you earn minus justifiable expenses) and must be paid in quarterly instalments (by 20th January, 20th April, 20th July and 20th

October) based on your earnings for the quarter. Once a year (in May/June) you're also required to make an annual tax statement for the previous calendar year – following this you may be entitled to a refund or required to pay extra tax. Most professions are required to charge (and then pay) 16 per cent VAT (*IVA*), although there are some exceptions. Income tax and VAT information is available from local tax offices listed below (where staff may not speak much English) or in Spanish only from the telephone helpline (☎ 901-121 224) or website (🖳 *www.aeat.es*). You may find it easier to consult a reputable tax adviser (*asesor fiscal*).

Tax offices on the Costa Del Sol can be found at:

Area One – The West

Marbella   Avda Jacinto Benavente 27   ☎ 952-824 994

Area Two – Central Costa Del Sol

Torremolinos   C/ Cruz 18   ☎ 952-380 606

Area Three – Malaga

Malaga   Avda Andalucía 2   ☎ 952-077 200

                   C/ Puerto 12 (Malaga East)   ☎ 952-600 351

                   C/ Parra 3, Alora   ☎ 952-497 200

Area Four – The East

Vélez-Málaga   C/ Romero Pozo 4   ☎ 952-503 000

Social Security

The self-employed must also register with the social security system and make monthly contributions. The monthly minimum contribution is currently €225.11 and the maximum around €2,575, which entitles you to sickness and temporary invalidity benefits, maternity benefits, health treatment under the public health system and a retirement pension. Within these limits, you can choose how much you pay but, if you're under 50, there are few advantages in paying more than the minimum amount; if you're over 50, you may consider paying a higher amount in order to qualify for a higher pension.

Information about social security payments and benefits is available from local social security offices listed below (staff may speak little English) or in Spanish only from the telephone helpline ☎ 900-616 200 or website 🖳 *www.seg-social.es*.

Area One – The West

Estepona   Avda Andalucía s/n   ☎ 952-802 373

Marbella   Pl Leganitos s/n   ☎ 952-771 599

Area Two – Central Costa Del Sol

Coín   Pl General Aranda 22   ☎ 952-450 191

Fuengirola   C/ Dr García Verdugo s/n   ☎ 952-581 303

Area Three – Malaga

Malaga   Avda Andalucía 31   ☎ 952-347 622

                   Alameda Capuchinos 79   ☎ 952-653 146

                   Pl Médico Zamudio 1, Alora   ☎ 952-496 121

Area Four – The East

Vélez-Málaga   C/ Dr Fernando Vivar 3   ☎ 952-500 948

Starting A Business

Starting up a business is a complex matter and you should seek professional help, particularly in deciding which business option is the best for you. There are several types of company in Spain, all requiring a minimum number of shareholders and minimum investment capital. Some also have accounting and auditing requirements. Tax obligations differ depending on the company, although all are subject to company tax currently levied at 35 per cent. Competent *gestorías* usually have a business advisor and tax advisors can also offer advice on setting up a company.

Buying Premises

Business premises (called a *local*) are often available on the Costa Del Sol, although most are bars, restaurants or shops. The majority of premises are sold on a leasehold basis (*traspaso*), which means you pay for the business lease plus rent to the landlord for the use of the premises. Leases may be for any length of time, although usually no less than 5 years and no more than 25, although most are renewable. The cost of the rent increases annually by the rate of inflation. When the lease is renewed, the rent may be increased by 20 per cent.

As the leaseholder you're responsible for the payment of local rates, utilities and possibly community fees incurred by the premises. You're permitted to sell the lease to a third party before it expires, although you must offer it to the landlord first and if you sell it to someone else, the landlord is entitled to commission (usually 20 per cent). Rental payments are usually made monthly in advance and most landlords require two months rent as a security deposit. If you're considering buying premises, don't undertake the purchase without proper legal advice.

Business premises for sale can be advertised through estate agents (some of which specialise in the sale of business premises), in the local press or even at the premises (the sign usually says 'Se Traspasa local').

Rock of Gibraltar

7

Health

One of the most important aspects of living on the Costa del Sol, or anywhere for that matter, is maintaining good health. One of the prime concerns of expatriates is the standard of the health service and medical staff. All foreigners must have medical insurance cover, public or private, and both systems have an excellent reputation on the Costa del Sol. This chapter looks at the public health system (including how to register) and private health insurance, and in addition provides details and information about health centres and hospitals, dentists and opticians, and chemists.

PUBLIC HEALTH SYSTEM

The public health system on the Costa del Sol is part of the Andalusian regional health service, the Servicio Andaluz de Salud (SAS). Under the system, residents who are pensioners or who contribute to the social security (*Seguridad Social*) system are entitled to free primary (being seen by a general practitioner/GP) and hospital medical treatment and to subsidised prescriptions (prescriptions are free for pensioners). The medical service on the Costa del Sol is generally very good and has an excellent reputation among foreign residents. However, health centres in some areas are overstretched, due to the fact that medical services haven't matched the rapid increase in number of residents over the last few years. Non-urgent operations are also subject to waiting lists, although these have been shortened dramatically in recent months.

You shouldn't expect medical staff to speak English – some may speak a little, but most don't. If your knowledge of Spanish is poor, you should take someone along with you to translate. Some health centres and hospitals offer translation services which are usually provided by a team of volunteer foreigners. The volunteers provide an excellent service, but you shouldn't rely on them in an emergency.

How To Register

EU Pensioners

In order to qualify for free medical treatment you should take form E-121 (issued in your home country) to your nearest social security office (Instituto Nacional de Seguridad Social/INSS – see below) and apply for a Spanish health card (*tarjeta sanitaria*), which will be sent later by post. Once a card has been applied for, you're entitled to free medical treatment and prescriptions. **If you need treatment before you receive your card, you should show the doctor or health centre the receipt given to you by the social security office.**

EU Visitors

Visitors should bring form E-111 with them from their home country. The form must be shown to medical staff if you require any medical treatment. If you don't have the form and need urgent medical treatment, you will be treated but you must pay for treatment. You may get a refund in your home country.

EU Residents

EU residents should bring form E-111 with them, which is valid for three months from the time of arrival. After three months if you've started work you should register with the social security system and apply for a social security/health card (*tarjeta sanitaria*). **If you don't plan to work, you will need private medical insurance.**

Note that an EU health card (similar to a credit card) will be introduced in EU countries from June 2004. The card will contain information (personal and social security details) about the holder, including the number and length of social security contributions. Holders of the card will no longer need forms E-111 and E-121.

Non-EU Residents

Non-EU residents must have proof of medical insurance cover (usually private) before they enter Spain in order to get a visa. If you find employment in Spain you should register with the social security system and apply for a social security/health card. **If you don't plan to work, you must continue with payments towards private medical insurance cover.** Information about your health card is available from ☎ 901-302 020 from 9am to 9pm Mondays to Fridays.

Social Security Offices

Social Security Offices (INSS) on the Costa del Sol are listed below. Offices are generally open from 9am to 1.30pm Mondays to Fridays. **Staff may not speak English.** Information is also available (in Spanish only) from the INSS telephone helpline ☎ 901-502 050 and website 🖳 *www.seg-social.es*.

Area One – The West

Estepona	Avda Andalucía s/n	☎ 952-802 373
Marbella	Pl Leganitos s/n	☎ 952-771 599

Area Two – Central Costa Del Sol

Coín   Pl General Aranda 22   ☎ 952-450 191

Fuengirola   C/ Dr García Verdugo s/n   ☎ 952-581 303

Area Three – Malaga

Malaga   Avda Andalucía 31   ☎ 952-347 622

                  Alameda Capuchinos 79   ☎ 952-653 146

                  Alora, Pl Médico Zamudio 1   ☎ 952-496 121

Area Four – The East

Vélez-Málaga C/ Dr Fernando Vivar 3   ☎ 952-500 948

Once you have your social security card you should register at your local health centre (see below). You're entitled to choose your doctor and if you have children (up to 14 or 16-years-old), you should choose a paediatrician as well. If you don't choose a doctor then the health centre will allocate you one.

Most health centres are open all day, although those in smaller towns and villages have reduced opening hours. Not all health centres provide emergency treatment and visits to doctors in health centres in small villages may not by appointment, but based on a first-come first-served basis. **Note that even if you have an appointment, you usually have to wait at least 20 minutes beyond your allocated time simply because appointments are given every 3 minutes regardless of how long they really take.** The SAS provides a 24-hour 'ask the doctor' telephone service for use in an emergency (☎ 902-505 060). **For life-threatening emergencies requiring an ambulance dial ☎ 061.**

Public Health Centres

Area One – The West

Benahavís   Avda Andalucía s/n   ☎ 952-855 360
                Open 9 to 11.30am Mondays to Fridays

Cancelada   Pl José Vázquez   ☎ 952-883 785
                Open 8.15am to 12.45pm Mondays to Fridays

Casares   C/ Peñón Redondo   ☎ 952-895 115
                              appointments only ☎ 952-855 360
                Open 8am to 3pm Mondays to Fridays

Estepona	C/ Cristóbal Colón 20, Casa del Mar	☎ 952-793 313
	appointments only ☎ 952-855 360
	Open 8am to 8pm Mondays to Fridays

Avda Juan Carlos I ☎ 952-801 084
appointments only ☎ 952-792 176
Open 8am to 8pm Mondays to Fridays

Istán C/ Azufaifo 12 ☎ 952-869 653
Open 8am to 5pm Mondays to Fridays

Manilva C/ Nueva 3 ☎ 952-892 451
Open 8am to 3pm Mondays to Fridays

Marbella Avda Las Albarizas, Las Albarizas ☎ 952-824 802
appointments only ☎ 952-828 836
Open 8am to 8pm Mondays to Fridays

Pl Leganitos 5, Leganitos ☎ 952-772 184
appointments only ☎ 952-828 801
Open 8am to 8pm Mondays to Fridays

C/ Pinsapo, Elviria ☎ 952-833 572
Open 11am to 3pm Mondays to Fridays

C/ Gustavo Bécquer 30, Nueva
Andalucía ☎ 952-818 734
Open 8am to 2pm Mondays to Fridays

Ojén C/ Alberca 4 ☎ 952-881 023
Open 9am to 5pm Mondays to Fridays

Sabinillas C/ Emilio Prado 1 ☎ 952-890 295
Open 8am to 3pm Mondays to Fridays

San Pedro Avda Príncipe de Asturias ☎ 952-787 700
appointments only ☎ 952-787 892
Open 8am to 8pm Mondays to Fridays

Area Two – Central Costa Del Sol

Arroyo De Urb Pueblo Sol s/n ☎ 952-440 404
La Miel *appointments only* ☎ 952-440 305
Open 8am to 8pm Mondays to Fridays

Alhaurín De Avda de España s/n ☎ 952-414 619
La Torre *appointments only* ☎ 952-410 482
Open 8am to 9pm Mondays to Fridays

Alhaurín El Grande	Virgen del Rosario 1	☎ 952-595 475
	appointments only	☎ 952-595 000
	Open 8am to 9pm Mondays to Fridays	

Benalmadena Village	C/ Cerrillo 2	☎ 952-449 167
	Open 8am to 3pm Mondays to Fridays	

Coín	Ctra Tolox	☎ 952-452 767
	appointments only	☎ 952-452 550
	Open 8am to 8pm Mondays to Fridays	

Fuengirola	C/ Antoñete, Los Boliches	☎ 952-463 622
	appointments only	☎ 952-584 849
	Open 8am to 8pm Mondays to Fridays	
	C/ La Unión, Las Lagunas (also serves	☎ 951-062 247
	Mijas Costa) *appointments only*	☎ 951-062 240
	Open 8am to 8pm Mondays to Fridays	
	C/ Dr García Verdugo (Fuengirola west)	☎ 952-468 835
	appointments only	☎ 952-584 848
	Open 8am to 8pm Mondays to Fridays	

La Cala	C/ Torreón	☎ 952-492 150
	Open 8am to 3pm Mondays to Fridays	

Mijas Village	Avda de México	☎ 952-485 404
	appointments only	☎ 952-590 513
	Open 8am to 3pm Mondays to Fridays	

Torremolinos	C/ Nerja, La Carihuela	☎ 952-053 213
	Open 8am to 8pm Mondays to Fridays	
	C/ Pablo Bruno, San Miguel	☎ 952-386 484
	Open 8am to 8pm Mondays to Fridays	

Area Three – Malaga

Malaga capital has around 16 health centres situated in the main districts, e.g. Ciudad Jardín, Limonar, El Palo, Puerto de la Torre etc. To find your nearest centre, telephone the SAS (☎ 902-505 060 – available 24 hours) or consult the SAS website (🖳 *www.juntadeandalucia.es/servicio andaluzdesalud*) under the section '*Información por centros*' and click on Malaga on the map.

Malaga	C/ Carmona, Alora	☎ 952-498 100
	appointments only	☎ 952-496 645
	Open 8am to 8pm Mondays to Fridays	

Bd San Rafael Alto, Cártama   ☎ 952-422 460
Open 8am to 2pm Mondays to Fridays

Area Four – The East

Caleta De Vélez Ctra Málaga, Almería.   ☎ 952-440 404
appointments only ☎ 952-440 305
Open 8am to 8pm Mondays to Fridays

Frigiliana   C/ Príncipe de Asturias   ☎ 952-533 123
Open 8.30am to 12.30pm Mondays to Fridays

La Cala   C/ Ancla s/n   ☎ 952-403 083
Del Moral   Open 8am to 8pm Mondays to Fridays

Maro   C/ San Miguel
Open 8 to 11am Mondays to Fridays
**Note that there is no telephone number for this
health centre.**

Nerja   C/ Carlos Millón   ☎ 952-523 131
Open 24-hours Mondays to Fridays

Rincón De   Avda Mediterráneo   ☎ 952-404 140
La Victoria   Open 8am to 8pm Mondays to Fridays

Torre Del Mar   C/ Eduardo Iglesias   ☎ 952-545 428
appointments only ☎ 952-542 396
Open from midnight to 10pm Mondays to Fridays

Vélez-Málaga   San Isidro, Norte   ☎ 952-549 261
appointments only ☎ 952-549 260
Open 8am to 9pm Mondays to Fridays

C/ Fernando Vivar, Sur   ☎ 952-502 008
appointments only ☎ 952-503 454
Open from midnight to 10pm Mondays to Fridays

PUBLIC HOSPITALS

All public hospitals provide 24-hour casualty and emergency treatment
(*urgencias*). Patients for non-emergency operations are entitled to choose
any public hospital within Andalusia – this is sometimes a useful way
of avoiding a long wait as some hospitals have shorter waiting lists
than others.

Area One – The West

Marbella   Hospital Costa del Sol, A-7 km 187
(opposite Los Monteros hotel)   ☎ 952-828 250
💻 *www.hcs.es*
Serves central and western Costa del Sol.

Area Two – Central Costa Del Sol

Torremolinos   Hospital Marítimo, Sanatorio 5   ☎ 951-032 000

Area Three – Malaga

Malaga   Hospital Ciudad Jardín/Carlos Haya,
Avda Jorge Silvela   ☎ 951-030 100
💻 *www.carloshaya.net*

Hospital Civil, Avda Carlos Haya   ☎ 951-030 300

Hospital de Especialidades Virgen de
la Victoria, Campus Universitario,
Teatinos   ☎ 951-032 000
💻 *www.activanet.es/clinico*

Hospital Materno-Infantil, Avda
Miraflores de los Angeles   ☎ 951-030 200
💻 *www.carloshaya.net*
This is a children's hospital.

Area Four – The East

Vélez-Málaga   Urb El Tomillar   ☎ 951-067 000
Serves the Axarquía region as well as the
eastern side of the coast.

Day hospitals (*Servicio de Atención Rápida* – but known as *SAR*), providing primary hospital care and some specialist out-patient treatments are currently under construction in Benalmadena, Estepona, Fuengirola and Nerja with completion expected from 2005 to 2006.

USEFUL NUMBERS

AIDS Helpline ☎ 900-850 100
Available 10am to 2pm Mondays to Fridays

Alcoholics Anonymous	☎ 952 218 211 This is the central office and most towns have local groups, some of which are English-speaking, listed in the local press.
Alzheimer's Association	☎ 952-390 902
Cancer Helpline	☎ 900-100 036
Drugs Helpline	☎ 900-200 514 Available 8am to 3pm Mondays to Fridays
Helpline For Women	☎ 900-200 999 Available 24 hours
Sex Advice For Young People	☎ 901-406 969 Available 10am to 2pm and 5 to 7.30pm Mondays to Fridays
Smokers Helpline	☎ 900-850 300

PRIVATE MEDICAL TREATMENT

Private medical treatment is a popular alternative to the public system with both Spaniards and foreign residents. Private treatment is expensive unless you have private health insurance and most private clinics won't provide free treatment under the conditions of the E-111 form.. There are numerous companies offering a range of private health insurance policies and a good choice of private clinics and hospitals. **Note that most private hospitals don't have the full range of facilities and services provided in public hospitals.**

Health Insurance Companies

Spanish Companies

The main companies operating in the area are:

● **Adeslas** – Offices in Estepona, Fuengirola, Malaga, Marbella, Torremolinos and Torre del Mar (☎ 902-200 200 , 🖥 *www.adeslas.es*);

● **Previsión Médica** – Offices in Alhaurín el Grande, Benalmadena Costa, Malaga, Marbella, Mijas, Nerja, Torremolinos, Torre del Mar and Vélez-Málaga (☎ 952-226 596 or ☎ 952-216 522, 🖥 *www.previsionmedica.es*);

● **Sanitas** – Offices in Estepona, Fuengirola, Malaga, Marbella and Torremolinos (☎ 901-100 210, 🖥 *www.sanitas.es*).

Foreign Companies

- **AXA PPP Healthcare** – 💻 *www.axappphealthcare.com*;

- **BUPA International** – 💻 *www.bupaspain.com*. On the Costa del Sol contact Mr J Williams by telephone or email (☎ 952-491 115, ✉ *bupa int@mercuryin.es*);

- **Exeter Friendly Society** – ☎ *www.exeterfriendly.co.uk*. In Spain contact Jennifer Cunningham by telephone or email (☎ 966-461 690, ✉ *jenniferc@teleline.es*);

- **International Health Insurance** – ☎ 952-471 204, 💻 *www.ihi.com*.

There are also numerous insurance brokers who can give advice on which company and which policy is right for you. Ask around for recommendations or look in the yellow pages under '*Seguros*' or '*Seguros Médicos*'. Many companies also advertise in the local press. Policies and prices vary enormously so it's important to shop around.

Private Clinics

Every town on the Costa del Sol can boast several private clinics and staff there usually speak English and possibly other foreign languages. Some clinics cater for specific nationalities, e.g. British or German. Facilities and services vary greatly from no more than a GP to several specialist doctors and X-ray testing and scanning facilities. Most clinics provide home doctor services and emergency medical treatment, although note that if a clinic doesn't have the facilities required you will be referred to or taken to a public hospital. Clinics generally belong to one or more health insurance schemes – your insurance policy should provide a list of participating members in the area. If you don't have a list, consult the yellow pages under '*Clínicas Médicas*'.

Specialist Private Clinics

There are numerous private clinics specialising in specific areas of medicine, particularly gynaecology, heart complaints and cosmetic surgery.

There have been several scandals recently on the Costa del Sol concerning clinics offering cosmetic surgery. Irregular practices included unregistered or under-qualified doctors or inadequate facilities. Several cases even involved operations under general anaesthetic without the supervision of an anaesthetist! Check the clinic and doctor you've chosen for cosmetic surgery is properly qualified and registered with the health authorities before committing yourself.

Private Hospitals

Fuengirola	Hospital Salus, Avda Clemente Díaz, Edif Puebla Lucía	☎ 900-444 999
Malaga	Clínica El Angel, C/ Corregidor Nicolás Isidro 16	☎ 952-045 000
	Clínica Gálvez, C/ Duque de la Victoria 8	☎ 952-213 664
	Parque San Antonio, Avda Pintor Sorolla 2	☎ 952-121 100
Marbella	Hospital Costa del Sol (A-7 km 187, opposite Los Monteros hotel). 🖳 *www.hcs.es* Although essentially a public hospital, the centre also serves private patients.	☎ 952-828 250
	Hospital Europa, Avda Severo Ochoa 24	☎ 952-774 200
Torremolinos	Clínica Santa Elena, Urb Los Alamos	☎ 900-210 414

Helicopter Rescue Service

Helicópteros Sanitarios is a company based in Puerto Banús, which provides emergency helicopter evacuation services to its members as well as a home doctor service and ambulances. Annual membership costs €93.15 for one person, €186.31 for a couple and €213.31 for a family. Further information is available from ☎ 952-816 767 and 🖳 *www.helicopterossanitarios.com*. See also **Emergency Numbers** on page 288.

DOCTORS

Many Spanish doctors with private practices speak enough English to understand and explain health problems. The level of English, however, tends to be lower in Malaga city, simply because the doctors there attend far fewer foreign patients than their colleagues in other locations on the coast.

Most private practices hold clinics in the afternoons (e.g. 5pm to 8pm) and few offer morning appointments.

CHEMISTS

Most places on the coast have at least one chemist (*farmacia*) and there are also several located at urbanisations along the coast. **Chemists are the only places you can buy medicines in Spain, although supermarkets and *parafarmacias* stock basic first-aid items such as antiseptic cream, plasters and lint.** Chemists also sell a wide range of non-medical wares such as cosmetics, baby food and equipment, toiletries and diet foods. Pharmacists are highly trained and provide free medical advice for treatment of minor ailments. If they cannot help, they will recommend a local doctor or specialist in the area.

Chemists are generally open from 9.30am to 2pm and from 4.30 or 5pm through to 8pm Mondays to Saturdays. There are duty-chemists that are open either 24-hours, from 9.30am to 10pm or from 10pm to 9.30am. **If you visit a duty-chemist you usually have to ring a bell and are dealt with through a hatch.** Lists of duty-chemists in the locality are posted on chemist windows, listed in the local press and can be found on the internet (🖳 *http://canales.diariosur.es/fijas/farmacias/farm*).

Listed below are 24-hour chemists on the Costa del Sol:

Marbella	Avda Ricardo Soriano 4
	Avda Ricardo Soriano 44
Rincón De La Victoria	Avda del Mediterráneo 93
	Avda del Mediterráneo 100
San Pedro	C/ Marqués del Duero 80
Torre Del Mar	Avda Los Manantiales (next to Supersol/Mercadona)

DENTISTS

The only dental treatment currently provided on the public health system is one annual check-up for children born after 1991. Contact your local health centre if you want your child to be included in the scheme. Otherwise, dental treatment must be included under a private health insurance policy or paid for directly. Many health insurance companies provide policies including dental treatment, although comprehensive dental policies are usually very expensive!

Numerous dentists, both Spanish and foreign, have practices on the Costa del Sol and most Spanish dentists speak English. **Note that a foreign dental**

practice may be more expensive than a Spanish one. All dentists should be registered and they must be able to prove this. Not all dentists provide a full range of treatments, a service provided in large clinics only. Some smaller practices do check-ups, crowns and fillings only, and many don't have in-house X-ray facilities. If you need a tooth extracted, you may have to visit a specialist. **Not all dentists treat children.**

Fees vary greatly and it's worth looking around before registering with a dental practice. Some surgeries operate a membership scheme (e.g. €100 a year) which includes check-ups, consultations, a scale and polish. Ask around for recommendations or look in the yellow pages under *'Clínicas Dentales'* or *'Dentistas: Odontólogos y estomatólogos'*.

Orthodontic Treatment

Orthodontic treatment tends to be carried out by specialist dentists only and not by general practices. Correction and cosmetic treatment is increasingly popular on the Costa del Sol and there are now numerous clinics operating in the area. If you or your child needs orthodontic treatment, visit several recommended practices and compare the different treatments and prices offered. There's usually a consultation fee (around €30) for which the dentist will offer a diagnosis and treatment plan. **Prices and treatment vary enormously for children's orthodontic treatment and it's not uncommon for dental practices to carry out unnecessary treatment or start treatment prematurely.**

OPTICIANS

There are numerous opticians on the Costa del Sol, some of which cater for specific nationalities and most have English-speaking staff. Ask around for a recommendation or look in the yellow pages under *'Opticas'*. Most opticians provide free eye tests and have a wide range of frames and lenses. There are several chains of opticians who periodically have special offers on certain types of glasses so it's worth shopping around.

OTHER MEDICAL SERVICES

Spanish and foreign specialists offer a wide range of services on the Costa del Sol such as acupuncture (*acupuncturista*), chiropody (*podólogo*), chiropractic (*quiropráctico*), osteopathy (*osteopatía*), physiotherapy (*fisioterapauta*) and psychology (*psicólogo*). **Although most specialists are highly qualified and experts in their field, the odd conman or 'quack' isn't uncommon on the Costa del Sol so, before putting your body in**

anyone's hands, you should make sure they're qualified and registered with the local health authorities. Many professionals advertise in the local press, although the best way to find someone good is to ask around for recommendations. A sure sign is if the professional in question has been on the coast for several years –usually only the best last!

Alternative medicine and treatments are also widely available. A good source of information on what's available are health shops (*herbolisterías*) and La Chispa magazine (⌨ *www.lachispa.net*), published bi-monthly and has a wealth of information on alternative living on the coast.

Granada

8

Education

A main concern of parents when considering relocation to the Costa del Sol is their children's education. There are several options available and the one you choose will depend on many factors such as your finances, short-term plans and whether you wish your child to have a Spanish education. The different options are discussed in this chapter, which also provides a directory of private and international schools on the coast as well as information on after-school and summer activities, and learning Spanish.

> Note that all schools on the Costa del Sol are currently heavily over-subscribed – state schools are over-crowded and private schools have long waiting lists. If you can, plan ahead and get your child on the waiting list as soon as possible.

SPANISH EDUCATION

Advantages

- Your child has the chance to learn Spanish and integrate into a different culture and society.

- Spanish state schools are free and Spanish private schools are considerably cheaper than international schools.

- Entrance to a Spanish university will be easier if your child has gone through the Spanish education system.

Disadvantages

- Learning Spanish can take children time and hold back their learning process.

- You will need to learn good Spanish too in order to communicate with the teachers (Spanish teachers don't necessarily speak English!).

Education is compulsory for all children between the ages of 6 and 16 in Spain, although places are now available at many schools from the age of 3 and most children tend to start their schooling early. Education consists of four main phases:

1. *Infantil* (from ages 3 to 6) where the emphasis is on learning social skills;

2. *Primaria* (from 6 to 12) which is divided into three cycles of two years;

3. *Secundaria* (from 12 to 16) which is divided into two cycles of two years, at the end of which students who have achieved set standards receive the School Leaver's Certificate;

4. *Bachiller* (16 to 18), similar to A Level or International Baccalaureate (IB) in other countries.

The standard of Spanish education is generally on a par with that in other western countries, although there are major differences in learning methods (the Spanish system favours learning by rote) and there are few extra-curricular activities. The vast majority of Spanish schools are co-educational.

School Holidays

School holidays consist of around two weeks at Christmas, one week at the end of February, one week for Easter and nearly three months in the summer (from around 20 June to 15 September), plus local and national bank holidays.

STATE SCHOOLS

Education in state schools (*colegio público*) is provided free from the ages 3 to 18 for all residents – **but you do have to pay for books and materials.** As in many countries, places at state schools are determined by catchment areas – to find out which school is in your catchment area ask at the local town hall. **Note that places at state schools in many localities are in short supply and you're unlikely to get a place at a school outside your catchment area.**

Registration

Registration for state schools on the Costa del Sol takes place in the spring (usually in April). In practice, however, children can be registered at any time of the year if there are places. To register your child you need:

● Your child's passport (original and photocopy);

● Your passport (original and photocopy);

● Proof that your child's vaccinations are up to date;

● Proof of residence or imminent residence (this is available from your local town hall and the certificate is called '*certificado de empadronamiento*').

If your child is starting secondary school from the third year upwards you also have to provide proof of their education record and in addition obtain a certificate from the Spanish Education Ministry to confirm this. **Comprehensive information can be obtained from Spanish consulates and embassies in your country of residence.** You are also recommended to refer to *Living and Working in Spain* (Survival Books) for more detailed information – see page 334.

Primary Schools

After-School Activities

Many primary schools now have an after-school activity programme, typically running from 4 to 6pm. Children who stay to lunch are supervised until the activities start. Bus travel isn't available after activities.

Curriculum

The curriculum includes Spanish, English, maths, natural and social sciences, music, art and physical education. Catholic religion is optional – the alternative to this is usually extra reading or studies.

Lunch

Lunch is provided by outside caterers in many schools after school day has finished, this is at extra cost (around €3 a day) and the quality is generally excellent. Lunch usually finishes at 3 or 3.30pm. If your child travels to school using the school bus service it makes no difference whether they stay for lunch or not, they are still able to use this service to get home.

Parent-Teacher Meetings

Time is allocated each week (known as *tutoría*) when parents can meet up with the teacher. Reports (*notas/evaluación*) are issued at the end of each term.

Timetable

Generally, 9 or 9.30am until 2 or 2.30pm. Children are given a 30-minute break, during which most of them eat a snack.

Transport

Free buses to and from schools are usually available in large catchment areas (e.g. Mijas Costa and Las Chapas/Elviria in Marbella), but not within towns.

Additional Information

The maximum number of children permitted in a class at primary school is 25 and children aren't required to wear a uniform.

Secondary Schools

Curriculum

In the first two years students do Spanish, English, maths, natural and social sciences, history and geography, IT, music, art and physical education. During the second two years students may opt for certain subjects including a second foreign language.

Parent-Teacher Meetings

Time is allocated each week (known as *tutoría*) when parents can meet up with the teacher. Reports (*notas/evaluación*) are issued at the end of each term.

Timetable

Generally, 8.15 or 8.30am until 1.30 or 3pm depending on the day of the week and time of the year. Students have a 30-minute break when most of them eat a snack.

Transport

Free buses to and from schools are available in large catchment areas (e.g. Mijas Costa and Las Chapas/Elviria in Marbella), but not within towns.

Additional Information

The maximum number of children permitted in a class at secondary school is 30 and children aren't required to wear a uniform. Lunch isn't usually available.

Learning Spanish

If you decide to send your child to a state school, it's vital to give them as much as support as possible with their Spanish AND you should learn to speak it yourself. Some schools have specialist teachers for foreign children, but there isn't enough help and children may have three extra lessons of Spanish a week at the most. If you want your child to make academic and social progress you should make provision for lessons outside school and actively encourage participation in activities with Spanish children. Some state schools on the coast are currently full of British children who speak little or no Spanish and they make little academic progress. Teachers don't usually speak English and although they may make an attempt to speak it to help a child, they're under no obligation to do so and must teach the rest of the children in the class in Spanish.

Many expatriates on the Costa del Sol are under the false impression that their children will learn Spanish quickly and easily in school. This may be the case for nursery-age children but older children struggle if they have no extra support.

PRIVATE SPANISH SCHOOLS

Around a third of school children in Spain as a whole attend private schools, but on the Costa del Sol (with the exception of Malaga) there's a shortage of private schools. Most of them have long waiting lists (some lists have more children on them than actually attend the school!) and it's difficult to get a place. Some private schools are subsidised by the government and are therefore considerably cheaper. Private schools tend to start at 9.30am and finish at 5 or 5.30pm (3pm in June and September). Uniform is compulsory and can be bought at Corte Inglés (in Malaga and Puerto Banús) or in specialist shops. Most schools provide lunch and some after-school activities. **Note that private Spanish schools tend not to admit children over the age of 6 who don't speak Spanish well.**

Area One – The West

Estepona   Colegio San José, La Cala   ☎ 952-800 148
Co-educational, 3 to 18. Lunch provided. Bus service
available from Sotogrande and Las Chapas, Marbella.

Marbella   Colegio Alborán, Urb Ricmar s/n   ☎ 952-839 645
Co-educational, 3 to 18. Lunch provided. Bus
service available from Marbella and Fuengirola.

Colegio Ecos (Catholic denomination),
Urb Elviria s/n   ☎ 952-834 864
Boys, 3 to 18. Lunch provided. Bus service
available from Estepona and Fuengirola/Mijas.

Colegio La Latina, Urb El Mirador 70   ☎ 952-770 352
Co-educational, 3 to 16. Lunch provided.

Colegio Las Chapas (Catholic
denomination), Urb Las Chapas s/n   ☎ 952-831 616
Girls, 3 to 18. Lunch provided. Bus service
available from Estepona and Fuengirola/Mijas.

Colegio San José, Urb Guadalmina Baja ☎ 952-883 858
Co-educational, 3 to 18. Lunch provided. Bus
service available from Elviria and Sotogrande.

Area Two – Central Costa Del Sol

Benalmadena   Colegio Maravillas (subsidised), Cortijo
de Torrequebrada, Arroyo de la Miel   ☎ 952-442 633
Co-educational, 3 to 18. Lunch provided. Bus
service available from Fuengirola and Guadalmar
(west side of Malaga).

Fuengirola   Colegio Salliver, Avda de Finlandia 4,
Urb Los Pacos   ☎ 952-474 194
💻 *www.colegiosalliver.com*
Co-educational, 3 to 18. Lunch provided. Bus
service available from Fuengirola west and centre.

Colegio San Francisco de Asís, C/Los
Patos, Urb El Coto   ☎ 952-473 424
Co-educational, 3 to 16 (subsidised). Bus service
available from within Fuengirola and Las Lagunas.

Torremolinos Colegio Los Rosales, Av Ricardo Gross 8,
Urb El Olivar   ☎ 952-435 072
💻 *www.colegiolosrosales.com*
Co-educational, 3 to 16 (secondary subsidised).
Lunch provided. Bus service available from
within Torremolinos.

Colegio Miramar, Pl Andalucía 2   ☎ 952-385 347
Co-educational, 3 to 16. Lunch provided.
Bus service available.

Area Three – Malaga

Malaga   Colegio Alfonso X, Avda Carlos
Haya 157   ☎ 952-272 543
Co-educational, 3 to 18. Lunch provided. Bus
service available and after-school activities.

Colegio Platero, Baja 23, Urb El Candado ☎ 952-291 148
Co-educational, 3 to 18. Lunch provided. Bus
service available.

Cerrado de Calderón, Flamencos 19,
Urb Cerrado de Calderón   ☎ 952-290 400
Co-educational, 3 to 18 (12 to 16 subsidised). Lunch
provided. Bus service available and boarding facilities.

Colegio El Atabal, C/Java 3, Urb Puerto
de la Torre   ☎ 952-431 543
Co-educational, 3 to 16 (subsidised). Lunch
provided. Bus service available.

Colegio Europa, Lope de Rueda 181,
Urb Puerto de la Torre   ☎ 952-431 100
Co-educational, 3 to 18. Lunch provided.
Bus service available.

Colegio Los Olivos, Julio Verne 8, Urb
Puerto de la Torre   ☎ 952-431 000
Co-educational, 3 to 18. Lunch provided.
Bus service available.

Malaga also has numerous religious denomination private schools. These
are listed in the yellow pages under '*Colegios Privados*'.

Area Four – The East

Rincón de la   Rincón Añoreta, Ctra de Macharaviaya,
Victoria   Urb Añoreta Golf, Rincón de la Victoria ☎ 952-972 311
    🖳 *www.rinconcolegio.com*
    Co-educational, bi-lingual education (Spanish/English),
    3 to 18. Lunch provided. Bus service available from
    Nerja and Benalmadena.

FOREIGN & INTERNATIONAL PRIVATE SCHOOLS

There's a good choice of foreign private schools on the Costa del Sol and the
majority are so-called international schools offering teaching through
English and following a British-based curriculum, sometimes with the
International Baccalaureate. Some offer the possibility of studying a parallel
Spanish curriculum for Spanish pupils or foreign pupils with an exceptional
level of Spanish. This is advantageous for foreign pupils who wish to study
at a Spanish university without having to validate their qualifications.

Advantages

- If you return to your home country, your child's studies won't have
  been interrupted.

- Children feel more familiar and less isolated if the teaching is in their native tongue.

Disadvantages

- The fees are high.

- The waiting lists are long.

- Children tend to grow up a cultural ghetto with little contact with Spanish society. In some schools little progress is made in learning Spanish.

Foreign private schools are heavily over-subscribed and waiting lists are years long in many cases. Some British schools on the Costa del Sol belong to the National Association of British Schools in Spain (NABSS – 💻 *www. nabss.org*), whose inspectors visit and approve the schools.

Foreign Private Schools

Foreign private schools on the Costa del Sol are listed below:

Elviria   *German School, Urb Elviria, s/n
             (between Marbella & Mijas Costa)   ☎ 952-831 417
             Co-educational, 3 to 18. Bus service available
             from Marbella and Fuengirola.

Fuengirola   Finnish School, José Salik 4, Urb
             Los Pacos   ☎ 952-476 193
             Co-educational.

             Norwegian School, Av Acapulco 11   ☎ 952-464 313
             💻 *www.norskeskolencostadelsol.com*
             Co-educational, 3 to 18.

             Swedish School, Av Ramón y Cajal 9   ☎ 952-475 076
             Co-educational, 3 to 18.

International Schools

The international schools mentioned below teach in English. Any schools offering the possibility of studying a parallel Spanish curriculum have a asterisk (*) beside them.

Area One – The West

Estepona   Bedes Grammar School, C/Esparragal
                  69, Urb Bel Air   ☎ 952-880 867
                  Co-educational, 2 to 18.

Marbella   *Aloha International School, Urb El
                  Angel, Nueva Andalucía   ☎ 952-814 133
                  🖥 *www.aloha-college.com*
                  Co-educational, 3 to 18. Bus service is available
                  from Fuengirola and Puerto Banus.

                  *Calpe International College, Ctra de
                  Cadiz km 171, San Pedro   ☎ 952-781 479
                  🖥 *www.calpecollegeschool.com*
                  Co-educational, 7 to 18.

                  *Calpe Jardin, C/ Los Eucalipos 60, Urb
                  Linda Vista Baja, San Pedro   ☎ 952-786 029
                  🖥 *www.calpejardin.com*
                  Co-educational, 3 to 8.

                  English International College, Urb
                  Ricmar s/n   ☎ 952-832 221
                  🖥 *www.eic.edu*
                  Co-educational, 3 to 18. Bus service available
                  from Fuengirola and Marbella.

                  *Swans International Primary School,
                  Urb El Capricho   ☎ 952-773 248
                  🖥 *www.swansschool.net*
                  Co-educational, 3 to 12.

San Pedro   King's College, C/G, Urb Nueva
                  Alcántara   ☎ 952-799 900
                  🖥 *www.kcsanpedro.org*
                  The school opens in September 2004 and will be co-
                  educational, 3 to 18 (up to Year 10 only when it first opens).
                  Capacity for 750 pupils.

                  Saint George's School, Avda Pablo Ruiz
                  Picasso 10   ☎ 952-786 606
                  Co-educational, 2 to 8.

Sotogrande   *Sotogrande International School, Cortijo
                  Paniagua, Apdo 15, Urb Sotogrande   ☎ 956-795 902
                  🖥 *www.sis.ac*

Co-educational, 3 to 18. Bus service is available from Nueva
Andalucía. The school also provides boarding facilities for
students over 10 years. Around 600 pupils.

Area Two – Central Costa Del Sol

Benalmadena   *Benalmadena International College,
C/Catamarán s/n, Urb Nueva
Torrequebrada   ☎ 952-561 666
🖳 www.bicbenal.com
Co-educational, 3 to 18.

*The British College, C/Guadalmedina,
Urb Torremuelle   ☎ 952-442 215
🖳 www.thebritishcollege.com
Co-educational, 3 to 18. Bus service available from
Churriana and Riviera del Sol.

Fuengirola   St Anthony's College, Camino de Coín
km5.25, Mijas Costa   ☎ 952-473 166
🖳 www.stanthonyscollege.com
Co-educational, 3 to 18. Bus service available from
Torreblanca and Fuengirola.

Torremolinos   *Sunnyview, C/Teruel 32, Urb Cerro
del Toril   ☎ 952-383 164
Co-educational, 3 to 18. Bus service
available from Torremolinos and Fuengirola.

Area Three – Malaga

Malaga   *International School of Malaga, Avda de
la Centaurea 8, Urb Cerrado de Calderón ☎ 952-204 810
🖳 www.interschoolmalaga.com
British education from 3 to 16 (18 in the near future).

*Sunland, Ctra Cártama- Pizarra,
Nueva Aljaima, Cártama Estación   ☎ 902-502 250
🖳 www.sunland-int.com
Co-educational, 3 to Year 7 (set to increase by one year
annually). Bus service available from Torremolinos,
Alhaurín El Grande and Malaga East.

Area Four – The East

Almuñecar   Almuñecar International School, Urb
Los Pinos s/n   ☎ 958-635 911
🖳 www.almunecarinernationalschool.org
Co-educational, 3 to 18. Buses from Nerja and Motril.

Other Schools & Courses

Private schools on the Costa del Sol, both Spanish and international, tend to put great emphasis on academic success and many schools have entrance tests. Standards are high and many international schools base their PR and marketing on the academic results achieved by their students. As a result less-academic or disinterested foreign teenagers usually cannot continue their studies at a private school and need to find an alternative. Possibilities are currently limited (this area is a niche market) and include the following:

● For teenagers aged 16 or over who speak Spanish, there's a wealth of opportunities in the *Formación Profesional/FP* programme for students who have completed their compulsory schooling and gained the School Leaver's Certificate (*Certificado de Graduado en ESO*). The programme includes practical training and academic study depending on the profession or trade chosen and lasts at least two years. Common choices on the Costa del Sol include IT, professions within the tourist industry, car mechanics and gardening. The widest range is offered in Malaga, although schools along the coast offer different trades and professions as well. Information about *FP* is available from Spanish secondary schools (*institutos*) and education departments of local councils.

● Some international schools, e.g. Benalmadena International College, offer a more practical curriculum parallel to the usual academic programme for less-academic minded students.

● The Tutorial Learning Centre based at Calahonda, Mijas Costa (Ctra de Cádiz km 197) offers tuition in a range of GCSE and A Level subjects. Students attend the centre for lessons only and classes are small. Further information can be obtained by calling ☎ 952-838 078.

● The Marbella Design School offers several courses in design (automotive, interior, furniture and graphic). The school is currently in Marbella (C/ Virgen del Pilar 4), but is moving to new purpose-built premises in Monda in spring 2005. Further information is available from ☎ 952-861 702 and 🖥 *www.designschool.com*.

AFTER SCHOOL ACTIVITIES

Parents with children at state schools where the school day finishes around 2pm often want to find something for their children to do during the afternoon. There's usually a good choice but most activities are based in towns and if you live in an urbanisation you may have to spend your afternoon ferrying children from one activity to another.

Information on different activities can be found in schools (who often offer a variety of after-school activities on the premises), from town halls and municipal sports centres, on local notice boards or in publications such as *Kids on the Costa* and *Sur in English*. **Bear in mind that places for municipal activities tend to be in short supply so you should apply early (usually in September).** Below is a brief summary of what's available for children.

Art & Crafts

If your child is artistically inclined, there's a vast range of activities, including painting and drawing, ceramics, crafts, dance (all types, but Spanish classical is predominant), drama and theatre. Classes are available in municipal centres or privately. In addition, music classes (singing and instruments) are offered at municipal music schools known as *conservatorios*.

Cubs, Scouts, Brownies & Guides

Cubs, Scouts, Guides and Brownies meet once weekly in Fuengirola in Las Rampas. For more information call ☎ 952-592 171.

Information Technology

Most Town Halls organise courses in IT including internet and web design for children.

Languages

Language courses are offered all over the Costa del Sol for all ages and levels. If your child is at a Spanish school, it's a good idea to enrol them at extra classes in Spanish after school. Municipal classes are available at subsidised prices, but places are quickly filled so you should enrol your children as soon as possible in September. Some schools offer extra Spanish classes in the afternoons. See also **Learning Spanish** on page 191.

Sports

Most towns have good municipal sports facilities (often including an indoor pool) where there's a wealth of sporting activities for all ages. Activities usually take place two or three times a week and charges are low (from €12 to €25 a month depending on the activity). Sport is taken seriously and children who do well are often offered the chance to become a member of the national federation and play at regional and national levels. There are numerous private sports clubs (particularly tennis) where standards are high, but so are the prices. Horse riding and golf classes are available up and down the coast, although they're also expensive.

Some towns specialise in the following sports:

- **Athletics** – Mijas and Torremolinos;

- **Basketball** – Malaga and Mijas Costa (Las Lagunas);

- **Football** – Most municipal sports centres have teams competing at local and regional level;

- **Gymnastics** – Benalmadena and Marbella;

- **Swimming** – Malaga (Club Mediterráneo) and Mijas Costa (Las Lagunas);

- **Tennis** – Malaga.

SCHOOL HOLIDAYS

As anyone with children at school in Spain knows, the summer holidays are **very** long (up to 15 weeks in some cases) and by May parents are frantically asking themselves the inevitable question: 'What shall I do with the kids this summer?'.

Summer Camps

Summer camps are available both at municipal and private levels, and many schools also organise camps during the summer. Camps last from one to two weeks depending on the children's ages and activities are usually based around sports, games and craft-type activities with the emphasis on getting out into the countryside – many camps are held in national parks in Andalusia. **Camps run by the municipal authorities are good value, but places are always in short supply and residents in the area are given priority.**

Summer Schools

Summer schools are held at many schools and generally run by private companies during July and August. Schools usually run in the mornings only and consist mainly of sport and other leisure activities. Some summer schools offer lunch and slightly longer hours but most are from 9.30 or 10am to 2 or 3pm. Costs vary tremendously and it's worth shopping around to compare both prices and what's on offer. **All summer schools should offer an insurance policy for the children and in the case of a private company, the company should be legally registered, so ask to see their fiscal number (*CIF*).**

Other Activities

Sports centres often run special summer courses in most areas and many private sports centres organise intensive courses in tennis or football during the summer.

Otherwise, there's always the beach...

HOME EDUCATION

Some parents prefer to educate their children at home instead of sending them to school and there are numerous private home tutors operating on the Costa del Sol. Some tutors co-operate with foreign schools in the area, which gives their pupils the possibility to take external exams at the school. Private tutors also offer after-school classes in Spanish, English or extra help in specific subjects. **One-to-one private classes can be expensive but you get what you pay for.** Experienced qualified teachers charge from €20 an hour. Ask around for personal recommendations or look in *Sur in English* in the small advertisements under 'Classes'.

LEARNING SPANISH

When you first arrive on the Costa del Sol you may be forgiven for thinking you're not in Spain at all because everyone's speaking English and when you try your best evening class Spanish to ask for "*4 lonchas de jamón*", the shop assistant replies in English.

> **You should make learning Spanish one of your first priorities since not only is it a beautiful language providing an insight into a unique culture, being able to speak Spanish is extremely useful and could be vital in an any emergency situation.**

The majority of non-British foreigners on the Costa del Sol make a concerted effort to learn Spanish and many speak it well. Many British, however, make little or no attempt to learn it, and it's common to come across a British expatriate who's been 'here' for years but can hardly manage more than a *'buenos días'*. In some areas of the coast you're more likely to need Spanish than others, but you should never rely on there being someone to speak English or to understand you.

Many expatriates would argue that you don't need to speak Spanish on a daily basis at all and it's true that many Spaniards in the tourist industry on the coast speak and understand enough English to answer basic needs. There are also thousands of fellow Britons providing services in English and some civil servants in councils and public administration speak English. To a certain extent you don't need Spanish and many people live here without speaking a word. **However, there are numerous situations where you do need Spanish – unless you're prepared to pay someone to accompany you interpret and translate.** Some of these situations include:

● In a medical emergency – you cannot rely on an interpreter being available.

● For dealings with public administration – communications from the tax office, local council, regional government etc., are all in Spanish staff – don't usually speak English.

● If your children are at a Spanish school, you need Spanish to speak to the teacher and to help your children with their homework or problems.

● Communicating with the locals and generally making an effort to integrate into Spanish society.

Like French and Italian, Spanish is a Romance language derived from Latin and Greek. It's not really a difficult language to learn the rudiments of and has the huge advantage of being phonetic so once you know how to pronounce each letter, you can pronounce any word correctly (unlike English, for example). Advanced Spanish, however, is more difficult and there are grammatical concepts, particularly tenses, that can tie even the most competent linguist in knots – but mastering a high level of Spanish isn't necessary for everyday life. You really just need a grasp of the basic tenses and vocabulary to express what you want and need.

Many expatriates claim they've tried to learn Spanish, but failed because they're too old or didn't have enough time. Many also claim that it's difficult to practise Spanish on the coast when so many people speak English. Both claims are true and to make a success of learning Spanish you need both time and patience. Usually if you make the effort to speak Spanish to a Spaniard, they will reply in Spanish.

Methods

There are numerous methods of learning a language from teach-yourself audio tapes or CD-ROMs to complete immersion classes in remote rural areas. All methods are available on the Costa del Sol and the most popular are the following:

- **Escuela Oficial De Idiomas (EOI)** – This official language school (run by the Junta de Andalucía) offers Spanish for foreigners at five different levels for two hours a day during the academic year. At the end of the course, successful candidates receive official certificates. **Courses are very popular so subscribe early.** The school also organises cultural visits throughout the courses, which are offered in Malaga, Marbella and San Roque. The EOI also offers courses in nine other languages. Cost: €61.65 (subscription fee) plus €38 per language studied. For further information contact the EOI, Paseo de Martiricos 26, Malaga (☎ 952-272 502, 🖳 *www.eoimalaga.com*).

- *Intercambio* – An economical and pleasant way to learn Spanish and a good way to meet new people is to organise an *intercambio* with a Spaniard interested in learning English. Usually you agree to speak Spanish for half of the meeting and English for the other half. Notice boards at your local town hall, supermarket or language school are good places to advertise for this.

- **Language Schools** – Spanish classes are available at language schools on the coast and a choice of levels is usually available. You may be able to choose how many lessons you want a week, although the minimum is usually three one-hour classes. Typical prices are from €130 a week for three hours daily. Language schools advertise in the local press or you can look in the yellow pages under *Centros de Idiomas* or *Escuelas de Idiomas* or ask around. A listing of language schools is also available on 🖳 *www.malagaweb.com/espanol/lang_schools.php*.

- **Local Spanish Classes** – Classes for foreigners are offered by most local councils and have the advantages of being cheap (they're usually subsidised) and giving you the chance to meet people in your area. Classes generally run from October to mid-June and there are usually several levels and times available. **Book early, however, because classes tend to be oversubscribed.**

- **Malaga University** – Spanish for foreigners is also offered by the university (the language school is in the centre of Malaga) at various levels for three or four hours per day for the whole academic year or for four months. Prices for four month courses start at €683 and for the academic year they start at €1,273. Summer courses are also available.

Courses are popular, particularly with overseas students. Further information is available from Malaga University, Cursos de Español para Extranjeros, Avda de Andalucía 24, 29007 Malaga (☎ 952-278 211 ▣ *www.uma.es/estudios/extranj/extranjeros*).

- **Private Teachers** – Spanish lessons are offered on a one-to-one basis and usually the teacher comes to your home or office. Private classes are usually advertised in the English-language press or on local notice boards. Expect to pay from €15 to €30 an hour for a private class.

Which ever method you choose, make sure you enjoy it and above all, keep at it – *Suerte!*

Marbella

9

Banks

There are numerous banks operating on the Costa del Sol, both Spanish and foreign, and most provide an efficient banking service. There are two main types of bank: clearing banks (*bancos*) and savings banks (*cajas de ahorro*), which are often the only banking facilities in small villages. The banking giants are the BSCH (often refered to as the Santander Hispano) and the BBVA. Other smaller Spanish banks are Banco Atlántico, Banco Popular and Banesto. The largest saving banks are La Caixa and Caja Madrid, although Unicaja (based in Malaga) is the one with the largest presence on the coast. Foreign banks with branches on the coast include Barclays Bank, Deutsche Bank, Lloyds TSB and Solbank. The Royal Bank of Scotland also operates at the main BSCH branches. Foreign banks operate in exactly the same way as Spanish banks and you shouldn't expect a branch of a foreign bank to behave in the same way as a branch in the UK. **Note that bank charges generally aren't lower at foreign banks, compared to a Spanish one and may in some cases be higher.** For a list of foreign banks, see page 199.

SPANISH & FOREIGN BANKS

Branches of banks are listed in the yellow pages under *Bancos* or *Cajas de Ahorros*. Further information on individual banks can be obtained by contacting the bank directly or by visiting the bank's website (click on *Oficinas* and choose Malaga province). Telephone numbers and website addresses for banks on the Costa del Sol are provided in the lists below.

Note that there is little difference between the services provided by a clearing bank and a savings bank (e.g. current accounts) – so you can choose either type for your personal or business use. For further details of banking in Spain refer to *Living and Working in Spain* (Survival Books) – see page 334.

Clearing Banks

Clearing banks provide similar services to those of savings banks.

- **Banco Atlántico** – 🖥 *www.batlantico.es* (English language option available);

- **Banco De Sabadell** – ☎ 902-323 777, 🖥 *www.bancsabadell.es* (English language option available);

- **Banco Español De Crédito** – ☎ 902-224 466, 🖥 *www.bbva.es* (English language option available);

- **Banco Popular** – ☎ 902-301 000, 🖥 *www.bancopopular.es* (English language option available);

- **Banco Zaragozano** – ☎ 901-123 321, 🖥 *www.bancozaragozano.es*;

- **Banesto** – ☎ 902-101 235, 🖥 *www.banesto.es* (language options are available in English, French and German);

- **Bankinter** – ☎ 902-365 563, 🖥 *www.bankinter.es* (English language option available);

- **BBVA** – ☎ 902-224 466, 🖥 *www.bbva.es* (English language option available);

- **BSCH** – ☎ 902-242 424, 🖥 *www.gruposantander.es* (English language option available).

Savings Banks

Savings banks provide similar services to those of clearing banks – including current accounts.

- **Bancaja** – ☎ 902-204 020, 🖥 *www.bancaja.es*;

- **Caja Granada** – ☎ 902-100 095, 🖥 *www.caja-granada.es*;

- **Caja Madrid** – ☎ 902-246 810, 🖥 *www.cajamadrid.es* (English language option available);

- **CajaMar** – ☎ 952-217 761, 🖥 *www.cajamar.es* (English language option available);

- **CajaSur** – ☎ 902-224 466, 🖥 *www.cajasur.es*;

- **CAM** – ☎ 902-100 112, 🖥 *www.cam.es* (English language option available);

- **La Caixa** – ☎ 93-404 6000, 🖥 *www.lacaixa.es* (English language option available);

- **Unicaja** – ☎ 902-224 466, 🖥 *www.unicaja.es* (language options are available in English and German).

Foreign Banks

- **Barclays Bank** – ☎ 901-141 414, 🖥 *www.barclays.es*;

- **Deutsche Bank** – ☎ 902-240 124, 🖳 *www.deutsche-bank.es* (**note that all post offices are Deutsche Bank agents**);

- **Halifax** – ☎ 902-310 100, 🖳 *www.halifax.es*;

- **Lloyds TSB** – 🖳 *www.lloydsbank.es*;

- **Solbank** – ☎ 902-343 999, 🖳 *www.solbank.es*.

Listed below are the foreign banks that can be found on the Costa del Sol.

Area One – The West

Barclays

Estepona	Avda España 106
Elviria	Pueblo Los Arcos, Ctra de Cádiz 191
Marbella	Avda Ramón y Cajal 1
Nueva Andalucía	Ctra de Cádiz 174
San Pedro	Ctra de Cádiz 170
Sotogrande	Pueblo Nuevo de Guadiaro

Deutsche Bank

Estepona	Avda Juan Carlos I
Estepona/ San Pedro	Urb Benamara, Ctra de Cádiz km 174
Manilva	Ctra de Cádiz, Conj Res San Luis 59
Marbella	Avda Ricardo Soriano 39 and Puerto Pesquero
Puerto Banús	Edif A2 Jardines
San Pedro	Lagasca
Sotogrande	Puerto Deportivo

Halifax

Marbella	Avda Ricardo Soriano 20, 4°A

Lloyds TSB

Marbella   Avda del Mar 7

Puerto Banús   Avda Rotary International 4, Edif Tembo Banús

Solbank

Estepona   Avda España 190

Estepona/   Urb Benamara, Complejo Gómez Barrio blq A
San Pedro

Elviria   CC Elviria

Marbella   Avda Ricardo Soriano 57

Nueva   CC Plaza
Andalucía

San Pedro   Pza Vista Alegre

Area Two – Central Costa Del Sol

Barclays

Benalmadena   Avda Antonio Machado 27

Calahonda/   Ctra de Cádiz 197.6
Calypso

Fuengirola   Avda Clemente Díaz

Deutsche Bank

Arroyo De   C/ Lanzarote 2
La Miel

Calahonda   Ctra de Cádiz km 196

Fuengirola   Avda de los Boliches 88 and Condes de San Isidro 45

Torremolinos   Pza de la Independencia 3

Halifax

Arroyo De   C/ Lanzarote 2
La Miel

Fuengirola   Avda Juan Gómez Juanito, Edif Milano 1, 103

Solbank

Alhaurín El Grande	C/ Cruz de la Misión 37
Arroyo De La Miel	Avda García Lorca 2
Benalmadena	Avda Antonio Machado
Calahonda	CC Los Cipreses
Fuengirola	Avda Clemente Díaz 4, Avda Mijas 2 and Avda de los Boliches 87
La Cala	Bulevard de la Cala
Torremolinos	Avda Palma de Mallorca 22 and Urb Playamar, Paseo Colorado 24

Area Three – Malaga

Barclays

Malaga	Avda Andalucía 8
	Sancho de Lara 5

Deutsche Bank

Malaga	Avda Andalucía 7 and C/ Larios 3

Halifax

Malaga	Alameda de Colón 9

Area Four – The East

Deutsche Bank

Nerja	Pza de la Ermita 4
Torre Del Mar	Avda Andalucía 104
Torrox	Ctra de Almería 2

Solbank

Nerja	Balcón de Europa 2
Torre Del Mar	Paseo de Larios 2

BANKING HOURS

All banks are open from 8.30am to 2pm Mondays to Fridays. In addition, clearing banks open on Saturday mornings from 8.30am to 1pm (from 1st October to 1st April) and savings banks are open on Thursday afternoons until 7pm (from 1st October to 1st April). Some branches have longer opening hours, such as the Unicaja branch at Malaga airport (open seven days a week) and the Santander branch in La Cañada shopping centre (open all day).

All banks are closed on both national and local holidays. **Banks in the main towns close early (at noon) for several days while the local *fiestas* are in progress, e.g. during the second week of June in Marbella and the first week of October in Fuengirola.**

Bureaux de change have longer opening hours (usually similar to shops) and some open continuously during the summer.

CHOOSING A BANK

Shop around before you choose a bank and compare bank charges carefully. **Bank charges are *very* high in Spain and even the simplest transaction such as a transfer costs at least €2.50 in charges.** Some banks offer special deals, e.g. fixed monthly charges regardless of number of transactions or a number of free transactions if you maintain a certain amount in your account. If you're a good client (i.e. one with a healthy bank balance) you should be able to negotiate a reduction in fees. Most banks have English-speaking staff and many publish leaflets and other information in English. Some will even send you statements in English. Foreign residents and tourists account for a significant part of banking business on the Costa del Sol and competition for clients is fierce. Banking is a very personal affair in Spain and most bank managers know their clients personally.

Most banks now offer online banking, a secure option allowing you to conduct most banking transactions whilst saving considerable time (bank queues are very long). ATMs also provide some services as well as cash withdrawal. Servicaixa ATMs (*Servired* networks) are particularly comprehensive: cash and cheques can be paid in, statements and transactions can be printed, tickets for cinema, theatre and concerts can be bought and you can recharge your mobile phone.

Opening An Account

It's easier to open an account in person (banks may require credit references if you open an account by post) and all you need is proof of identity and proof of an address in Spain.

Non-Residents

Banking regulations are the same for both residents and non-residents, but non-residents can only open a non-resident euro account or a foreign currency account. **Charges tend to be higher for non-resident accounts**, but there are few differences in services offered.

Residents

Residents need to provide proof of residence in Spain, usually in the form of a residence permit or certificate of residence from the police. It's difficult to open a resident's account without some official proof of residence in spite of the fact that EU nationals employed in Spain no longer require a residence permit – banks still need to see the official stamp! This requirement is expected to be abolished in late 2004.

BANKING BY INTERNET

There are several internet/telephone banks in Spain (they only operate via the internet or telephone), which offer interest on current accounts (around 3 per cent) with immediate access to your money as well as the usual banking services. The most popular is ING Direct (☎ 901-020 901, 🖥 *www. ingdirect.es*) owned by the European banking giant, ING Nationale-Nedenlanden who have just moved into the mortgage market offering very low interest rates and zero or nominal commission for most transactions. Other internet banks are Patagon (☎ 902-365 366, 🖥 *www.patagon.es*) owned by BSCH and Uno-e (☎ 901-111 113, 🖥 *www.uno-e.es*) owned by BBVA and Telefonica.

MORTGAGES

Mortgages are available from most Spanish and foreign banks on the Costa del Sol, and there's currently fierce competition for clients. Banks generally lend up to 80 per cent (90 per cent in some cases) for residents and up to 60 per cent for non-residents. Shop around as rates and commission vary tremendously. **Note that you cannot usually get a mortgage for property on land classed as rural and banks are extremely reluctant to lend to anyone over 65.**

Mortgage Brokers

There are numerous mortgage brokers on the coast who will do the shopping around for you and find you the best mortgage for your circumstances. **Before committing yourself to a broker (and definitely** before parting with any money), check his credentials and make sure he's registered with the local authorities as a business.

CREDIT & DEBIT CARDS

Credit and debit cards are generally accepted by most businesses, although some smaller shops don't take credit cards and you will find that some shops are reluctant to take cards and may offer a discount for cash. Inland and in villages cash may be the only form of payment. Visa and Mastercard are the most accepted credit cards. If you have an American Express or other card you should enquire in advance whether it's accepted. **Note that most establishments ask for photographic ID (residence card, passport, driving licence) if you pay with a card.** Debit cards issued by Spanish banks cannot be used abroad, nor can they be used for internet shopping other than with Spanish businesses.

Stolen Cards

If your card is lost or stolen, you should either inform your bank branch or telephone the appropriate number (see below) as soon as possible after you detect the loss or theft. **If your card is stolen, you should also report this to the police and obtain a written report from them so that you're not liable for purchases made with the stolen card.**

- **4B (Mastercard, Visa, Visa Electron)** – ☎ 913-626 200;

- **American Express** – ☎ 915-720 303;

- **Red 6000** – ☎ 915-965 335;

- **Servired** – ☎ 915-192 100.

COST OF LIVING

The Costa del Sol is no longer as cheap as it was and the arrival of the euro has pushed prices up spectacularly with some items going up by more than 50 per cent. When it comes to certain items such as property and fresh food and vegetables, prices on the coast are among the highest in Spain. It is, however, still possible to live fairly cheaply and some things such as eating out and alcohol are still very cheap compared to the UK. Prices vary from area to area with the highest prices on the coast found in Marbella, Puerto Banús and Sotogrande, and the cheapest in Malaga city and inland. If you want to spend less, shop, have coffee and eat out where the locals do. No sensible resident is going to pay €2 for a coffee when down the road you can enjoy a cup for €1! Imported foods are expensive and it pays to buy Spanish products rather than imported ones, e.g. a packet of imported biscuits costs at least €1.50 whereas a packet of Spanish biscuits costs from €0.60. A litre of fresh local milk costs around €0.75 and a litre of fresh imported milk costs €1.50.

Although prices vary around the coast expect to pay from €0.80 to €1.50 for a coffee, from €6 to €8 for a '*menú del día*' and €5 for a cinema ticket. **Note that beach bars are generally expensive and that many businesses (particularly restaurants and bars) put their prices up in high season.** For information on property prices see **Chapter 5**.

The Puente Nuevo, Ronda

10

Leisure

The Costa del Sol offers numerous leisure possibilities for all ages and tastes, and the fine climate lends itself to a wealth of activities on the beach, in the country or up in the mountains. This chapter aims to provide a guide to what you can do in your spare time.

Information about opening times and prices was correct in February 2004, but they're subject to change and you should double check before making a long journey to visit somewhere.

FINDING OUT WHAT'S ON

An excellent source of information about activities and what's on is the local tourist office where you will find a wealth of useful information and leaflets about local attractions and events. Tourist offices are usually open from 9.30 or 10am to 2pm and from around 4pm to 7.30 or 8pm Mondays to Saturdays. Hours are longer in the summer when many offices open on Sunday morning as well.

Tourist Information Offices are listed below (many of the website addresses are the town council's site, which also include tourist information).

- **Alhaurín De La Torre** – Town Hall, ☎ 952- 413 529, 🖳 *www.aytoalhaurindelatorre.es*;

- **Alhaurín El Grande** – Town Hall, Pza del Convento, ☎ 952-491 275, 🖳 *www.alhaurinelgrande.net*;

- **Alora** – Avda de la Constitución 102, ☎ 952-498 380, 🖳 *www.ayto-alora.org*;

- **Benalmadena** – Avda Antonio Machado 14, ☎ 952-442 494, 🖳 *www.benalmadena.com*;

- **Cártama** – Town Hall, Pza de la Constitución 3, ☎ 952-422 126, 🖳 *www.cartama.ws*;

- **Coín** – C/ Pedro González Domínguez, ☎ 952-453 211, 🖳 *www.ayto-coin.es*;

- **Estepona** – Avda San Lorenzo 1, ☎ 952-801 086, 🖳 *www.infoestepona.com*;

- **Fuengirola** – Pso Santos Rein 6, ☎ 952-467 457, 🖳 *www.fuengirola.org*;

- **Gibraltar** – ☎ 9567-74982;

- **Istán** – C/ Empedrada 32, ☎ 952-869 603, 🖳 *www.istan.es*;

- **Malaga** – Airport ☎ 952-048 484 (ext 586); Avda de Cervantes 1, ☎ 952-604 410;

- **Manilva** – C/ Villa Matilde, ☎ 952-890 845, 💻 *www.manilva-costadelsol.com*;

- **Marbella** – Pza de Los Naranjos, ☎ 952-823 550;

- **Mijas** – Avda Virgen de la Peña, ☎ 952-485 900, 💻 *www.mijas.es*;

- **Nerja** – C/ Puerta del Mar 2, ☎ 952-521 531, 💻 *www.nerja.org*;

- **Ojén** – Pza Andal 1, ☎ 952-881 519, 💻 *www.webojen.org*;

- **Pasaje De Chinitas** – 4, ☎ 952-213 445, 💻 *www.ayto-malaga.es*;

- **Rincón De La Victoria** – C/ Granada 2°B, ☎ 952407 768, 💻 *www.rincondelavictoria.com*;

- **San Pedro** – N-340 km 170.5, ☎ 952-781 360, 💻 *www.marbella.es*;

- **Sotogrande** – N-340 km 135, Torreguadiano, ☎ 956-616 866, 💻 *www.ayuntamientodesanroque.es*;

- **Torremolinos** – Pza de Borbollón 1, ☎ 952-372 956, 💻 *www.ayto-torremolinos.org*;

- **Torrox** – Bulévar 79, bajo, ☎ 952-530 225;

- **Vélez-Málaga** – Avda de Andalucía 119, ☎ 952-541 104, 💻 *www.ayto-velezmalaga.es*.

Most town councils publish a monthly guide to cultural and sports events in the area, which is usually available from tourist offices and town halls. The local press publishes a weekly summary of events and the local Spanish newspapers publish daily events bulletins. Concerts and plays are usually advertised on notice boards and hoardings.

AQUARIUMS

Benalmadena Centro De Mar, Avda Antonio Machado
83, Benalmadena Costa   ☎ 952-577 784
Aquarium, museum, video presentation and shop. Open 8am to 2pm from Mondays to Saturdays. Price: €4 adults, €3 children (4 to 14) and pensioners.

Sea Life, Puerto Marina,
Benalmadena Costa   ☎ 952-560 150
🖥 *www.sealife.es*
Variety of aquariums showing marine life from different parts of
the world including the biggest shark collection in Europe and a
unique sea horse breeding scheme. Shop and restaurant.
Open 10am to 10pm daily. Price: €8.50 adults, €6.50 children
(4 to 12), €7 pensioners. **Note that you can buy a combined
day ticket including entrance to Sea Life and Tivoli (see
page 228).**

Selwo Marina, Parque de la Paloma,
Benalmadena Costa   ☎ 902-190 482
🖥 *www.selwomarina.com*
A sea life zoo with daily dolphin and sea lion shows. Shop
and restaurant. Open 10am to sunset daily. Price: €12 adults,
€8 children.

Malaga   Aula Del Mar, Cofradía de Pescadores,
Avda de Heredía 35 (near the port)   ☎ 952-229 287
Aquarium, museum and marine investigation centre. The
centre also treats injured marine life. Open 10.30am to
2.30pm Mondays to Saturdays. Price: €4 adults, €3 children
and pensioners.

BEACHES

The Costa del Sol has a good selection of beaches ranging from long
stretches of sand to tiny pebbled coves depending on the area. None of the
beaches are particularly wide and the tide never really goes out more than
a couple of metres except on windy or stormy days. Most municipal
beaches are cleaned daily from March to the end of September and some
localities (e.g. Marbella) clean their beaches all year round. Lifeguard
services (some with first aid points) are available on many beaches during
July, August and part of September, and some localities have teams of
beach patrollers walking the beaches as well. Outdoor (cold!) showers are
available on many beaches and some have toilets, showers and changing
facilities. **Beaches in many towns have access for wheelchairs.**

Beaches are very busy in the summer months, particularly on Sundays
when local families flock to the beach together with plenty of relations,
huge tents, food for thousands and tonnes of equipment. It's not
uncommon to see tables laid with a tablecloth, cutlery, plates and glasses
with a television and/or radio near by. These families arrive at around
noon and pack up late in the evening. **Unless you enjoy having no more
than a square metre to yourself on the beach, it's best to stay at home on
Sundays in the summer!** On the other hand, many beaches are almost

deserted in the autumn and winter months when you can walk for miles and sunbathe in peace.

There are no private beaches on the Costa del Sol and access to the beaches is good and well signposted from the A-7 – signs usually say '*Acceso Público a la Playa*' (public access to the beach). Parking facilities are limited in some places and in the summer parking attendants operate in many car parks. You're not obliged to pay them, although many people do.

Area One – The West

Beaches to the west of the Costa del Sol are generally sand or small pebbles and not all are well-maintained outside high season. **Beware of sea urchins in rocky areas.**

Generally speaking the best sandy beaches in the area are found on the east side of Marbella stretching from Los Monteros to the Don Carlos hotel. Estepona and Marbella have good beaches with excellent facilities, most of which has disabled access.

Area Two – Central Costa Del Sol

Mijas Costa has few good beaches apart from the sandy bay at La Cala – **beware of steep shelving.** The other beaches are narrow, often rocky with sea urchins and are rarely cleaned out of season. Fuengirola, Benalmadena and Torremolinos all have good clean municipal beaches with excellent facilities.

Area Three – Malaga

Malaga's beaches are concentrated on the east side of the city where the Playa de la Malagueta, Los Baños del Carmen and the Playa del Palo are situated. **The sand is grey and occasionally there are problems with pollution from the nearby port**, but in general the beaches are well-maintained and clean.

Area Four – The East

There are several long grey sandy beaches on the east side and Nerja has many isolated coves, some of which, particularly those near Maro, are protected natural areas and vehicle access is prohibited. **The sand is coarse, and beaches in some parts aren't well-maintained out of season.**

Nudist Beaches

Nudism is generally not officially permitted on beaches on the Costa del Sol, except on the beaches listed below. On a few other beaches the authorities may turn a blind eye, but bear in mind that if you go nude on a beach where nudism isn't officially permitted, you risk problems with the police if other people on the beach complain. Going topless on beaches is permitted and is quite common, although some beach clubs don't allow it. **If in doubt, ask.**

Official Nudist Beaches

Area One – The West

Estepona   Arroyo Vaquero/Costa Natura
Costa Natura is the Costa del Sol's only nudist resort.

Marbella   Artola-Cabopino (to the west side of the tower)

Area Two – Central Costa Del Sol

Benalmadena   Benalnatura, Ctra de Cádiz km 218

Area Four – The East

Torre Del Mar   Almavate-Bajamar

Beaches On The Atlantic

Some of the best beaches in Europe are found on the Atlantic coast on the Costa de la Luz, about two hours from Malaga. The beaches west of Tarifa (one of the world's windsurfing meccas) are almost without exception long stretches of wide golden sands often backed by spectacular dunes. The best beaches are Punta Paloma, Bolonia (also home to the Roman ruins of the town of Baelo Claudio), Playa de Zahara de los Atunes and Playa de Zahora. Some of the beaches are isolated and facilities vary greatly. In the winter, few beach bars open. **Note that some areas are owned by the military and access may be restricted.** Bear in mind that the Atlantic coast is **extremely** windy and, when the wind blows hard, conditions on the beach are unbearable for all except windsurfers! **Check the weather before you make the journey.**

Beach Bars

Beach bars (*chiriguitos*) are an essential part of the Costa del Sol's beaches and there are few stretches of beach without at least one. Beach bars range from little more than a snack bar to full-scale restaurants offering sports equipment hire as well as food and drink. Most have loungers and sunshades on the beach for hire (from €3 to €6 a day), and the upmarket ones provide waiter service for lounger users. Food ranges from the ubiquitous burger and chips, to paella and other fish dishes. **Note that beach bars are by no means cheap and a meal for four at some can cost as much as in a good restaurant.** Drinks and ice creams can be particularly expensive. If in doubt, ask to see the price list first. In the summer beach bars get very crowded and, if you want a table or lounger, make sure you book early. Popular beach bars are also crowded at weekends and public holidays throughout the year.

Beaches bars open at around 11am or noon until the small hours daily during the summer months. Many close in the winter and others open just for lunch and dinner. The ones that remain open all year may close for holidays in the quieter months (e.g. in November or January).

Beach Clubs

Several hotels on the coast have beach clubs. Some are for hotel guests only, but others also admit day guests. Beach clubs have at least one swimming pool, loungers, bar and restaurant facilities and access to the beach. Towels are usually provided. **Beach clubs aren't cheap and even if entry is free, you will pay through the nose for a drink.**

Beach Rules

- All litter should be disposed of in bins or taken home;

- Camping is prohibited on all beaches on the Costa del Sol;

- Fishing is permitted only in certain areas;

- Vehicles aren't allowed on the beach;

- Dogs are prohibited on most beaches all year round. If they're allowed it's usually from October to March only;

- Beach bars with sports equipment (pedalos and jet skis) must have an entry and exit lane marked by coloured buoys in the sea. **Swimming is prohibited in this lane.**

The Sea

Average sea temperatures are around 15°C (55°F) from November to June and 20°C (68°F) from July to October, although, because of the proximity to

Atlantic currents, the water is often cooler. Some people pride themselves on the fact that they bathe daily throughout the year, but most residents don't go in before May or after September! The water is generally clean and in the summer months the water is tested weekly and only rarely in the last few years has bathing been prohibited for health reasons. Occasionally, however, strong currents or storms bring rubbish and sewage to the shore. The Mediterranean is generally a much calmer sea than the Atlantic, but you should never underestimate the power of the sea. **Every year at least one bather drowns on the Costa del Sol.** On windy days, waves can be extremely strong with powerful undercurrents. Some beaches shelve very quickly from the shore and you can be out of your depth after just two metres. On beaches with lifeguard services a coloured flag is flown indicating the state of the sea:

- Green – good conditions for bathing;

- Yellow – exercise caution;

- Red – bathing is prohibited.

Always respect the lifeguard's decisions and obey all instructions. Keep an eye on children at all times.

Jellyfish

Note that jellyfish are sometimes found near the shore in late summer and autumn, and although their sting isn't fatal, it's painful! If you're stung, wash the sting with fresh water (from a shower on the beach) and apply cream (sun cream is quite effective). **If you're badly stung or have an adverse reaction, go to the nearest lifeguard station or doctor.**

Sea Urchins

Several beaches on the Costa del Sol are home to colonies of sea urchins (particularly beaches with rocky areas). **Sea urchin spines are poisonous and extremely painful to humans, although they're not fatal.** In areas where you see sea urchins, you shouldn't go barefoot. If you do tread on one, try not to walk on that foot and bathe it in warm water and vinegar, either at home or at a lifeguard post. Then wipe the affected area with antiseptic lotion before trying to take out as many spines as possible. You won't be able to remove all the spines (most break before you can get them out), but if they're not painful you can leave them to come out on their own rather like splinters.

Parking

Most beaches have parking facilities nearby and the these are for public use unless the parking area is part of a hotel or complex. In the summer at some car parks there may be a car park attendant who guides you to a parking space and probably expects a fee for this (around €1). **The fee should be paid at your discretion and you're under no obligation to pay for parking in a public area near the beach unless you're in a blue zone in a town.**

BOAT TRIPS

Several companies offer boat trips leaving from the various marinas on the coast (mainly Puerto Marina in Benalmadena, Fuengirola port and Marbella port) to another location on the coast. **Before you get on, make sure the company (and boat) have comprehensive insurance and are legally registered.**

Benalmadena	Costasol Cruceros	☎ 952-444 881
To Fuengirola	💻 *www.costasolcruceros.com*	
	Several trips daily (each one takes around one hour). Price for a return ticket €10 adults and €3.50 children.	

Benalmadena To Malaga

Benalmadena	Costasol Cruceros	☎ 952-444 881
To Malaga	💻 *www.costasolcruceros.com*	
	One trip daily on Mondays and Thursdays (takes around 75 minutes). Price for return ticket €11 adults and €4.50 children.	
Marbella To	Don Jorge	
Puerto Banús	Trips from Marbella to Puerto Banús and back, leaving several times daily. Trip takes 30 minutes. Tickets available from hotels in Marbella or from the Don Jorge boat in Marbella port.	

Marine Life Spotting

As well as boat trips from one locality to another, you can also go on a dolphin or whale-sighting trip. The Strait of Gibraltar are home to several large colonies of Common and Striped Dolphins, and small whales are also visitors. Sightings from boat trips are common, although not guaranteed, and there are several companies offering trips out to the Strait to see dolphins. If you take a trip from Gibraltar or Tarifa you're more likely to see dolphins than on a trip from Fuengirola, because the dolphins tend to congregate nearer the Strait themselves. Note that trips are cancelled in bad weather – telephone the company to check before setting out on a long journey. **Before getting on a boat, check the company (and boat) are registered and has adequate insurance.**

Companies offering dolphin-sightings include:

Fuengirola   Submarine Vision   ☎ 679-554 067
Catamaran boat trips with underwater glass cabins to view
marine life. Dolphins are often viewed. Trips leave daily from
Fuengirola port and last one hour.

Gibraltar   Nautilus   ☎ 9567-73400
🖳 *www.dolphin.gi*
Trips out to the Strait in a Nautilus semi-submersible
allowing you to see the dolphins underwater. Trips run from
Marina Bay, Gibraltar

Whale & Dolphin Safaris   ☎ 956-173 537
🖳 *www.dolphinsafarispain.com*
This company claims a 95 per cent sighting rate and runs
several trips daily from La Línea (near the Gibraltar border).

Tarifa   Whale Watch España (between
Marbella and Malaga)   ☎ 956-627 013
Daily trips from Tarifa (Café Continental, Paseo de la
Alameda) by reservation only.

CASINOS

A list of casinos that can be found on the Costa del Sol is given below.

Benalmadena   Casino Torrequebrada, Avda del Sol   ☎ 952-446 000
🖳 *www.torrequebrada.com*
Dinner and/or show plus entrance to the casino. €62 for dinner
and show. €30 for show only. Open all year from 9pm to 5am.
Slot machines open from 4pm to 9pm. **Note that entrance is
for over 18-year-olds only, passports must be shown and
formal dress worn.**

Marbella   Casino Nueva Andalucía, Hotel
Andalucía Plaza, A-7 km 181 (opposite
Puerto Banús)   ☎ 952-814 000
Open all year from 6pm to 5am. Entrance: €4. **Note that
entrance is for over 18-year-olds only, passports must
be shown and formal dress worn.**

Sotogrande   Casino San Roque, A-7 km 124 (west
side of Sotogrande)   ☎ 956-780 100
🖳 *www.casinosanroque.com*
Dinner and/or show plus entrance to the casino. Open all year
from 9pm to 5am. **Note that entrance is for over 18-year-
olds only and passports must be shown.**

CINEMAS

Films In Spanish

The Costa del Sol has a good selection of cinemas, although many of the multi-screen complexes tend to show blockbuster films only and it can be difficult to see an alternative or minority film. Tickets can be bought in advance from most cinemas by phone or internet. **Note that there's a surcharge for this service (around €0.60 per ticket).** The following locations have cinemas showing films in Spanish:

Area One – The West

Estepona	Cines Veracruz (four screens) *www.cinentradas.com*	☎ 902-221 622
Marbella	Puerto Banús (seven screens) *www.cinentradas.com*	☎ 902-221 622
	La Cañada (nine screens) *www.servicaixa.es*	☎ 902-333 231
Puerto Banús	Cine Gran Marbella *www.cinentradas.com*	☎ 902-221 622

Area Two – Central Costa Del Sol

Coín	La Trocha shopping centre (on the A-355 from Cártama) This cinema will have seven screens when it opens in late 2004.	
Benalmadena	Cinebox Benalmar (seven screens) *www.cinentradas.com*	☎ 902-221 622
Fuengirola	Multicines Alfil (eight screens) *www.cinentradas.com*)	☎ 902-221 622
	Cine Miramar, A-7 opposite the castle (12 screens) *www.cinesur.com*	☎ 902-221 622

Area Three – Malaga

Malaga	Alameda Multicines, C/ Córdoba 13 (two screens) Usually shows non-blockbuster films.	☎ 952-213 412

Albéniz Multicines, C/ Alcazabilla 4
(four screens)   ☎ 902-221 622
💻 *www.cinentradas.com*

Andalucía, C/ Victoria 2 (one screen)   ☎ 902-221 622
💻 *www.cinentradas.com*

Astoria, Plaza María Guerero
(one screen)   ☎ 902-221 622
💻 *www.cinentradas.com*
Multicines Larios, Larios centre
(ten screens)   ☎ 902-221 622
💻 *www.cinentradas.com*

Multicines La Rosaleda, Rosaleda centre
(12 screens)   ☎ 902-221 622
💻 *www.cinentradas.com*

Victoria, Plaza de la Merced (one screen)   ☎ 902-221 622
💻 *www.cinentradas.com*

Yelmo Cineplex, Plaza Mayor (20 screens) ☎ 902-221 622
💻 *www.cinentradas.com*

Area Four – The East

Rincón De   Yelmo Cineplex (16 screens)   ☎ 902-221 622
La Victoria   💻 *www.cinentradas.com*

Vélez-Málaga   Cinesur El Ingenio (12 screens)   ☎ 902-221 622
                    💻 *www.cinentradas.com*

Films In English

The following cinemas show films in English, usually with Spanish subtitles. Films in English are usually indicated by a V.O. (*versión original*) next to the title and are generally recent films. Note that only three new releases are shown per week (often the same one in different cinemas) and if you want to see a particular film, you may have to see it in Spanish or wait until it comes out on video and DVD.

Area One – The West

Puerto Banús   Cine Gran Marbella   ☎ 902-221 622
                    💻 *www.cinentradas.com*
                    One film a week, usually in the afternoon session
                    (around 5pm)

Area Two – Central Costa Del Sol

Fuengirola   Cine Miramar (opposite the castle)   ☎ 902-221 622
💻 *www.cinesur.com*
This cinema shows one or two films a week and there are
several showings daily.

Area Three – Malaga

Malaga   Plaza Mayor   ☎ 902-221 622
💻 *www.cinentradas.com*
One film per week with several showings daily,

Area Four – The East

Vélez-Málaga   El Ingenio   ☎ 902-221 622
💻 *www.cinentradas.com*
This cinema shows one film a week, matinée and
early evening showings only.

Films clubs such as 'Luis Buñuel Cineclub' based at the Instituto Río Verde
in Marbella and the Veracruz cinema in Estepona also have original version
showings of older films (no new releases). See the local press for details.

EATING OUT

The Costa del Sol offers a wide variety of places to eat out and there's
something to suit all budgets and tastes from €6 for a *menú del día* in a local
bar to a gourmet meal costing more than €100 a head in a top restaurant.
Eating out is a popular pastime on the coast, both with locals and foreigners,
mainly because it's a relatively cheap option – a family can eat out for as little
as €35 in a restaurant. Weekends and public holidays are generally very busy
and Sundays are particularly busy from 2pm. Unless you arrive early (e.g.
before 2pm for lunch and before 8.30pm for dinner) you should book in
advance. The Spanish generally eat late – lunch is from 2pm (3pm in the
summer) and dinner from 9pm (10pm in the summer).

There's a huge choice of eateries on the Costa del Sol and below is a summary.
The best way to find a good meal is to ask friends for recommendations or
try out local restaurants. The quality of food is generally good at most places
and it's difficult to go wrong, although not impossible, but if you have a poor
meal the chances are it won't break the bank and you needn't go back!

Local Bars

Some people claim there are more bars in Spain than people – this may be
an exaggeration, but there are certainly bars are everywhere. Most offer

breakfast (rolls and pastries) and lunch, usually a *menú del día* consisting of two home cooked courses plus bread, a drink and fruit, which costs from €6 depending on the food and venue. Some bars offer *tapas* in the evening. Most bars are cheap and cheerful, and the best are usually packed during opening hours and if you want lunch, you should arrive before 2pm to get a table. The best bars offer good food and value for money. To find the best, look around a town centre at lunchtime and see which ones are full.

There are also many bars run by foreigners (usually British) where you can get the ubiquitous all-day English breakfast, snacks and other meals.

Restaurants

Restaurants are obviously more up market and expensive than bars, although the food isn't always better quality! Food tends to cost from €3 for a starter, from €5 for a main course and from €3 for a dessert, although many have special offers for two-course lunches or set-menus. All have wine lists, but note that the majority include Spanish wine only or a very limited choice of foreign wine. Some restaurants specialise in fish dishes, or a Spanish regional gastronomy such as Basque, Catalan or Galician.

Beach Restaurants

Beach restaurants (often known as *chiringuitos*) are an essential part of Costa del Sol living and are found on most beaches in the area. Many specialise in fish dishes, and paella and sardines (*espetos* – cooked on an open wood fire) are favourites. Beach restaurants are popular and get very crowded at weekends and in July and August. Prices have gone up in recent years at beach restaurants where it's generally no longer cheap to eat, but most are in pleasant locations and have 'beach' terraces.

Ventas

Typically Spanish venues, *ventas* are found in the country, usually outside a main town and often in the middle of nowhere. They offer country food, usually home cooked and often of excellent quality, at reasonable prices in rustic surroundings. Most have tables outside as well as inside and are extremely popular especially at weekends. Saturdays in May and June are particularly busy with large parties of locals celebrating first communions or christenings. Some *ventas* also do wedding banquets.

Fast Food

For those in a hurry, take-away options on the Costa del Sol include:

● **Burgers & Chips** – Burger King and McDonald's offer take-away purchases. Several McDonald's have a drive-in facility (which they call 'McAuto') for the 'ultimate' in convenience food.

- **Chinese & Indian Food** – The majority of Chinese and Indian restaurants (there are lots) do take-away as well as in-house meals.

- **Fish & Chips** – No British expatriate scene could be without its fish and chips, and the coast has several 'frying tonight' venues, most of which claim to offer 'the real thing' – complete with grease!

- **Jacket Potatoes** – In the evenings, it's common to see a take-away jacket potato stall on seafronts or in busy squares. Potatoes are usually served with just salt and butter (no baked beans!).

- **Pizza** – Most pizza restaurants on the coast offer take-away (pizza, pasta and drinks) and you can phone most of them to order in advance. Some companies offer home-delivery (e.g. TelePizza).

- **Sandwiches & Baguettes** – Available from most cafés and bars. The specialist baguette company, Pans & Company, has several branches on the Costa del Sol, where you can eat in or take-away.

- **Tapas** – Found at most bars or at specialist venues such as Gambrinus, Lizarrán and Cañas y Tapas, all of which have several branches along the coast.

Local Food

The Costa del Sol is famous for its seafood dishes, and in particular, fried fish known as *pescaíto frito*, in the form of squid rings, sardines (often cooked on an open fire on the beach) and anchovies (called *boquerones* – the name for anyone born in Malaga!). Anchovies from Rincón de la Victoria waters (*boquerón victoriano*) are particularly prized for their taste and smaller size. Many fish restaurants offer a large platter of different types of fried fish called a *fritura malagueña*. Larger fish are also available and fish baked encased in sea salt crystals is a local delicacy – surprisingly the fish doesn't taste at all salty.

Inland, fish is also on offer, although meat dishes tend to predominate. Local beef and pork are excellent and some restaurants also offer game such as venison (*venado*), wild boar (*jabalí*) and partridge (*codorniz*). Malaga sauce, creamy and made with Malaga wine and raisins, accompanies some pork dishes. Pork products such as *chorizo* and black pudding (*morcilla*) are popular fried and served with chips, fried eggs and fried green peppers, a dish that's often called '*plato de los montes*' (mountain dish). **You have to be hungry to finish it.**

Locally-grown vegetables and fruits, particularly salads and avocados, form part of many restaurants' menus. Malaga salad (*ensalada malagueña*) is made with potatoes, oranges and cod dressed in olive oil. Fried aubergines with wild honey are another local delicacy.

Local desserts include almond pastries, ice cream with Malaga wine and raisins, custard-apple mouse and cheese cake.

Foreign Food

Cuisine from just about every nationality is represented on the Costa del Sol where there are Chinese, Indian, Italian, Japanese, Moroccan and Thai restaurants in most large localities. Other nationalities such as Colombian, French, Greek, Indonesian and Russian are also represented, although you may have to travel further afield to sample the food.

Eating Out With Children

Children are generally welcome at most restaurants and bars along the coast, although it's probably best to avoid 'posh' restaurants if there are children in your party. Many restaurants have children's menus (usually for those under 12) or you can order half-portions of a main course. Most restaurants and bar will heat up baby food or a bottle if you ask. Some restaurants provide colouring pencils and paper for children and a few have outdoor swings or climbing frames.

¡*Qué aproveche*! (Enjoy your meal!)

EVENING & DAY CLASSES

There are plenty of opportunities to learn new skills and activities on the coast during the afternoons and evenings. Local councils run numerous courses such as Spanish and other languages, sporting activities, art and crafts, cookery, computing and internet skills, and dance. Courses are offered to all ages and generally run twice or three times a week from October to June. Advantages of courses offered by local councils include subsidised prices and the chance to integrate with the local community and speak Spanish. Courses are usually very popular and you need to book early to get a place. Information is available from town halls, sports centres and tourist information offices.

Courses are also run privately by professionals and local clubs. Check the local press and notice boards for information.

FAIRS & FESTIVALS

Festivals (*fiestas*) and fairs (*ferias*) form an essential part of cultural and social life in the whole of Spain, but Andalusia is world-famous for its particularly colourful and lively celebrations, and the Costa del Sol has its own fair share. Every village and town has its annual fair lasting from one or two days to a whole week. They're usually held on the local saint's day (*patrón* or *patrona*) when the saint is usually paraded through the streets or a pilgrimage (*romería*) is organised to the local shrine.

All localities have two local holidays a year (for dates see **Local Holidays** under each locality in **Chapter 4**) as well as national holidays. Festivals are a great occasion for all the family (tourists and foreigners are usually welcome) when celebrating goes on for hours and often until the next day. Bullfights, fireworks, concerts, recitals and competitions are all part of most fairs. **There's rarely any violence or serious crime, although pickpockets and bag snatchers are common at the fairgrounds of the main fairs.**

In large towns the main celebrations last around a week and have several sections. The streets and bars and restaurants in the old quarter are decorated and celebrations (drinking and dancing) take place during the day. At night the fun moves to the fairground where in one section there are purpose-built premises (*casetas*) where drinking, eating and dancing goes on, and in the other there are typical fairground attractions, mainly for children and young people. Most *casetas* are privately-owned and you need an invitation or to be a guest in order to enter. Some, however, are public and usually run by the local council or local political parties. Council *casetas* often put on shows or concerts.

It's common for locals to spend a whole night in a *caseta* and it's not unusual to spend more than €100 on food and drink a night (treating others is an essential part of the *feria* spirit). Fairground attractions are also expensive and each ride costs from €2. Some localities have a special children's night during the week when rides are cheaper. During *feria* week, normal life grinds almost to a halt and many businesses and shops in the locality close or work only in the mornings and banks close at noon. **Some schools also close or strongly 'recommend' that children take the time off!** The main fairs and festivals on the Costa del Sol are listed below:

Fairs

- **Alhaurín De La Torre** – San Sebastián (20th January for three days);

- **Alhaurín El Grande** – May Fair (27th and 28th May);

- **Alora** – San Paulino (beginning of August);

- **Benahavís** – Virgen del Rosario (10th to 15th August);

- **Benalmadena** – Virgen de la Cruz (mid August);

- **Cártama** – Nuestra Señora de los Remedios (22th to 26th April);

- **Casares** – Fiesta de la Barriada Secadero (third week of July);

- **Coín** – Main fair from 10th to 15th August;

- **Estepona** – Main fair 3rd to 10th July;

- **Frigiliana** – San Antonio (13th June);

- **Fuengirola** – Virgen del Rosario – 2nd week in October;

- **Istán** – San Miguel (end of September for three days);

- **La Cala De Mijas** – main fair takes place in the second week of July;

- **La Cala Del Moral** – Main fair takes place from 4th to 7th July;

- **Las Lagunas (Mijas Costa)** – Main fair takes place in the first week of June;

- **Malaga** – Main fair is in mid-August commemorating the incorporation of Malaga into the kingdom of Castille in 1487;

- **Manilva** – Santa Ana (26th July);

- **Marbella** – San Bernabé (mid June);

- **Mijas** – Virgen de la Pena (mid September);

- **Monda** – San Roque (mid August);

- **Nerja** – Virgen de las Augustias and San Miguel (8th to 12th October);

- **Ojén** – San Dionisio Aeropajita (9th to 12th October);

- **Rincón De La Victoria** – Main fair takes place at the end of August;

- **San Pedro** – Main fair takes place around 19th October;

- **Torre Del Mar** – Santiago and Santa Ana (end of July);

- **Torremolinos** – San Miguel – 3rd week in September;

- **Torrox** – October Fair (4th to 7th October);

- **Vélez-Málaga** – San Miguel (end of September).

Festivals

Carnivals

Most towns have a carnival, usually during a week in February before Shrove Tuesday, with fancy-dress competitions and parades. The highlight of the celebrations is the 'Burial of the Sardine' (*Entierro de la Sardina*) marking the end of revelries and the beginning of Lent.

Holy Week

Holy Week (*semana santa*) processions mark the main religious celebrations in Spain and most localities on the Costa del Sol have at least one procession. The biggest and best are in Malaga whose Holy Week celebrations are famous countrywide. Processions start on Palm Sunday and continue until Easter Sunday with the most dramatic and solemn on Maundy Thursday and Good Friday. Huge ornate floats depicting images from the Passion (usually a crucified Christ or weeping Mary) are carried through the streets by penitents dressed in long purple robes, often with pointed hats, followed by women in black carrying candles. Drums and trumpets play solemn music and occasionally someone spontaneously sings a mournful *saeta* dedicated to the floatas it makes its way slowly round the streets. Malaga's most famous parades are the '*Cristo de la Legión*' and the '*Cristo del Perdón*' whose float is followed by a recently-released prisoner, granted pardon by the float's brotherhood.

San Juan

Many localities celebrate the summer solstice which falls on St John's day on 21st June with parties and purifying bonfires on the beach.

Virgen Del Carmen

The Virgen del Carmen is the patron of fishermen and in July most coastal localities celebrate a safe year's fishing by parading the her image in a procession of boats along the coast.

FUN PARKS & ATTRACTIONS

Antequera   Las Navillas Adventure Park (3km
                   outside Antequera)   ☎ 952-031 301
A large adventure centre set in the spectacular countryside
near the El Torcal mountain range where a variety of activities
are available for all ages (there's a crèche for children under 5)
including archery, climbing, paintball, quad biking and looking
after animals. Accommodation and restaurant facilities are
available on site.

Benalmadena   Benalmadena Cable Car, Arroyo de la Miel
                  (situated next to Tivoli World)   ☎ 902-190 48
💻 *www.teleferico.com/benalmadena*
This cable car takes you to the top of Calahorro peak (769m
high) – it takes 15 minutes and once you're there, options
include hiking and cycling routes (cabins can carry bikes),
donkey rides, birds of prey demonstrations as well as
spectacular views. Open daily from 10am (wind conditions
permitting). Price for return ticket: €10 adults, €7 children (4 to
12) and pensioners. The price includes donkey ride.

Tívoli World, Avda de Tívoli, Arroyo
de la Miel   ☎ 952-577 016
💻 *www.tivolicostadelsol.com*
The coast's oldest theme park and an institution in itself with
numerous fairground rides catering for a wide range of ages.
There are also shows and concerts in the summer. There are
bars and restaurants on site. Open from 11am to 9pm
November to March inclusive, 4pm to 1am during April, May,
15th to 30th September to October inclusive, 6pm to 3am
during July and August, and from 5pm to 2am during June and
1st to 15th September. Price €4.50 entrance (rides are extra).
**Note that you can buy a combined day ticket including
entrance to Tivoli and Sea Life (see page 212).**

Malaga   Finca De La Concepción, Ctra de Las
                  Pedrizas (on the way out of Malaga
                  on the A-45)   ☎ 952-252 148
Beautiful botanical gardens with many unique species of plants.
Spring is particularly stunning when the huge wisterias flower.
Open Tuesdays to Sundays 10am to 5.30pm. Price: €2.85
adults, €1.45 children (aged 6 to 16) and pensioners.

Malaga Tour   ☎ 952-363 133
✉ *busturistmalaga@terra.es*
A unique way to see the city on an open top bus stopping at 12
sights of interest in Malaga including the cathedral, Picasso
museum, Alcazaba fortress and the port. Tickets priced €11.50
for adults and €5.50 for children are valid for 24-hours and you
can get on and off the bus as many times as you like in that
time. Reduced prices are available for Malaga residents.

Marbella	Funny Beach, A-7 km 184 (east end of Marbella) ☎ 952-823 359

Marbella Funny Beach, A-7 km 184 (east end
of Marbella)   ☎ 952-823 359
💻 *www.funnybeach.net*
Open daily from 10.30am to 11pm. The park offers several
attractions including karts and trampolines. Price depends on
the attraction.

Nerja Nerja Caves, Ctra de Maro (on the east
side of Nerja, accessible from the
A-7 bypass).   ☎ 952-529 520
💻 *www.cuevasdenerja.com*
A fascinating collection of caves discovered in 1959. The caves
run for some 4.3km, although only a third of them are included
in the visit, and include spectacular stalactite and stalagmite
formations. The annual festival of opera and ballet is held in the
caves in July. The caves are open daily from 10am to 2pm and
from 4 to 6.30pm. Price : €5 adults and €2.50 children (6 to 12)
and pensioners. Children under the age of 6 enter free.

MUSEUMS

Benalmadena Archaeological Museum, Avda Juan
Luis Peralta 49, Benalmadena village ☎ 952-448 593
Interesting selection of archaeological finds from the area.
Open Mondays to Fridays 10am to 2pm and 4 to 7pm.
Entry is free.

Malaga Aircraft Museum, Malaga airport ☎ 952-048 176
Displays and models illustrating the history of aircraft and
flying. Open Mondays to Thursdays and Saturdays 9am to
1pm. Entry is free, but visits are by appointment only.

Centro de Arte Contemporáneo (CAC),
C/ Alemania   ☎ 952-120 055
💻 *www.cacmalaga.org*
A newly opened and popular museum of modern art situated
in the restored market building near the river. Exhibitions
change frequently and the museum intends to be a showcase
for new artists in the region. There's also an interesting
permanent exhibition. Open 10am to 8pm Tuesdays to
Sundays. Free entry

Dolls House Museum, C/ Alamo 32 ☎ 952-210 082
💻 *www.museocasitasvoriaharras.org*
A collection of some 50 dolls houses dating from 1850 to 1976.
Open Tuesdays to Sundays 10.30am to 1.30pm and from 5.30
to 8.30pm. Price: adults €5, children €3.

Museum of Popular Arts & Traditions,
C/ Mesón de la Victoria, Pasillo de
Santa Isabel 10   ☎ 952-217 137
An interesting selection of artefacts and displays showing how people used to live and work. Open Mondays to Fridays 10am to 1.30pm and 5 to 8pm, and Saturdays from 10am to 1pm. Price: €2 adults, €0.60 children under 14 and pensioners.

Picasso Museum, Palacio de Buenavista,
C/ San Agustín 8   ☎ 902-443 377
🖳 www.museopicassomalaga.org (for information)
                              (Uniticket) ☎ 901-246 246
🖳 www.unicaja.es (to make a booking)
A newly opened and highly acclaimed museum set in the surroundings of a XVI century palace and housing more than 200 works by the Malaga-born painter in the permanent collection. There's also a temporary exhibition and shop and restaurant. Open Tuesdays to Saturdays from 10am to 8pm (until 9pm on Fridays and Saturdays, closed Mondays). Price: €8 adults, €4 children and pensioners over 65 for the whole museum, and €6 adults and €3 children and pensioners over 65 for the temporary exhibition only. Children under 10 enter free. The museum is highly popular and it's best to pre-book tickets. **Discounts aren't available if you book online.**

Marbella   Bonsai Museum, Parque Arroyo de la
Represa (near the suspension bridge),
Avda Dr Maíz Viál.   ☎ 952-862 926
A large collection of bonsai trees, many of which are unique specimens. Open daily from 10.30am to 1.30pm and from 5 to 8pm. Price: €3 adults and €1.50 children.

Museum of Contemporary Spanish Prints
(Museo del Grabado Español Contemporáneo),
Antiguo Hospital Bazán, C/ Hospital
Bazán (old quarter of Marbella)   ☎ 952-765 741
Interesting collection of prints housed in a beautifully restored old building. Open Tuesdays to Saturdays from 10am to 2pm and 6 to 9pm. Price: €2.50 adults and €1 pensioners. Free entry for children under 14.

Mijas   Museum of Popular Traditions (Casa-Museo),
Plaza de la Libertad 2, Mijas village   ☎ 952-590 380
Selection of artefacts and displays showing how people used to live in Mijas and the surrounding area. Open daily 10am to 2pm and 6 to 9pm. Free entry.

Ojén   Wine Museum, C/ Carreras 39   ☎ 952-881 453
This old distillery now houses displays on the history of Malaga's different wines and spirits. Guided visits in English, French and Spanish are available. Open daily 11am to 3pm and 5.30pm to 9.30pm. Entry is free.

NATURAL PARKS

Malaga province has several natural parks offering the chance to enjoy some spectacular scenery, often in complete peace and quiet. Many parks are busy at weekends and holidays, but if you're prepared to walk some distance it's easy to get away from the crowds. **Natural parks are highly protected areas and some sections have restricted or prohibited access.** In some areas of the parks the number of visitors is limited daily and you may have to book beforehand. Most parks organise guided or semi-guided tours and walks during the year. Information is available from the park or from the regional authorities on the Andalusian tourist website (☎ *www.andalucia.org*).

Parque Ardales

Situated to the north-west of Malaga in beautiful natural surroundings, including the Guadalhorce river gorge and extensive pine forests. Activities include watersports on the reservoir, hiking, rock climbing and caving. The area has a campsite and several rural accommodation options. For more information call ☎ 952-458 046.

Parque National De Las Nieves

Situated to the north of Marbella and east of Ronda, these spectacular peaks include the highest in the province, Torrecilla (1,917m/6,326ft) and offer numerous possibilities for walking and climbing. The area is home to unique fauna including several species of birds of prey and the Spanish mountain goat. **Beware of fog and changeable weather conditions (including snow!), and if you plan to go on a long hike, you should leave your intended itinerary with the park's guards if possible.** Limited accommodation is available in the villages on the park's boundaries such as Istán, Yunquera and Tolox. For the visitor centre or general information contact ☎ 952-877 778.

Parque National Montes De Malaga

Situated to the north of Malaga city these attractive pine-covered mountains offer numerous possibilities for walking and trekking. The park authorities also offer guided walks and visits to the area. For the visitor centre or general information contact ☎ 952-041 169 or ✉ *pn.montesde malaga@cma.caan.es*.

Parque National Torcal De Antequera

Situated to the south of Antequera, are the Torcal rock formations where wind and rain have carved spectacular shapes into the karst rock forming deep gorges and towering peaks. There are several itineraries to walk round and the area has attractive views of the surrounding countryside. Accommodation is available in nearby Villanueva de la Concepción and Antequera. For the visitor centre or general information contact ☎ 952-031 389.

Parque National Sierra De Grazalema

Situated in the far west of the province, this park is one of the most stunning in Spain with abundant vegetation (Grazalema has Spain's highest rainfall) and picturesque white villages. The park is also home to a wide range of fauna and the Pinsapo pine tree, found only in this part of Spain and Morocco. Accommodation is available in the park or in the surrounding villages such as Grazalema and Zahara de la Sierra. For the visitor centre or general information contact ☎ 952-716 063, ✉ *pn. grazalema@cma.junta-andalucia.es*.

Other Parks

In addition to the parks mentioned above, the Costa del Sol is also within relatively short driving distance of numerous other natural parks, such as Cazorla in Jaén, Doñana in Huelva, Sierra Nevada in Granada, Cabo de Gata in Almería and Sierras de Andújar in Jaén. **It takes at least three hours to reach these parks so it's best to go for a weekend or longer.**

NIGHTLIFE

If you're a night owl (and the Spanish generally are) possibilities on the Costa del Sol are endless and range from theme pubs to some of the most sophisticated nightclubs in Europe. Most localities have a good selection of nightclubs open until the small hours, but the most famous are *Olivia Valere* and *Oh! Marbella* in Marbella, and *Pachá* in Plaza Mayor (see page 233). Opening hours are usually from 10 or 11pm to 3 or 5am. Many clubs have a dress code and you may be required to show identification on entry. Some clubs open in the summer months only. Entry fees range from nothing to up to €50 – if you have to pay to get in the first drink is usually included in the price. **Drinks are usually very expensive in clubs, e.g. from €10 for a spirit plus mixer.**

Live Music

You can hear live music of almost any sort on the coast at different venues. Classical music concerts are given regularly by the Malaga Philharmonic

Orchestra at the Cervantes theatre in Malaga (see **Theatres** on page 234) during the season from October to June and other national and foreign orchestras also include the Costa del Sol in their tours.

There are numerous bars and clubs that offer live music as part of their nightly entertainment and you can hear live jazz (Malaga has an annual jazz festival in the autumn), local bands and singers, and flamenco. Expatriate crooners singing cover versions are popular entertainment at foreign bars and pubs. Needless to say, some are better than others.

Spanish singers and bands play regularly on the coast and top international soloists and bands occasionally give concerts, particularly during the summer months. Recent visitors have been Elton John, Supertramp and Van Morrison. Tickets for concerts are usually on sale at local record shops, tourist offices and at Corte Inglés.

If you're into making your own music, lots of bars and clubs offer karaoke nights or jam sessions.

Flamenco Dancing

You can watch flamenco dancing at numerous venues on the coast and many bars and restaurants offer a flamenco show as part of the evening's entertainment, although the quality of dancing varies tremendously and recorded music is played. The best and most authentic offering live singing and music, is found at specialist venues, known as *tablaos*, e.g. *Bona Dea* in Marbella, *Taberna Flamenca Pepe López* in Benalmadena and *Vista Andalucía* in Malaga.

Concerts and recitals are also put on regularly at different venues around the coast, including *Teatro Cervantes* in Malaga and, perhaps surprisingly, Tívoli in the summer months. The village of Ojén celebrates its renowned annual festival of flamenco singing (*cante jondo*) in August. True *aficionados* may be interested in joining one of the many flamenco clubs (*peñas flamencas*) active on the coast. Flamenco dancing is also very popular with young children and there are several academies in most towns.

Plaza Mayor

The Plaza Mayor, situated near Malaga airport (Parador del Golf exit from the A-7), is a purpose-built leisure complex built in typical Andalusian style with narrow alleyways, squares and fountains, and consisting of some 60 restaurants and cafés, numerous bars and nightclubs, a 20-lane bowling alley and 20-screen cinema. The complex, which has proved hugely popular with both residents and tourists, is open daily from 10am to 3am. There's ample parking as well as bus and train services. For more information contact the website (🖥 *www.plazamayor.es*).

SOCIAL CLUBS & ORGANISATIONS

The cosmopolitan nature of the Costa del Sol has spawned a wide variety of clubs catering for just about every activity and nationality, ranging from bridge to square dancing, cycling and football, from the Conservatives abroad to Labour clubs, and from American to South African social clubs. There are also chapters of global social clubs such as the Lions Club, the Inner Wheel and Toastmasters International. Charitable and self-help organisations such as Alcoholics Anonymous, Cudeca (cancer care) and Lux Mundi also operate on the coast.

Many clubs advertise their activities and venues in the local press (*The Costa del Sol News* has particularly comprehensive listings) or on local notice boards. Some town councils (e.g. Torremolinos) have a database of clubs and associations in their area. A comprehensive listing of clubs is also available from 🖥 *www.andalucia.com/entertainment/clubs/home*. Children's activities are often posted on school notice boards and in the bi-monthly publication, *Kids on the Costa*.

Spanish speakers also have the option of joining a local club, of which there are many. These clubs are often subsidised by the local council and provide low-cost sports activities and social occasions. Pensioners are particularly well catered for and most towns have a social centre known as the *Hogar del Jubilado* or *del Pensionista*. Local town councils can provide information. If you cannot find a club for your particular needs, why not start one?

University Of The Third Age

Older residents may be interested in the University of the Third Age (U3A) which has centres in Fuengirola and Marbella. A variety of courses, lectures and travel activities are offered in two terms from September to July. Information is available from 🖥 *www.u3acostadelsol.org*.

THEATRES

A good choice of plays and concerts is offered at venues around the coast and most towns have an extensive cultural programme, mostly in Spanish, although some events are in English. Theatre can be seen in English, mainly at Salón Varietés in Fuengirola (see below) and numerous foreign-language theatre groups and clubs on the coast also perform regularly at different locations. See the local press for details.

Theatres are located at the following venues:

Area One – The West

Marbella   Parque de la Constitución
The open-air auditorium in the main park offers a programme of theatre, dance and music during the summer months.

Parque   ☎ 952-903 159
The *Teatro Ciudad de Marbella* offers a year-round programme of theatre, music and dance, usually in Spanish. Tickets can be bought by telephone or at the Corte Inglés in Puerto Banús.

Area Two – Central Costa Del Sol

Fuengirola   Salon Varietés Theatre   ☎ 952-474 542
🖥 *www.salonvarietes.org*
Situated in central Fuengirola this is one of the coast's oldest and offers an extensive year-round programme of theatre, dance and musicals in English. Events are popular so book early for good seats.

Palacio de la Paz
Offers an extensive range of theatre and recitals throughout the year including the annual Festival of Musicals held in July/August. For information on events see the town's website (🖥 *www.fuengirola.org*) or enquire at the tourist office.

Mijas   Mijas hold an annual international theatre festival in July.

Area Three – Malaga

Malaga   Teatro Cánovas, Plaza del Ejido s/n   ☎ 952-260 611
🖥 *www.teatro-canovas.org*
This modern theatre situated near the Ejido campus offers an extensive range of dance, music and theatre mainly for young people and children.

Teatro Cervantes   ☎ 952-224 109
🖥 *www.teatrocervantes.com. (for information)*
                                        (*Uniticket*) ☎ 9501-246 246
🖥 *www.unicaja.es (to make a booking)*

Malaga's main theatre situated in the centre of the old quarter offers a year-round programme of music, opera, dance and theatre, mostly in Spanish, although occasionally foreign companies perform. The theatre is the main stage for the Malaga Philharmonic Orchestra. The annual jazz festival is held here in the autumn. **Acoustics are excellent, but the theatre's small and demand for seats is high so you should book as early as possible.** Prices range from €12 for celestial (and very uncomfortable) seats to €75 for seats in the circle. Tickets for opera tend to be more expensive.

Area Four – The East

Nerja   Cultural Centre, C/ Granada 45   ☎ 952-523 863
💻 *www.nerja.net*
Nerja's cultural centre and auditorium offer an extensive range of activities such as dance, music and theatre productions as well as courses and master classes. The annual International Music Festival and Flamenco Festival are also held here.

WATER PARKS

Note that the parks get very crowded in July and August when queues for attractions are very long. It is also advisable (sensible!) to wear plenty of high-factor sunscreen.

Mijas   Parque Acuático Mijas, N-340 Fuengirola
(opposite Dunnes Stores and Mijas
cinema)   ☎ 952-460 404
💻 *www.aquamijas.com*
Water fun for all ages. Open during the summer only from 10am to 6 or 8pm. Price: approximately €12.50 adults, €7.50 children (4 to 12), €5 pensioners. Discounts are available after 3pm, for two-day tickets and for season tickets. Restaurant and snack facilities on site. Ample parking.

Torre Del Mar   Aquavelis, Urb El Tomillar   ☎ 952-542 758
💻 *www.aquavelis.com*
A new water park with plenty of fun attractions. Open in the summer months from 11am to 6pm (7pm in July and August). Price: approximately €17 adults, €13 children. Discounts available for season tickets. Buses leave frequently from Malaga and Nerja for the park.

Torremolinos   Parque Acuático Aquapark, C/ Cuba 10   ☎ 952-388 888
One of Spain's first water parks and the biggest on the coast. Water fun for all ages. Open in the summer months only from 10am to 6pm (7pm in July and August). Price: approximately €16 adults, €11.20 children.

WILDLIFE PARKS & ZOOS

Estepona   Selwo Safari Park, A-7 km 162.5 (east
side of Estepona)   ☎ 902-190 482
🖳 *www.selwo.es*
A huge safari park with many animals and birds in natural
surroundings. The visit – **allow the whole day** – includes rides
on safari jeeps and shows. The park has several restaurants
and shops. Open from 10am to sunset daily (night visits are
possible during the summer). Price: €17 adults, €11 children
and pensioners. Tickets available on site, at hotels, travel
agents, Corte Inglés and Portillo bus stations. Buses to Selwo
run from Malaga with stops at main towns daily and from
Algeciras on Sundays only.

Fuengirola   Fuengirola Zoo, C/ Camilo José Cela 6   ☎ 952-666 301
(near the bull ring and cinema)
Many animals in unusual settings. Open 10am to sunset (night
visits in the summer) daily. Price: €9.50 adults, €7 children
(4 to 12) and pensioners. Special discounts are available for
visitors visiting Fuengirola by train. Information is available
from the station.

Torremolinos   Crocodile Park, C/ Cuba 14   ☎ 952-051 782
✉ *cocophil@activanet.es*
More than 300 crocodiles, plus a museum and crocodile
nursery. Open 10am to 7pm daily. Price: €7.50 adults,
€5.25 children (4 to 12) and pensioners.

OTHER PLACES TO VISIT

The Costa del Sol is situated in one of Spain's most varied regions,
Andalusia, home to some of the country's most beautiful cities and most
spectacular scenery. Andalusia's main cities are: Córdoba (187km/117mi
from Malaga) with its unique mosque and archaeological remains at the
ruined city of Medina Zahara; Granada (130km/81mi from Malaga), home
to the Alhambra and Generalife (Spain's most visited tourist attraction);
and Seville (220km/138mi from Malaga), the archetype of a true
Andalusian city with its white narrow streets lined with orange trees. All
are well worth a visit (if not several) and can be visited in a day, but it's
better to go for a weekend. Other towns and cities of note in the region
include: Antequera, Baeza, Cadiz, Jerez and Ronda as well as the white
villages in the province of Cadiz and the mountain villages of the
Alpujarras in Granada and Almeria.

Days trips to most of the above locations are available from the coast and
prices start at around €30 including the coach and tour and entrance fees.

Most trips offer lunch for an extra price. Trips usually leave early in the morning and return in the evening. **Note that although the sun may be shining on the coast, it can be considerably cooler inland especially in Ronda and Granada where temperatures can be very low in the morning and evening – take warm clothing.** Tickets for day trips can be bought at most travel agents and hotels. Information on the various destinations can be found at tourist offices on the coast or from the Andalusia tourist website (🖥 *www.andalucia.org*). Good guide books to the region are *Andalucía* (Lonely Planet), *Andalucía: The Rough Guide* (Rough Guides) and *Inside Andalucía* by David Baird (Santana).

If you're travelling independently to Granada and plan to visit the Alhambra, you should pre-book tickets. Tickets are available from ☎ 902-224 460 (☎ +34 915-379 178 from abroad) and 🖥 *www.alhambra* tickets.com.

Gibraltar

The Rock of Gibraltar is a popular day trip from the Costa del Sol (the journey takes about 90 minutes from Malaga) and offers several tourist attractions including cable car rides to the top of the rock and duty-free shopping. Duty-free allowances are 200 cigarettes, one bottle of spirits and 200 litres of petrol, plus any other purchases to the value of €175 (€90 for the under 15s). Gibraltar is also a popular shopping destination for residents who cannot do without British food. **You need your passport to enter and leave Gibraltar, and if you enter by car you may have to queue up for hours at the border control in order to leave.** Coach trip passengers go through border control on foot. Day trips from the coast cost around €10 for the coach trip only and from €22 for a guided tour of the rock.

Note that the border does get closed from time to time – Spain closed its side in November 2003 for the best part of the day when the P&O cruise ship 'Aurora' docked at Gibraltar.

Morocco

If you're feeling adventurous, why not travel across to Morocco? Day trips to Tangier are feasible from both Algeciras and Tarifa (the catamaran ferry takes 30 minutes), and tours leave daily from the coast to Chauoen, a mountain village in the north and Tangiers. Day trips cost around €50 and trips lasting several days around €300. Most travel agents and tour operators offer longer trips to Morocco visiting the cities of Casablanca, Fez, Marrakech or Rabat. Flights are available from Malaga to Rabat and Marrakech.

DNAC is a company specialising in unique personalised trips to Morocco with top class accommodation, gourmet food and visits to both tourist haunts and places off the beaten track. DNAC organises à la carte trips to many destinations in Morocco including the main cities and the Sahara. Further information is available from ☎ 610-841 665 and 🖳 *www.dnac.net.*

Puerto Banús

11

Sports

The Costa del Sol's, climate and comprehensive facilities make it possible to participate in many different types of sport. Golf, sailing and tennis, however, remain the most popular. This chapter covers the different sporting activities on the coast.

MUNICIPAL SPORT

If you speak some Spanish and want the chance to integrate into local society, it's a good idea to join a sports club or group at your local sports centre. Municipal centres also offer the opportunity to join sports federations and to compete at regional and national levels. Costs are usually low (and subsidised for residents in many cases) and annual membership may be available. A wide variety of classes are offered throughout the day (usually 10am to 2pm and 4 to 8pm) Mondays to Saturdays – evenings tend to be the most popular. Some activities are very popular and heavily over-subscribed (e.g. football and swimming) so you need to book a place early.

Ask at your local town hall for information on sports venues and activities available in your area. Municipal sports centres typically offer aerobics, athletics, badminton, basketball, football, gymnastics, handball, judo, karate, rhythmic gymnastics, swimming, tai chi, tennis and yoga. Most centres also have a gymnasium and sauna. **Note that all swimmers must wear swimming caps.**

The Malaga Sports Board (Patronato de Deportes de Málaga) can also provide information (☎ 952-261 316).

ATHLETICS

Athletics is increasing popular on the Costa del Sol where there are several athletics tracks, the most important of which are the track in Torremolinos and the one at the Mijas racecourse. An athletics stadium is currently under construction near the Martín Carpena sports stadium in Malaga in preparation for the 2007 European Athletics Cup. Running is extremely popular and there are numerous races held at towns all over the coast throughout the year. The Malaga half-marathon takes place in the spring. The Costa del Sol also has a Harriers Hash club.

FOOTBALL

Football is very popular on the Costa del Sol and there are numerous pitches, mostly municipal. Leagues operate at local, provincial and regional level for amateur players of all ages. Children may join the Spanish football federation and play with teams in the federation leagues. 'Football Schools' consisting of several days intensive football training and play are held at some sporting venues and schools in the school holidays. Check the local press for details.

Football Teams

Malaga CF is the area's top football team and is currently maintaining its place in the first division with aspirations to join the Champions League. Malaga CF's home matches offer the chance to see some of the best footballers in the world and brief moments of glory such as Malaga's 5-2 victory over Barcelona in November 2003! The team's home stadium at the Rosaleda in Malaga is currently undergoing extensive restoration and will eventually seat 33,000 spectators. Malaga's second team, Malaga B, plays in the second division. For more information contact the Rosaleda Stadium (☎ 952-614 210) or visit the team's website (🖳 *www.malagacf.es*).

Local teams play in provincial and regional leagues with varying degrees of success!

GOLF

With over 40 golf courses along its stretch, not for nothing is the Costa del Sol also known as the 'Costa del Golf'. The combination of quality courses, some of which rank among the best in Europe, with a pleasant all-year climate has led to a boom in the demand, particularly from Northern European golfers – especially when they are rained (or frozen!) off courses in their home countries during the winter months. As a consequence, the Costa del Sol now rates as one of the best places in the world for golf tourism and in 2004 was voted the world's fourth best golf destination by the International Association of Golf Tour Operators.

Below is a directory of the main golf courses on the coast together with contact information and an approximate idea of green fees. **Bear in mind that winter is high-season on the golf courses and prices are often lower in July and August.** Some prices may include buggy fees. Several golf courses are only for members only, although increasing numbers of courses now offer 'pay and play' facilities – it's advisable to check before going to play. At present there's only one municipal course at La Cañada near Valderrama, although Mijas has advanced plans for the construction of one near the village.

Area One – The West

Estepona

Atalaya, Benahavis   ☎ 952-882 812
Two 18-hole, par 71 and par 72 courses, designed by Von
Limburger. Green fees around €90.

Club de Golf El Coto   ☎ 952-801 357
One 9-hole, par 27 course. Green fees around €18.

El Paraiso   ☎ 952-883 846
One 18-hole, par 72 course, designed by Kirby and Gary
Player. Green fees around €65.

Golf Estepona   ☎ 952-113 081
One 18-hole, par 72 course, designed by José Luis López.
Green fees around €55.

Los Flamingos, Cancelada   ☎ 952-889 150
🖳 *www.flamingos-golf.com*
One 18-hole, par 72 course and 9-hole, par 36 course, both
designed by Antonio García Garrido. **A second 18-hole, par
72 course known as the Gran Flamingo will open during
2004**. Green fees around €95.

Monte Mayor, Cancelada   ☎ 952-113 088
One 18-hole, par 71 course, designed by José Gancedo.
Green fees around €85

Manilva

La Duquesa   ☎ 952-890 425
One 18-hole, par 72 course, designed by Robert Trent Jones.
Green fees around €60.

Marbella

Cabopino Golf   ☎ 952-850 282
One 18-hole, par 71 course, designed by Juan Ligues Creus, at
Artola. Green fees around €132 for two players.

Greenlife Golf   ☎ 952-839 142
One 9-hole course plus one 18-hole, designed by Greenlife, at
Elviria Hills. Home to the Powerlife Learning Centre. Green
fees from €20 to €32.

Guadalmina Golf   ☎ 952-883 375
Two 18-hole courses and one 9-hole course, designed by
Javier Arana and Follco Nardi, at Guadalmina Alta. Green fees
around €60.

La Zagaleta   ☎ 952-855 450
🖳 *www.lazagaleta.com*
One 18-hole, par 72 course, designed by Bradford Benz, on
Ronda road. Course is open to residents and guests of the
estate only.

Los Arqueros   ☎ 952-784 600
One 18-hole, par 72 course, designed by Seve Ballesteros, on Ronda road. Green fees around €60.

Marbella Golf Club   ☎ 952-830 500
One 18-hole, par 72 course, designed by Robert Trent Jones, at El Rosario. Green fees around €70.

Rio Real   ☎ 952-765 733
One 18-hole, par 72 course, designed by Javier Arana, at Rio Real (east of the city). Green fees around €80.

Santa Clara Golf   ☎ 952-850 111
One 18-hole, par 71 course, designed by Enrique Canales, east Marbella (near the hospital). Green fees around €90.

Santa Maria Golf   ☎ 952-831 036
One 18-hole, par 72 course, designed by Antonio García Garrido, at Elviria. Club house offers many facilities. Green fees around €70.

Nueva Andalucía

The urbanisation of Nueva Andalucía, just to the west of Marbella and directly opposite Puerto Banús, is home to Golf Valley, where five top-class golf courses (see below) are located within easy reach of one another:

Aloha   ☎ 952-907 085
💻 *www.clubdegolfaloha.com*
One 18-hole, par 72 course and one 9-hole course, designed by Javier Arquana, at Nueva Andalucía. Green fees from May to September only are around €85.

Dama de Noche   ☎ 952-818 150
One 9-hole course, designed by Enrique Canales, at Nueva Andalucía. For the real golf enthusiast since the course is floodlit and open 24-hours! Green fees around €25.

La Quinta   ☎ 952-762 390
💻 *www.laquintagolf.com*
One 27-hole course. Green fees around €72.

Las Brisas   ☎ 952-810 875
One 18-hole, par 72 course, designed by Robert Trent Jones, at Nueva Andalucía. Green fees around €120.

Los Naranjos   ☎ 952-815 206
One 18-hole, par 72 course, designed by Robert Trent Jones, at Nueva Andalucía. Green fees around €80.

Sotogrande

Alcaidesa Links (near La Línea)   ☎ 956-791 040
💻 *www.alcaidesa.com*
One 18-hole, par 70 course, one of the coast's only two links
courses, designed by Peter Allis and Clive Clark. Green fees
around €70.

Almenara (near Valderrama)   ☎ 956-582 000
One 27-hole course, designed by Dave Thomas. Green fees
around €60.

La Cañada (near Guadiaro)   ☎ 956-794 100
A municipal 9-hole, par 35 course, designed by Robert Trent
Jones. Green fees around €48.

Reserva de Sotogrande   ☎ 956-582 027
One 18-hole, par 72 course, designed by Cabell Robinson
and newly opened in 2003. Green fees around €120.

San Roque Old Course (near San Roque)   ☎ 956-613 030
One 18-hole, par 72 course, designed by Dave Thomas,
and within easy reach of Gibraltar. Green fees
around €80.

San Roque New Course (near
San Roque)   ☎ 956-613 030
One 18-hole, par 72 course, designed by Perry Dye and
Severiano Ballesteros, and within easy reach of Gibraltar.
Green fees around €80.

Golf Sotogrande   ☎ 956-785 014
💻 *www.golfsotogrande.com*
One 18-hole, par 74 course plus a 9-hole course, designed by
Robert Trent Jones and generally agreed to be one of the most
beautiful courses on the coast. Green fees around €150 (€160
during January).

Valderrama   ☎ 956-791 200
💻 *www.valderrama.com*
One 18-hole, par 72 course, designed by Robert Trent Jones
and Europe's top golf course. Green fees around €250
Mondays to Fridays and €275 at weekends.

Area Two – Central Costa Del Sol

Alhaurín

Lauro Golf, Alhaurín de la Torre   ☎ 952-815 206
One 18-hole, par 72 course, designed by Falco Nardi.
Green fees around €80.

Benalmedana   Torrequebrada, Benalmadena Costa   ☎ 952-412 767
One 18-hole, par 72 course and one 9-hole course course,
designed by José Gancedo. Green fees around €46.

Mijas Costa   Calanova
One 18-hole course currently under construction and
expected to be finished by the end of 2004.

La Siesta, Calahonda   ☎ 952-933 362
One 9-hole course, designed by Enrique Canales. Green
fees around €17.

Miraflores, Urb Miraflores   ☎ 952-931 960
One 18-hole, par 70 course, designed by Falco Nardi.
Includes a high quality driving range. Green fees
around €55.

Mijas Golf Valley

The verdant valley running from Mijas Costa to La Cala includes several
top golf courses (see below) and has been christened 'Mijas Golf Valley'.
There are advanced plans to create a further three courses (Altavista, Banos
del Puerto and La Manzanilla) by 2005/06.

Alhaurín Golf, Alhaurín El Grande   ☎ 952-595 970
Two 18-hole, par 72 courses and one 9-hole course, designed
by Severiano Ballesteros. Green fees around €65.

La Cala   ☎ 952-669 033
Two 18-hole courses, par 72 and 73, designed by Cabell
Robinson. Includes the David Leadbetter Golf Academy on site.
**A third course is currently under construction with the first
9-holes expected to ready by the end of 2004 and the
complete 18-hole course by 2005.** Green fees around €65.

Mijas Golf   ☎ 952-476 843
Two 18-hole courses, par 71 and 72, designed by Robert
Trent Jones,. Green fees from €50 to €70.

Santana Golf & Country Club   ☎ 952-472 436
A new 18-hole course, par 72, designed by Cabell B. Robinson.
Green fees around €80.

Area Three – Malaga

Malaga   El Candado, El Palo   ☎ 952-299 340
One 9-hole course, designed by Carlos Fernández Caleya.
Green fees around €25.

Parador del Golf (near Malaga airport) ☎ 952-381 255
One 18-hole, par 72 course, designed by Tom Simpson.
**The first course to be built on the Costa del Sol some 70
years ago and one of the only two links courses on the
coast.** Green fees around €54.

Guadalhorce, Cártama ☎ 952-179 378
One 18-hole course and one 9-hole, par 72 course, designed
by Kosti Kuronen. Club also includes facilities such as
swimming pool, tennis courts and recreation areas. Green fees
around €52.

Area Four – The East

Rincón De   Añoreta Golf   ☎ 952-404 000
Le Victoria   One 18-hole, par 72 course, designed by José Mª
Cañizares. Green fees around €66 for two players.

Vélez-Malaga   Baviera Golf, Caleta de Vélez   ☎ 952-555 015
🖳 *www.bavieragolf.com*
One 18-hole, par 71 course, designed by José Mª
Cañizares. Green fees around €45 for two players.

HORSE RACING

The Costa del Sol Racecourse (*Hipódromo de la Costa del Sol*) is situated in
El Chaparral in Mijas Costa and can be accessed from La Cala village (El
Limonar roundabout) or from Myramar in Fuengirola (turn-off opposite
the castle). The course is one of the best in Spain with top quality racing,
including the annual Mijas Cup race and is a popular venue with foreign
residents. Racing takes place on Sunday from noon in the winter and on
Saturday evenings from 10pm in the summer. The racecourse is open
daily (guided visits are available) and there are gym and athletics
facilities onsite. Riding lessons are also available. For more information
contact the racecourse by telephone (☎ 952-592 700) or via their website
(🖳 *www.hipodromomijas.com*).

HORSE RIDING

There are numerous riding schools (*picaderos* or *establos*) situated on the
Costa del Sol and riding lessons and guided rides in the country are
available. Horse riding is expensive and costs around €20 for adult
beginners in a group (€40 individually) and €15 for children. Some schools
organise horse rides in the surrounding countryside at weekends. **Check
that the school has adequate third-party insurance.**

One of the coast's main horse riding venues is the School of Equestrian Art (*Escuela de Arte Ecuestre*) in Estepona which organises competitions, events and shows as well as offering riding lessons for all levels and ages. The school is located on the N-340 Ctra de Cádiz Km. 159, Río Padrón alto, s/n. More information is available by telephone or fax (☎ 952-808 077, ▤ 952-808 078).

KARTING

Campillos   Campillos Karting
An international karting circuit will open here sometime towards the end of 2004..

Malaga   Malaga Indoor Karting, C/ Ortega y
Gasset 335, Pol Ind San Luís   ☎ 952-330 041
⊠ *indoorkarting@terra.es*
Andalusia's only **indoor** karting track including a professional timing system. Open all year round from 4pm to midnight Mondays to Fridays and from 2pm to 1am at weekends. Prices (including helmet and overalls): €10 adults for seven minutes and €6 children for six minutes. The track has bar and restaurant facilities.

Mijas   Mijas Karting Club, Ctra de Coín, Mijas
Costa (behind the BP petrol station)   ☎ 952-581 704
Two karting circuits (children, junior and formula competition). Open all year round from 10am. The track has bar and cafeteria facilities.

QUAD BIKING

Quad biking can be found at the Fuengirola Diving Centre (Fuengirola port). Quad biking trips are available from one hour to a whole day to various locations on the Costa del Sol. Price: €50 for adults, €40 for children (5 to 12) for one hour and includes helmets, boots, overalls and gloves. Open all year from 10am to sunset. More information can be obtained by telephone (☎ 676-771 120) or on the internet (▤ *www.rentaquad.com*).

SKIING & ICE SKATING

The Costa del Sol claims to be one of the few places in the world where you can ski in the morning and sunbathe on the beach in the afternoon. The area's nearest ski resort is situated in the perpetually snow-covered Sierra Nevada mountains some 200km (125mi) north in the province of Granada. **Sierra Nevada is a very popular resort and is packed at weekends and during the Christmas period.** The journey from the coast to the slopes takes around two hours by car (allow for longer at weekends when roads near the resort are often gridlocked).

The resort, centred around the village of Pradollano, offers around 70km (44mi) of pistes with 30 runs. The highest is the Olympic Run (*Pista Olímpica*), starting at 3,400m (11,155ft); on clear days there are breathtaking views of the Mediterranean coast and Morocco. The village has ample accommodation in hotels and apartments, and there are also numerous restaurants and shops, including ski equipment hire. There's undercover parking for 2,800 vehicles and outside parking for 1,000. During the skiing season (early December to April) snow is guaranteed as the resort has an extensive network of snow-making machines. Sierra Nevada is Europe's southernmost resort and the sun is very strong on the slopes even when the temperatures are low. **Wear plenty of high factor sunscreen.**

Prices for a one-day ski-lift pass (*forfeit*) are from €24.70 to €33 for an adult and from €14.80 to €19.80 for a child (depending on the season).

Discounts are available in low season and for passes that are for a period of four or more days. Sierra Nevada also offers snow boarding, ice skating, tobogganing, snowmobiles and dog-sledges.

Information and weather conditions are available in English and Spanish from ☎ 958-249 119 and 🖳 *www.cetursa.es*; bookings can also be made. The Sierra Nevada website (🖳 *www.sierranevadaski.com*) also provides comprehensive information.

Ice Skating

Benalmadena is currently constructing the coast's only ice rink (it will be an indoor one) next to the new indoor swimming pool in Arroyo de la Miel. It is due to open in late 2004.

SWIMMING

There are numerous indoor and outdoor pools on the coast and swimming is a popular sport. Municipal indoor pools, which are mostly Olympic size are situated at Coín, Fuengirola, Malaga (several), Marbella, Mijas (Las Lagunas), Torremolinos and Vélez-Málaga. Municipal pools offer classes for both children and adults, training and public swimming. Two swimming clubs, Mijas and the Real Club Mediterráneo in Malaga, have produced national champions. Classes cost from €15 a month for three hours a week. **Note that a swimming cap is compulsory.**

Indoor Pools are currently under construction in Alhaurín de la Torre, Benalmadena (due to be finished in late 2004) and Estepona (due to be finished shortly).

Several sports clubs on the coast have indoor pools. **Most hotels (three star and over) have outdoor pools, most of which are unheated and suitable only for swimming from May to October.**

TENNIS & OTHER RACKET SPORTS

Tennis is extremely popular on the Costa del Sol where there are numerous tennis clubs. Clay, hard and fast courts are available and prices for court hire vary tremendously, e.g. from €4 to €30 an hour. Most municipal sports centres offer tennis lessons for adults and children – **prices for these are very reasonable (e.g. €15 a month for three one hour classes a week), but classes are often large.** Private clubs charge from around €6 to €30 an hour for classes. Tennis clubs organise regular tournaments for all ages and standards, and there are also several provincial and regional competitions. Many urbanisations have private tennis courts for residents' use. The main private tennis clubs on the Costa del Sol are listed below. Municipal tennis courts are usually located at Municipal Sports Centres.

Area One – The West

Estepona	Atalaya Park Hotel, Ctra de Cádiz km 168.5 ☐ *www.atalaya-park.es*	☎ 952-889 000
	Bel Air Tennis Club, Urb Bel Air	☎ 952-883 221
	Club de Tenis Estepona, Urb Abejeras	☎ 952-801 579
	Mansfield's Tennis Club, Urb Benavista	☎ 952-888 106
Marbella	Club El Casco, Urb El Rosario ☐ *www.elcasco.com*	☎ 952-837 651
	Club Nuevo Alcántara, Urb Nuevo Alcántara, San Pedro	☎ 952-788 315
	Don Carlos, Don Carlos Hotel, Ctra de Cádiz km 192 ☐ *www.hotel-doncarlos.com*	☎ 952-831 140

El Madroñal Country Club, Ctra.
Ronda km164   ☎ 952-785 307

Hofsass Tennis, Urb Elviria   ☎ 952-835 249
🖳 *www.hofsaesstennis.com*

Life Tennis Centre, Ctra de
Cádiz km 193.7   ☎ 952-834 913

Los Granados Tennis Club, Puerto Banús ☎ 952-818 662

Los Monteros, Los Monteros Hotel, Ctra
de Cádiz km 187   ☎ 952-771 700
🖳 *www.monteros.com*

Manolo Santana Racquets Club, Ctra de
Istán km 2   ☎ 952-778 580
🖳 *www.manolosantana.net*

Marbella Playa, Ctra de Cádiz km 189   ☎ 952-831 345
🖳 *www.fuertehoteles.com*

Puente Romano Tennis Club, Hotel
Puente Romano, Ctra de Cádiz km 177.5 ☎ 952-820 900
🖳 *http://es.marbellaclub.com/tennis2*
**One of the largest clubs on the coast and where Davis
Cup and ATP matches have been played.**

Sotogrande   Octagon Beach Club (next to
Sotogrande port)   ☎ 956-615 614

Sotogrande Racquet Centre, El
Cucurucho Beach Club, Pº del Parque   ☎ 956-796 233

Area Two – Central Costa Del Sol

Benalmedena   Club de Golf Torrequebrada, Ctra de
Cádiz km 220   ☎ 952-442 742

Mijas Costa   Calahonda, Club del Sol   ☎ 952-939 595
🖳 *www.tenniscostadelsol.com*

Lew Hoad, Ctra de Mijas km 3.5   ☎ 952-474 858
🖳 *www.tennis-spain.com*

	Miraflores Tennis Club, Urb Miraflores, Ctra de Cádiz km 199	☎ 952- 932 006
	Riviera, Aztec Tennis Club	☎ 952-934 477
Torremolinos	Club de Tenis La Colina, Urb La Colina	☎ 952-051 237

Area Three – Malaga

Malaga	Club El Candado, Urb El Candado	☎ 952-299 340
	Club Deportivo Calderón, Centaurea 6	☎ 952-203 444

Area Four – The East

Nerja	Club Andaluz, Urb Capistrano	☎ 952-520 948
Torre Del Mar	Club de Tenis El Capitán, Urb El Capitán	

Other Racket Sports

Badminton and squash are both played on the Costa del Sol, although neither is as popular as in other countries, e.g. the UK. There are badminton and squash courts at some tennis clubs (see above) and Mijas has a badminton team who compete at regional and national level. Paddle tennis, played on a smaller court with wooden rackets, is a popular sport and many hotels have courts.

WATERSPORTS

You can do just about every imaginable watersport on the Costa del Sol where there are several marinas with sailing clubs as well as other clubs specialising in watersports. Conditions for watersports are usually excellent all-year round. The following provides a guide to some activities on or in the water.

Boating

The Costa del Sol offers wonderful opportunities for boating, which is a popular pastime. The possibilities range from luxury power boats or yachts to modest dinghies. If you don't own a boat you can hire one from most marinas, by the hour, day or week. **Note that for larger vessels you may need a licence and/or experience.** If you own a boat it must be moored at one of the coast's many marinas (see below). **Note that legally you can only keep fishing boats on beaches and only then in designated areas.** Fishing trips (short and deep-sea) are also available from most fishing ports and marinas. For information on boat trips and dolphin and whale watching see page 217.

Marinas

Area One – The West

Estepona   Puerto de la Duquesa (west of Estepona)
Berths for 328 boats.

Puerto de Estepona (west of the town)
Mooring available for 443 boats.

Marbella   Marbella marina (in the centre of the town – the fishing port is further east)
Has 337 berths.

Puerto de Cabopino (situated on the far east of Marbella)
Small with 169 berths.

Puerto Banús Puerto Banús marina
The area's most famous marina and one of the largest with mooring for some 915 boats. **Marbella's rich and famous dock here.**

Sotogrande   Sotogrande port
One of the most attractive in the area and has 548 berths.

Area Two – Central Costa Del Sol

Benalmadena   Puerto Marina
The Costa del Sol's largest marina and has mooring for some 960 boats, including private mooring for owners of apartments on the artificial islands.

Fuengirola   The port is in the central part of town and has mooring for 225 boats. **The cheapest berths are found here.**

Area Three – Malaga

As well as the huge port where some of the world's largest cruise ships dock, Malaga also has two small marinas.

Malaga	Club Mediterráneo Has 40 berths.
	Puerto Deportivo El Candado (east of the city) This is the base for the sailing club.

Area Four – The East

Vélez-Málaga	Caleta de Vélez Has 238 moorings.

Diving & Snorkelling

Although the Mediterranean waters around the Costa del Sol aren't particularly rocky or deep, conditions are good for diving, especially if you're a beginner as the relatively calm seas and gentle tides make diving easier. There are a surprising number of marine species around the Costa del Sol, but more adventurous divers may wish to explore the waters east of Nerja (e.g. Salobreña or Motril) or nearer the Strait where there are several wrecks. **To dive in Spanish waters you need a permit (around €7), available from diving clubs and schools (see below).** Hunting with spears or harpoons is prohibited. If you want to learn to dive, most diving clubs and schools on the coast offer tuition leading to the world-recognised PADI qualification.

Even if you're an experienced diver, never dive alone and make sure you have above water support when diving.

Diving Clubs

Diving clubs are found at the following locations:

Benalmadena Costa	Sol Dive Charters, Pueblo Evita, Avda Erasa	☎ 626-071 784
Marbella	Diving Marbella, Puerto Deportivo, Local 4 🖳 *www.divingmarbella.com*	☎ 952-902 304
Nerja	Club Nautico Nerja, Avda Castilla Pérez 2	☎ 952-524 654
	Nerja Diving, Playa Burriana	☎ 952-528 610
Torremolinos	Simply Diving, C/ Carmen Montes, Edif El Cortisollo, 4	☎ 952-058 651

Surfing & Windsurfing

When the wind blows conditions are ideal for surfing and windsurfing, and there are several surfing clubs on the coast, although the waves can hardly ever be classed as 'rollers', but some beaches (e.g. those at Estepona and Cabo Pino) make good practice grounds for beginners. The best place near the Costa del Sol for wind and kitesurfing is undoubtedly Tarifa, classed as one of the world's top windsurfing destinations, and 108km (67mi) from Marbella and 158km (99mi) from Malaga – the journey takes from between 90 minutes and two hours.

Tarifa's excellent sandy beaches (e.g. Playa Chica, Río Jara) and above all, almost permanent gale, make ideal conditions for windsurfing and kitesurfing. The surfing season starts at Easter with the Toro Andaluz race and the Ballentines Championship is also held here. **The surfing scene is huge in the town where there are numerous shops, clubs and meeting places.**

Further information is available via the internet (🖳 *www.tarifa.net* and 🖳 *www.tarifainfo.com*) where information on accommodation and the town is also available.

Other Watersports

There are numerous other watersports on the Costa del Sol. Waterskiing, rides on inflatables and jet-ski rides are offered by beach bars, beach clubs and sports stands on beaches. **Make sure the owner has a licence and adequate insurance for all sports, particularly for jet-skis – in the summer of 2002 several people were killed or badly injured in jet-ski accidents and legislation has since been tightened up.**

Parascending can be done at Fuengirola port all year round. For more information telephone ☎ 630-131 234.

For those who like to stay firmly on dry land or get seasick even in the calmest waters, watching watersports or strolling round the marinas is a good substitute!

Ronda

12

Shopping

Shopping facilities on the Costa del Sol have improved beyond all recognition over the last few years and there's now an excellent choice of both large and small shops, national and international chain stores, hypermarkets and supermarkets. Imported goods, including an excellent range of foreign food, are available in most areas. This chapter looks at where to shop on the Costa del Sol for specific items and includes lists of markets and shopping centres.

FOOD

Fresh Produce

Spain has a fantastic variety of home-grown fresh produce available all year round, although many fruit and vegetables are seasonal and out-of-season produce tends to be imported. Many varieties of tropical fruit are now grown on the Costa del Sol, such as avocados and mangos, and most fruit and vegetables are grown in the area. Fish and shellfish are available in abundance, much of it caught locally. Fresh fish isn't usually for sale on Mondays, however, as fishermen don't work on Sundays. Fresh meat tends to be Spanish and of excellent quality. Pork and veal are particularly good.

As well as at indoor markets (see page 263), fresh produce can be bought in shops in towns where there are butchers' (*carnicerías*), greengrocers' (*fruterías*), bakers' (*panaderías*) and grocers' (*ultramarinos*). Produce in these shops is usually good quality and value. Supermarkets also sell fresh produce, although the quality may be inferior. A recent survey of food stores in Spain found that the best fruit, vegetables and fish are found in small shops, but the best meat is found in both small shops and supermarkets.

Foreign Food

There's generally a good variety of foreign food available at supermarkets on the Costa del Sol and many 'foreign' products, e.g. cereals and biscuits, are actually produced in Spain. British and German products are the easiest to find, although there may not be much choice, particularly between brands. Not all supermarkets stock foreign foods, although you can usually find what you need at Supersol supermarkets, hypermarkets (not in Malaga) and specialist foreign food shops (e.g. Islandia) or foreign-run supermarkets. Some people travel to Gibraltar to the Safeway supermarket, where many British foodstuffs can be bought.

Bear in mind that foreign food, particularly if imported, is expensive and there may be a cheaper Spanish equivalent, although there are no Spanish baked beans!

Britbuys is a company specialising in British foodstuffs, which you can buy online. Postage and packaging is extra, and the minimum order is €30. The company has a huge range of products (more than you find in most supermarkets on the coast) and offers special goodies for Christmas and Easter. Products aren't cheap, but if you're craving a bar of Turkish delight or need some wholemeal bread flour, you may be tempted to look at the website (🖳 *www.britbuys.com*).

Markets

Markets (*mercadillo*) are an essential part of life on the Costa del Sol and at the larger ones (Fuengirola's Tuesday market claims to be the biggest) you can buy just about everything, usually very cheaply – especially if you haggle. Markets are usually open from 9am to 2pm. If a public holiday coincides with market day or it's raining, the market probably won't take place. Markets are popular and can get very crowded; keep your belongings safe and your money well protected, as pickpockets may be about. The following is a list of the general markets that take place on the Costa del Sol during the week. An asterisk denotes markets selling crafts and second-hand goods or car boot sales.

Mondays	Manilva (fairground)
	Marbella (around the bull ring)
	Torrox Costa (Plaza Almedina)
Tuesdays	Fuengirola (fairground)
	Mijas village (municipal market)
	Monda (C/ Los Huertos)
	Nerja (C/ Antonio Ferrandiz Chanquete)
Wednesdays	Alhaurín de la Torre (Urb El Limonar)
	La Cala (fairground)
	Estepona (Avda Juan Carlos)
	Istán
	Rincón de la Victoria (Paseo Marítimo)
Thursdays	Alhaurín el Grande

	Frigiliana (near the by-pass)
	San Pedro (Saladillo)
	Torre del Mar
	Torremolinos (El Calvario)
	Vélez-Málaga (Avda Europa)
Fridays	Arroyo de la Miel (next to Tívoli World)
	Benalmadena village (Plaza Pedro Aguacil)
	Sabinillas (fairground)
Saturdays	Coín (fairground)
	* Fuengirola (fairground)
	La Cala (fairground)
	Las Lagunas, Mijas Costa
	* Puerto Banús (around the bull ring)
	San Pedro (Diana centre)
Sundays	* Arroyo de la Miel (Tívoli grounds)
	* Coín (fairground)
	* Duquesa (port)
	* Estepona (port)
	* Fuengirola (port)
	Malaga (near the football stadium)
	* Marbella (fairground)
	* Nerja (end of C/ Antonio Millón)
	* Sabinillas (fairground)
	* Sotogrande (port)
	* Torremolinos (next to the football ground)

Indoor Markets

The best place to buy fresh produce is at an indoor market – most towns have one – open Mondays to Saturdays from 8.30 or 9am to 2pm. The best produce is available first thing, although bargains may be available at closing time. Shop around the different stalls – some sell top-quality produce at top prices and others sell cheaper inferior quality produce. A good guide to the best stalls is the queues! Haggling is acceptable, although not for individual items but rather as a reduction in your final price (stall holders often round down to the nearest euro) or a special price if you buy more. Shopping in indoor markets is an enjoyable experience and not one to be done in a hurry, as all stallholders and customers want to discuss local and national affairs! The following is a list of indoor markets on the Costa del Sol.

Area One – The West

Estepona   C/ Castillo

Marbella   C/ Benavente

Area Two – Central Costa Del Sol

Benalmadena   C/ Las Flores

Fuengirola   Mercacentro (opposite the railway station)

                  Mercado Los Boliches (C/ Salinas)

Torremolinos Pza del Mercadillo

Area Three – Malaga

Each district has its own indoor market, but the central ones are:

Malaga   Mercado Central (Pza Arriola)

                  Mercado Merced (next to Cervantes Theatre)

Area Four – The East

Nerja   Pza Ermita

Torre Del Mar C/ el Río

Vélez-Málaga Carrera San Francisco

Local Shops

There are numerous small shops on the coast selling food and, although prices here are generally more expensive than supermarkets, the quality is better, as is the service. They also give you a good chance to practise your Spanish! Local shops generally open from 9.30 or 10am to 1.30 or 2pm and from 4.30 or 5pm to 8 or 8.30pm Mondays to Fridays and on Saturday mornings.

Supermarkets

There are several supermarket chains on the coast. Opening hours are usually 9, 9.30 or 10am to 8.30 or 9pm Mondays to Saturdays. Some supermarkets open on Sundays in the summer and during the Christmas and Easter holidays. The main supermarkets are:

- **Corte Inglés** – In Malaga and Marbella. Food here is generally of good quality and more expensive than in other supermarkets. Many own-brand products of good quality are stocked, as well as some foreign produce. Further information is available from ☎ 901-122 122 and 🖥 *www.elcorteingles.es* (online shopping available with delivery to certain areas).

- **Mas** – Mas supermarkets offer reasonable quality at low prices and have branches in Benalmadena, Malaga and Nerja. Further information is available from ☎ 900-180 551 and 🖥 *www.supermercadosmas.com*.

- **Mercadona** – Reasonable quality at inexpensive prices with many own-brand products in favour of other brands. Stores often have their own parking facilities (free if you make a purchase). There are numerous stores on the coast and inland. Further information is available from ☎ 902-113 177 and 🖥 *www.mercadona.es* (online shopping available with delivery to certain areas).

- **SuperCor** – Part of the Corte Inglés chain (see above), these new large supermarkets sell a limited range of clothes, shoes and household items as well as offering services such as travel agents. SuperCor stores are currently at Benalmadena Costa, Coín (CC La Trocha), Fuengirola (Los Boliches), San Pedro and Sotogrande. Further information is available from ☎ 901-122 122 and 🖥 *www. elcorteingles.es*.

- **Supersol** – Reasonable quality at average prices with some own-brand products and a good choice of foreign food products. Supersol have branches at numerous locations on the coast and inland.

Supersol's owners (the Dutch company Ahold) are currently selling the Supersol chain in Spain, although as yet there isn't a buyer. Several supermarket chains have expressed an interest, including Carrefour and El Corte Inglés.

Discount Stores

There are numerous so-called discount stores on the Costa del Sol where products are sold at lower prices than in supermarkets. Discount stores tend to display produce in boxes rather than on shelves and there's little choice of brand. They are, however, inexpensive and offer good value in basics such as pasta, flour and cleaning products. Note that you must pay for plastic bags in most discount stores (€0.05 each) and queues for the checkout can be very long.

Discount stores on the coast include the following:

- **Día** – Discount supermarkets with many own-brand products. There are stores in Fuengirola, Malaga (several) and Marbella. Free parking is provided. Further information is available from ☎ 902-453 453 and 🖳 *www.dia.es*.

- **Lidl** – Discount supermarket with mainly German produce also selling some clothing and household goods. There are stores in Coín, Malaga (several), Marbella, Mijas Costa (in Calahonda and Ctra de Mijas) and Nerja. Free parking is provided. Further information is available from ☎ 902-243 222 and 🖳 *www.lidl.es*.

- **Makro** – Wholesale only and you must have a card to buy here, although cards are easy to obtain if you have a business or are self-employed. The single store is on the N-340 km near the airport. Further information is available from 🖳 *www.makro.com*.

- **Plus** – Discount supermarkets with many own-brand products. Stores in Benalmadena, Fuengirola, Malaga, Marbella, Rincón de la Victoria, Torremolinos and Vélez-Málaga. Free parking is provided. Further information is available from ☎ 901-102 202 and 🖳 *www.plus-supermercados.es*.

Hypermarkets

The large shopping centres on the Costa del Sol usually include a hypermarket selling just about everything for the home (although the choice of furniture is usually limited) as well as food, clothes and footwear, books and music, and toys. Hypermarkets also offer a range of services such as home delivery and discount cards. Most hypermarkets have in-store cafeterias or restaurants and travel agents'. Hypermarkets are generally open from 10am to 10pm Mondays to Saturdays and are open on Sundays in July and August and during the Christmas and Easter holidays. **Note that you need a €0.50 or €1 coin for trolleys.**

The main hypermarkets on the Costa del Sol are:

- **Alcampo** – Part of the French company, Auchan, with many own-brand products. There are stores at La Cañada shopping centre in Marbella and in Motril. The La Cañada store offers home delivery to the Marbella area only and supervised childcare is available for the under-tens. Free parking is available. Further information can be found on 🖥 *www.alcampo.es.*

- **Carrefour** – Carrefour has branches in the Alameda, Los Patios and La Rosaleda shopping centres in Malaga, in Estepona and in Rincón de la Victoria. A French company with a huge presence throughout Spain and usually with excellent special offers. Free parking is available. Further information is available from ☎ 902-202 000 and 🖥 *www.carrefour.es.* Online shopping is available with delivery to certain areas.

- **Eroski** – Belonging to a Basque company, this is the only fully Spanish hypermarket chain in the country, with stores in the Larios shopping centre in Malaga (two hours' free parking), CC El Ingenio in Vélez-Málaga and the Parque Miramar shopping centre in Fuengirola (free parking). Special emphasis is placed on consumer rights and the company also offers an excellent online magazine (🖥 *www.consumer.es*), free to email subscribers. Further information is available from ☎ 902-540 340 and 🖥 *www.eroski.es.* Online shopping is available with delivery to certain areas.

- **Hipercor** – Hipercor branches can be found in Malaga (Ctra de Cártama km 2, free parking) and Puerto Banús (two hours' free parking for El Corte Inglés card holders). A new Hipercor is due to open in Las Lagunas, Mijas Costa at Easter in 2005. Hipercor is part of the Corte Inglés group and offers quality food and products at higher prices than other hypermarkets. Further information is available from ☎ 901-122 122 and 🖥 *www.elcorteingles.es/hipercor.* Online shopping is available with delivery to certain areas.

Hypermarkets and supermarkets are popular places for pickpockets and thieves. Don't leave your bag or wallet unattended, especially when you're at the checkout or packing your car. Women on their own or with children are favourite targets.

CLOTHING & FOOTWEAR

Chain Stores

Numerous clothing and footwear chain stores operate on the Costa del Sol and the following is a list of the main shops you can expect to find in most high streets and shopping centres.

Clothing For Adults

The main clothing stores are listed below, but you may also find other well known clothing stores (e.g. Dorothy Perkins, Evans, Miss Selfridge).

- **Benetton** – Italian fashion for women. Good for knitwear. Note that some Benetton stores are franchise shops and it may be difficult to return or exchange an item if you bought it in a different store.

- **Berska** – Mainly women's fashion, although there are a few lines for men. Casual wear aimed at the young and teenage market.

- **Cortefiel** – Men and women's fashion. Casual and smart. Good for quality knitwear, coats and suits. Generally better quality and more upmarket than Zara and Mango.

- **Mango** – Women's fashion. You have to be pretty slim to get into most of the garments!

- **Massimo Dutti** – Men and women's fashion. Casual and smart. Good quality and more expensive than Zara.

- **Pull & Bear** – Mainly men's fashion, although there's a small women's section. Casual wear predominates. Inexpensive and good for basics such as T-shirts and sweaters.

- **Springfield** – Men's fashion. Good value casual and smart wear with average quality.

- **Women's Secret** – Women's nightwear, swimwear and underwear at reasonable prices.

- **Zara** – Men and women's fashion. Spain's flagship fashion store where lines change frequently. Good value casual and smart wear, although quality can be poor and clothes usually only last for a season. Note that women's clothes are designed for those on the slim side and men's clothes don't fit tall men.

Clothing For Children

- **Benetton** – Most Benetton stores stock clothes for children from 0 to 12 years. Clothes are expensive, but the quality is generally good.

- **Charanga** – This local firm has several stores on the coast and sells inexpensive clothes for 0 to 16-year-olds. Good for basics such as jeans, sweaters and T-shirts.

- **El Corte Inglés** – A good choice for 0 to 16-year-olds. Good brands as well as designer labels. Prices range from reasonable to very expensive. Quality is generally good.

- **Dunnes** – Children's wear including footwear for 0 to 16-year-olds. Good for basics. Inexpensive but clothes only last for one season.

- **Hypermarkets** – Hypermarkets such as Alcampo, Carrefour and Hypercor sell good basics such as trousers, tracksuits and underwear at reasonable prices.

- **Mayoral** – A local firm with several stores on the coast stocking clothes for 0 to 16-year-olds. Good quality and reasonable prices.

- **Zara** – Clothes and footwear for 0 to 16-year-olds. Reasonable prices, but quality is average.

Department Stores

Details of the two main department stores that can be found on the Costa del Sol are given below.

El Corte Inglés

Spain's largest department store company and one of the country's most profitable has several branches on the coast (and more are planned or under construction). The store offers a good choice of fashion, including own-brand lines (Easywear and Gold Coast) and national and international brands such as Burberry, Dior, DKNY, Episode and Tommy Hilfiger. Good for knitwear and basics, and there are good bargains in the sales.

Dunnes

The Irish department store has several branches on the coast (Fuengirola, Malaga in the Larios centre, Mijas Costa and CC El Ingenio in Vélez-Málaga) and provides cheap fashion for men and women. Good for basics at reasonable prices.

Designer Stores

Many national and international designers are represented on the Costa del Sol and some have their own stores, such as Adolfo Dominguez, Ana de Sousa, Armani and Versace. Puerto Banús has the best selection of designer clothes and El Corte Inglés department stores sell some lines.

Footwear

Shoe shops (*zapaterías*) abound on the Costa del Sol and there's an excellent choice of casual and smart footwear to suit all tastes and budgets. It's worth shopping around and comparing prices, but bear in mind that not all shoes are leather. It's worth stocking up on several pairs during the sales, when many shoe shops offer huge discounts (up to 50 per cent). Note that it's difficult for women with feet size 41 or over to find a good choice of shoes.

Children's Shoes

Shoe shops in Spain don't generally stock children's shoes as well as adults'. Children's shoes are usually sold in specialist shops. Most towns have one or two shops where you can buy children's shoes. El Corte Inglés department stores have a good selection of children's footwear and Dunnes and Zara also sell some. Note that shops usually don't measure children's feet (you will be asked their size) and there's usually only one width fitting.

HOUSEHOLD GOODS

A list of the main stores selling household goods on the Costa del Sol is given below.

- **Casa** – Several branches on the coast specialising in inexpensive items for the home including decoration, linen, kitchenwear and small items of furniture.

- **Dunnes** – Dunnes stores stock inexpensive items for the home, including linen, accessories, kitchenwear and some garden furniture. Dunnes stock linen in British sizes for British-made duvets and pillows.

- **El Corte Inglés** – Everything you need for the home, and catering for all tastes and budgets.

- **Zara Home** – The recently created home section of the fashion store sells mainly household linen and accessories at reasonable prices.

Furniture

Furniture stores (*tiendas de muebles*) are everywhere on the coast and most have a good selection of furniture at a range of prices. Some stores cater for budget furnishing only and offer to furnish a two-bedroom apartment for €3,000. Most have frequent special offers and discounts, which are advertised in the local press. Some self-assembly furniture is available from hypermarkets and DIY stores (see page 273), and for those who love spending hours assembling bits of furniture with complicated instructions IKEA opened a store in Seville in January 2004 (Ctra de Huelva, Castilleja de la Cuesta, 🖥 *www.ikea.es*).

Household Appliances

Generally most household appliances from another European country will work on the Costa del Sol with just a change of plug, but you should check with an electrician beforehand. Televisions and videos from the UK don't usually work in Spain (you can get a picture but no sound – see page 307) and if you bring a washing machine from the UK you will need to block the hot water intake since washing machines in Spain heat their own water rather than taking it from the hot water system.

Appliances can be bought from specialist shops, department stores and hypermarkets. Special offers and discounts are frequent and most outlets offer credit facilities. Note that some shops don't include installation of a new appliance or removal of an old appliance in the price.

BOOKS

There's generally a shortage of good book shops on the coast, although the situation has improved greatly in recent years and more large towns can now boast at least one good book store. Hypermarkets also stock a selection of books. English-language books are available at specialist shops (see below) and a limited selection (usually paperback bestsellers) can be found at some large supermarkets and newsagents. Otherwise you can buy online from one of the many internet book shops, such as Amazon (🖥 *www.amazon.co.uk* or *www.amazon.com*), The Book Place (🖥 *www.thebookplace.com*) or WH Smith (🖥 *www.whsmith. co.uk*) and have the books delivered by post. There are also second-hand book shops in most areas, where you can purchase or exchange English-language books.

Main book shops on the coast are listed below:

Area One – The West

Marbella

El Corte Inglés, Puerto Banús
A good selection of books, including a limited number of
English-language books.

FNAC, La Cañada shopping centre
🖳 *www.fnac.es*
The large FNAC store stocks an excellent range of books and
can order practically anything. A selection of English-language
books (children's, fiction and non-fiction) are available. Books
can also be ordered online.

Bookworld España, C/ Las Palmeras
25, San Pedro   ☎ 952-786 366
A large selection of English-language books as well as cards
and wrapping paper. Ordering service available.

Area Two – Central Costa Del Sol

**Arroyo De
La Miel**

Librería Internacional, Avda de la
Constitución, local 18-1   ☎ 952-564 104
Good selection of foreign language books.
Ordering service available.

Fuengirola

Bookworld España, Pso Santos Rein
(opposite the railway station)   ☎ 952-664 837
A large selection of English-language books as well as cards
and wrapping paper. Ordering service available.

Librería Teseo, Avda Juan Gómez
Juanito 15   ☎ 952-473 413
A good selection of books, including some
English-language. Good ordering service. Children's
story-telling on occasional Saturdays.

Librería Tiempo, Maestra Angeles
Azplazu 1   ☎ 952-588 677
Small book shop with a good range of books.

Area Three – Malaga

Malaga has several good book shops, although they're quite small and
crowded, usually offering a limited selection of English-language books.

Malaga

El Corte Inglés, C/ Hilera   ☎ 952-211 999
The ground floor section has a wide range of books,
including an excellent selection for children.

Librería Cervantes, Pza de la
Constitución 3 Librería Rayuela,
C/ Cárcer 1   ☎ 952-219 697
The main book shop.

Librería Rayuela, Pza de la Merced 1   ☎ 952-219 697
The language section of the above bookshop.

Paideia, C/ Pinzón 3.   ☎ 952-219 196
Educational books.

Proteo-Prometeo, Puerta de la
Buenaventura 3-6   ☎ 952-217 736
🖳 *www.libreriaproteo.es*

Area Four – The East

Nerja   WH Smiffs, C/ Almirante Ferrandiz 10   ☎ 952-523 102
English-language books available as well as an
ordering service.

Torre Del Mar   Pasatiempo, C/ Infantes 30   ☎ 952-543 703
Ordering service for English-language books.

MUSIC

The best selection of CDs and tapes of all types of music can be found in El
Corte Inglés department stores and in FNAC in the La Cañada shopping
centre, although many small music shops offer good selections.
Hypermarkets also sell music but usually only pop or a very limited choice
of other types of music. Music shops on the coast are listed below. At most
shops you can order CDs or tapes and buy tickets for local concerts.

Area One – The West

Estepona   Discos Lollypop, C/ Castillo 3   ☎ 952-802 966

Marbella   Disco 2000, Ramón y Cajal 2   ☎ 952-770 708
✉ *disco2000@jet.es*

Area Two – Central Costa Del Sol

Fuengirola   Disco Precio, C/ Miguel de Cervantes 2   ☎ 952-461 514

Discos Euterpe, Pza de la Constitución 11   ☎ 952-479 993

Discos Euterpe, Avda de los Boliches 72 ☎ 952-470 392
✉ *euterpex@teleline.es*

Area Three – Malaga

Malaga	Chill House, Alarcón Luján 5	☎ 952-221 870
	Disco Pat, C/ Atarazanas 1	☎ 952-223 341
	Gong Discos, Larios Centre and Malaga Plaza 🖥 *www.gongdiscos.com*	☎ 952-369 137
	Groove Records, Pza Federico Alba Varela 69 ✉ *djscraggy@hotmail.com*	☎ 952-348 800

Piracy is *big* business in Spain and it's common to be approached by someone selling pirate CDs on the beach or while you're sitting in a bar. Pirate CDs are cheap (around €3 compared to at least €10 in the shops), but the sound quality may be poor AND THEY'RE ILLEGAL and damaging to the recording business. Don't feel you're helping the seller by buying one – most proceeds go to the big fish at the top running the piracy operation and exploiting the sellers.

DIY MATERIALS

There are numerous places where you can buy DIY materials on the Costa del Sol and, although many people favour the large specialist stores, it may be worth asking at your local ironmonger's (*ferretería*) or household supplies shop (*droguería*) for the item you need – it's often cheaper and much more convenient.

Builders' Merchants

Large orders of building material can be made through builders' yards, although you might get a better discount if you order through a builder rather than in person. Delivery is usually extra.

Chain Stores

The Costa del Sol has two large DIY stores: Akí on the west side of Malaga near Los Patios shopping centre and Leroy Merlín in the La Cañada shopping centre. Both offer a comprehensive range of DIY and gardening equipment, including items of furniture and machinery. Note that, although these stores have a good choice, they aren't always the cheapest and it's worth shopping around.

Local Shops

Ironmongers sell a wide range of DIY materials as well as numerous other items for the home. You can usually buy small objects such as nails or bolts by weight or number rather than having to buy a whole packet. *Droguerías* sell paint and brushes, etc. Some larger shops may deliver and most will offer a discount on a large order. Pinturas Andalucía has several branches on the Costa del Sol and offers a large selection of paint and painting equipment as well as tools and some DIY equipment.

Warehouses

Most towns have several warehouses (*almacén*) specialising in building material, tiles or plumbing and electrical goods. Warehouses are generally situated on the outskirts or in industrial areas (*polígono industrial*). Most have a good selection on display and in stock; other items can usually be ordered within a week. Delivery is normally extra unless you have a very large order, and most warehouses will offer a discount if you ask. Prices vary greatly and it's worth shopping around and comparing prices – especially if you plan to buy a lot.

SHOPPING CENTRES

Until relatively recently there were no shopping centres (*centros commerciales*/CC) on the Costa del Sol except for Cristamar in Puerto Banús and the now-closed Marbell Centre in Marbella. Over the last few years, however, shopping centres have started to spring up all over the coast, a tendency that looks set to continue, as the regional government has now lifted its moratorium on their construction.

Centres are generally open from 10am to 10pm Mondays to Saturdays and open on Sunday during July and August (except in Malaga) and during the Christmas holidays. Parking is usually free or you have a number of free hours (e.g. three).

Shopping centres are very popular, especially in the evenings and at weekends. Christmas is particularly crowded and queues to get in and out of car parks can be kilometres long.

Thieves love shopping centres, and people are victims of theft everyday. A favourite trick is to distract you as you're loading your car while an accomplice steals something. Keep your car doors locked while unloading shopping and when returning your trolley. Don't leave belongings unattended even for a few seconds and watch out for pickpockets in crowds. Women on their own or with children are favourite targets.

The major shopping centres on the Costa del Sol are listed below.

Area One – The West

Marbella   CC La Cañada (on the A-7 Marbella bypass, Ojén exit)
This award-winning centre was greatly extended in 2003 and houses a multi-screen cinema, Oxigene fitness centre, Alcampo hypermarket, FNAC book and audio store, two large furniture stores and numerous chain stores (mainly clothes), including several British chains, as well as other shops selling accessories, toys and household goods. There's a good choice of places to eat and cafés. Free parking is available on site. Next to the centre are Boulanger (household appliances), Leroy Merlín (DIY centre) and Norauto (car parts and repair). La Cañada is one of the coast's most popular centres and gets very crowded in the afternoons and on Saturdays.

San Roque Golf Resort (A-7 km at San Roque)
A large shopping centre is currently under construction (expected to be finished by July 2004) at the entrance to the Golf Resort. It will house a variety of chain stores and designer shops as well as a supermarket.

Area Two – Central Costa Del Sol

Coín   La Trocha
This large centre around 2km from Coín on the A-355 from Cártama opens in 2004 and houses a Supercor supermarket (part of the El Corte Inglés chain), Moreno Rivera (furnishing and appliances) and 50 other stores, mainly fashion chain stores, accessories and snack bars and restaurants. There's also a multi-screen cinema. Parking is free and local schoolchildren are planting the car park with trees native to the Guadalhorce Valley.

Fuengirola   Parque Miramar (A-7 opposite the castle)
This new centre (opened in spring 2004) houses an Eroski hypermarket, a multi-screen cinema, numerous chain stores (mainly clothes) and a selection of places to eat.
Work will begin on the second part of the centre in 2004 and this section will house large stores specialising in furniture, decoration and DIY.

Area Three – Malaga

Malaga

CC Larios
Situated near the bus station in one of Malaga's up-and-coming areas, the Larios centre houses a multi-screen cinema, Eroski hypermarket, Dunnes store, a large furniture store as well as numerous chain stores (mainly clothes and sports). There are several cafés, snack bars and restaurants on site and there's also a good choice in the main square outside the centre. Parking is free for the first three hours.

CC La Rosaleda
Situated in the north of Malaga near the Rosaleda stadium and the Materno hospital, this centre houses a multi-screen cinema and Carrefour hypermarket, as well as numerous chain stores (mainly clothes and sports). There are several cafés, snack bars and restaurants. Parking is free.

CC Malaga Plaza
This small centre, situated behind El Corte Inglés, is attractively designed and has many shops, including La Oca (household goods), Oboe (furniture), Virgin Megastore and several fashion chain stores. Parking is available. There's a restaurant downstairs.

Plaza Mayor (A-7, Parador del Golf exit, near the airport)
Although it isn't strictly a shopping centre, there are advanced plans to extend the leisure complex by some 10,000m^2 to include numerous small shops. Plaza Mayor currently houses a gift shop and a Nike factory shop as well as a vast choice of places to eat.

Area Four – The East

Rincón De La Victoria

CC Rincón de la Victoria
This new shopping centre (La Cala del Moral exit from the A-7) houses a Carrefour hypermarket, numerous fashion outlets, household and design shops, and places to eat. Ample parking is available.

Vélez-Málaga

CC El Ingenio
This large centre opened in 2001 (next to the Vélez-Málaga exit from the A-7), is well designed and has ample parking, much of which is in the shade (very welcome in the summer). Shops include an Eroski hypermarket, Dunnes store, numerous fashion and accessory stores, and places to eat. There's also a multi-screen cinema, one of which shows a film in English.

SHOPPING ABROAD

Gibraltar

Many expatriate residents go shopping in Gibraltar (about one hour's drive from Marbella and one and a half from Malaga), where you can make considerable savings (depending on currency exchange rates) on cigarettes, petrol, food, luxury goods (e.g. perfumes) and various consumer items. Although Gibraltar has its own currency (Gibraltar pounds), euros and sterling are also accepted. If you pay in euros, however, the exchange rate is usually poor.

You can also buy British medicines that are unavailable in Spain. British chain stores in Gibraltar include Safeway (a large supermarket), Marks & Spencer, The Body Shop and Early Learning Centre. Duty-free allowances are listed below.

If you go to Gibraltar, you need your passport, which must be shown on entry and exit, and car papers if you enter by car. There are often long delays for vehicles entering Spain from Gibraltar, so it may be better to park on the Spanish side of the border in La Línea and get a bus or taxi (or walk) into Gibraltar. Make sure to lock and secure your car against theft, as cars are sometimes stolen while their owners are in Gibraltar! You can also go by coach on one of the many day trips organised by tour operators on the coast. These leave from numerous points along the A-7 and cost around €10. Coaches don't have to queue long to cross the border.

Duty-Free Allowances

● 200 cigarettes;

● One bottle of spirits;

● 200 litres of petrol;

● Purchases to the value of €175 (€90 for the under 14s).

Nerja

13

Miscellaneous Matters

This chapter includes miscellaneous information, of all which is useful to anyone living or staying on the Costa del Sol, namely (in alphabetical order) information on foreign church services, climate, consulates, crime, geography, libraries, pets, residence permits and registering as a resident, services, telephone (fixed and mobile, and internet connections and cafés), and utilities (electricity, gas and water) and refuse collection.

CHURCHES

There are numerous foreign churches on the Costa del Sol. The following is an alphabetical listing of churches and services.

Baptist & Evangelical

Arroyo De La Miel	Arroyo Baptist Church Sundays at 5pm.	☎ 952-563 184
Benalmadena	Triton Hotel Sundays at 11am.	☎ 952-486 820.
Calahonda	Baptist church Sundays at 10am.	☎ 952-930 458
Fuengirola	Hotel Club Puerta del Sol Sundays at 11am.	☎ 952-467 394
	Ark premises, Las Rampas Sundays at 11am.	☎ 952-582 518
	Evangelical Church, Los Boliches Sundays at 2.45pm.	☎ 952-448 763
Marbella	Buenas Noticias church Sundays at 11.30am.	☎ 952-932 216
Mijas	Words of Power Evangelical church Several meetings a week.	☎ 952-485 052
Nerja	Fellowship of the King Sundays at 10.30am.	☎ 958-658 439
Sotogrande	Hotel Royal Golf, N-340 Sundays at 11.30am.	☎ 615-226 084
Torre Del Mar	New Cáritas Halls Sundays at 11.30am.	☎ 952-544 548

Torremolinos   Evangelical Community Church   ☎ 952-622 680
Sundays at 11am.

Catholic

Catholic churches in large towns usually hold a daily service and several at weekends in Spanish only. The following churches hold services in English.

Arroyo De   Main church
La Miel   Saturdays at 1pm.

Benalmadena   Virgen del Carmen church   ☎ 952-473 705
Costa   Sundays at 10am.

Calahonda   Ermita de San Miguel   ☎ 952-932 838
Sundays at 11.30am.

Fuengirola   St Joseph's Chapel, Las Rampas   ☎ 952-474 840
Daily at 11am, Sundays at 10am and 11am.

St Andrews' Chapel, Los Boliches
Saturdays at 5.45pm.

Marbella   International Mass Church
Sundays at 11.30am.

Torre Del Mar   Lux Mundi Ecumenical Centre   ☎ 952-543 334
Saturdays at 5pm (6pm in summer).

Church Of England

Benalmadena   Residencia Hogar Marymar chapel
Costa   Sunday mornings.

Calahonda   Ermita de San Miguel
Sunday mornings.

Coín   Cristo church
Second Thursday of the month at 10.30am.

Estepona   Corazón de María   ☎ 952-805 775
Second and fourth Sundays of the month at 9.30am.

Fuengirola   St Andrew's church, Los Boliches   ☎ 952-472 140
Sundays at 11.30am and Wednesdays at 9am.

Malaga	St George's Church in the British Cemetery Sundays at 11am.	☎ 952-219 396
Nerja	San Miguel church Sundays at 11.30am.	☎ 952-525 406
San Pedro	Corazón de María, Cancelada Second and fourth Sundays of the month at 9.30am.	☎ 952-805 775
Sotogrande	Old School Chapel Second and fourth Sundays at 11.30am.	☎ 956-795 062.
Torre Del Mar	Lux Mundi premises Sundays at 10.30am.	☎ 952-400 030

Church Of Scotland/Presbyterian

Fuengirola	Lux Mundi Sundays at 10.30am.	☎ 952-584 652

Dutch Evangelical

Fuengirola	Skandinaviska Turistkyran Sundays at 9.30am.	
Torremolinos	Holland Huis Sundays at 11.30am.	

Jehovah's Witnesses

Fuengirola	Kingdom Hall, C/ Núñez de Balboa Tuesdays at 7.30pm and Sundays at 11am.	☎ 952-469 082
Malaga	Don Juan de Austria 18 Sundays at 4pm, Mondays at 7.15pm and Fridays at 8pm.	
San Pedro	Kingdom Hall Sundays at 11am and Tuesdays at 7.30pm.	☎ 952-811 415
Torre Del Mar	Islas del Sol Sundays at 5pm.	
Torremolinos	Edif Apolo 1, Avda Sorolla Sundays at 11.30am and Wednesdays at 7.30pm.	☎ 952-051 571
Torrox Costa	Kingdom Hall, Urb Costa de Oro Sundays at 11am and Wednesdays at 7pm.	☎ 952-526 740

Methodist

| Sotogrande | Old School Chapel near Paniagua
First and third Sundays in the month. | ☎ 956-795 062 |

Muslim

Fuengirola	Sohail Mosque Fridays at 2.30pm.	☎ 952-473 916
Malaga	Malaga Mosque, C/ San Agustín 11 Fridays at 2.30pm.	☎ 952-228 595
Marbella	King Abdulaziz Mosque Fridays at 2.30pm.	☎ 952-774 143

CLIMATE

The Costa del Sol has one of the world's best climates and more than 325 days of sunshine a year. Seasonal weather is described below.

Spring

Spring is generally pleasant with average temperatures of around 20°C to 24°C (68°F to 75°F) during the day. April, May and June are often the best months. Rainfall is occasional and it usually doesn't rain after the end of May.

Summer

Summer is warm and sunny. The temperature rises in July and August, when it's often over 30°C (86°F). Note that some areas of the Costa del Sol are often several degrees warmer, particularly when the hot dry wind (known as *terral*) blows from the north. Areas most likely to be affected by this wind, which can blow for several days at a time, are valleys such as Fuengirola, Benalmadena and Malaga city. It rarely rains in summer.

Autumn

Autumn is warm and sunny, although rainfall can be frequent and is sometimes torrential. September and October are usually pleasant months.

Winter

The lowest temperature is usually around 12°C (54°F), although in an exceptional year it may fall lower and very occasionally there's snow on the highest mountains. (In winter 2003 there was a sprinkling of snow on La Concha peak near Marbella for the first time in many years.) The daytime temperature often rises to 20°C (68°F). Note, however, that, although daytime temperatures may be high, you need some form of domestic heating. Rainfall can be frequent and is often torrential, although bad weather rarely lasts for more than three or four days at a time.

Flooding and flash floods are common during torrential rain, and dry river or stream beds can turn into fast flowing currents within a matter of minutes. If it's raining, don't attempt to cross a river or stream on foot or by car (even if it's a four-wheel-drive vehicle) as you can easily be swept away.

In winter 2004 two foreigners were drowned in the Mijas countryside whilst attempting to cross a river during heavy rainfall.

Flooding is common in low-lying areas along the Guadalhorce Valley, although floods can occur anywhere, e.g. Fuengirola and Vélez-Málaga in spring 2003.

Wind

The Costa del Sol can be a very windy place, particularly the western end around Estepona and Sotogrande. Prevailing winds, from the Atlantic (known as *poniente*) and from the Mediterranean (*levante*), can be strong and usually blow for several days at a time. The *levante* is dry in winter and humid in summer, and the *poniente*, humid in winter and refreshingly cool in summer. *Levante* storms in winter often cause severe damage along the sea front. The wind from the north, known as *terral*, is dry and cold in winter, and dry and scorching in summer. Occasionally the wind blows from the south in the summer (*siroco*), bringing sand from the Sahara desert.

Local Variations

Most of the Costa del Sol enjoys much the same pleasant climate, although there are slight local variations. The western side of the coast is generally cooler in summer than the rest of the region because it's fanned by Atlantic breezes, which don't reach the rest of the coast. All areas claim to have the best climate and many also claim a particular microclimate, but it's generally agreed by the experts that Marbella city has the best climate in the area. Local variations are as follows:

The West

The area around Sotogrande and Estepona is generally wetter and windier than the rest of the Costa del Sol, as this area is directly influenced by weather on the Strait of Gibraltar. Not far inland from Estepona is Grazalema, Spain's wettest place.

The East

The area from Malaga eastwards is generally warmer throughout the year than the rest of the Costa del Sol because the Atlantic breezes don't reach the area. This is an advantage in winter, but not in the summer. Malaga itself can be particularly hot in July and August.

Inland

All towns and villages away from the coast are colder in winter and hotter in summer. The difference can be more than 5°C (9°F). In mountain villages, frosts are common in the winter.

CONSULATES

Consulates from numerous countries are represented on the Costa del Sol and most have their offices in Malaga. Consulates provide useful services for foreigners in Spain, including passport renewal and information. Consulate hours are usually 9am to 2pm Mondays to Fridays and consulates close on public holidays (both Spanish and those of their home country).

Austria	Alameda de Colón 26, Malaga	☎ 952-600 267
Belgium	C/ Compositor Lehmberg 5, Malaga	☎ 952-399 907
Canada	C/ Cervantes, Edif Horizonte, Malaga	☎ 952-223 346
Denmark	Avda Garriga Sansó 23, Benalmadena	☎ 952-448 450
Finland	C/ Blasco de Garay 7, Malaga	☎ 952-212 435
France	C/ Duquesa de Parcent 8, Malaga	☎ 952-226 590
Germany	C/ Mauricio Moro Pareto 2, Malaga	☎ 952-363 591
Greece	C/ Salitre 16, Malaga	☎ 952-311 847

Iceland	Pso Marítimo 91, Fuengirola	☎ 952-661 200
Ireland	Avda Los Boliches, Fuengirola	☎ 952-475 108
Italy	C/ Palestina 3, Malaga	☎ 952-306 150
Netherlands	Avda Carlota Alessandri 33, 1°F, Torremolinos	☎ 952-380 888
Norway	C/ Blasco de Garay 7, Malaga	☎ 952-210 331
Philippines	C/ Marqués de Larios 4, 2°, Malaga	☎ 952-222 757
Saudi Arabia	C/ Mauricio Moro Pareto 2-2°, Malaga	☎ 952-310 358
Sweden	Alameda de Colón 26-8, Malaga	☎ 952-604 383
United Kingdom	C/ Mauricio Moro Pareto 2-2°, Malaga	☎ 952-352 300
United States	Avda Juan Gómez 8, 1°C, Fuengirola	☎ 952-474 891

CRIME

In general, the crime rate for the Costa del Sol is low for Spain, although petty theft from property and cars is common in the summer, and some areas are more susceptible to crime than others. Malaga city has a higher crime rate than the rest of the coast, although police statistics show that the rate for most types of crime in the capital decreased by at least 7 per cent during 2003, mainly thanks to increased police presence.

To prevent petty crime, you should do the following:

Property

● Always lock your property when you're out, even if you just pop to the swimming pool. This is particularly important if the property is on a holiday complex – groups of gypsy women operate on the coast and 'specialise' in stealing from holiday property.

● Fit your property with an alarm connected to a security company (don't bother with just an alarm, as no one takes any notice of ringing alarms). Fit your windows with grilles or security windows.

- Don't carry large amounts of cash around (most insurance companies will only refund up to €100 in cash) and don't leave your handbag out of sight, even next to your feet while you're having a coffee.

Cars

- Never leave valuables in your car, particularly if you're driving a hired car.

- Fit your car with an alarm and, better still, a steering-wheel lock. This is especially important if you have an expensive or rare model, as many cars on the Costa del Sol are stolen to order.

- Lock your car at petrol stations when you're filling up or paying.

- At petrol stations and in car parks, watch out for people asking for directions or claiming you've got a flat tyre. While you're distracted, an accomplice could be helping himself to your belongings.

Violent crime is rare despite the Costa del Sol's international reputation for mafia crime, which is highly publicised and dramatised by the media. Although there are occasional shootings between rival gangs, most people are completely unaffected by mafia violence, which rarely intrudes on everyday life. The British tabloid press has nicknamed the Costa del Sol the 'Costa del Crime' because of the number of British criminals who took refuge here during the 1980s. An extradition treaty between the UK and Spain has more or less put a stop to this and, in any case, criminals are likely to have such a low profile you won't see them!

Reporting A Crime

If you're the victim of a crime on the Costa del Sol, you should report it to the police, not least in order to make a claim on your insurance. You can report a crime in the following ways:

- **In Person** – At the local Policía Nacional station at any time. There are interpreter services at most police stations on the coast, but these may not be available when you wish to make your claim, which must be made in Spanish. Queues can be long.

- **By Telephone** – A relatively easy and quick way of reporting a crime is by phoning ☎ 902-102 112 (cost of a local call). Some staff speak English (although you may have to wait until one is available). You report the crime and are given a reference number. You then go to your local police station after 10am the following day and within 72 hours of making the report with the reference number and sign the report.

● **By Internet** – Crime report forms are available on the internet (🖳 *www. policia.es*) in several languages. You fill in the form online and, when you send it, you receive a reference number. You then go to your local police station after 10am the following day and within 72 hours of making the report with the reference number and sign the report.

> Note that if you're reporting a violent crime or can identify the criminal by name, you cannot make a report by telephone or internet, you must do this in person.

EMERGENCY NUMBERS

● **Ambulance Service**   ☎ 061

● **Fire Brigade**   ☎ 080

● **General Emergency Number**   ☎ 112

● **Police**

   – **Civil Guard**   ☎ 062

   – **Local Police**   ☎ 092
     (individual police station numbers are listed in **Chapter 4**)

   – **National Police**   ☎ 091
     (see also **National Police Stations** on page 298)

● **Sea Rescue**   ☎ 900-202 202

GEOGRAPHY

The Costa del Sol has some dramatic scenery, as most of the coastline is fringed by high mountain ranges, including the Sierra Bermeja behind Estepona, the Sierra de las Nieves (whose peaks rise to 3,000m/9,900ft and form the backdrop to Marbella), the Sierra de Mijas behind Fuengirola and Benalmadena, and the high mountains of the Axarquía range, which flank much of the Eastern Costa del Sol.

Most of the coast is green and lush (mainly thanks to intensive watering) and there are large wooded areas, mostly of pine and cork oaks. The far west of the coast is the least developed, where there are still large stretches of virgin countryside dotted with cork oaks and cattle. The eastern region is a centre for tropical fruit farming, vast areas being planted with avocados, custard apples and mango trees.

LIBRARIES

Spain has one of the poorest provisions for libraries in the EU, and the Costa del Sol is no exception. You shouldn't expect to find the range of books and lending facilities you may be used to in your home country, particularly if you come from the UK. The situation is improving, however, and libraries on the coast are becoming better stocked and more user-friendly. There are public libraries in all areas – in separate buildings in larger towns but often within the Casa de la Cultura in smaller places.

Public libraries stock Spanish-language books and offer a selection of newspapers and magazines, CDs and DVDs. Most also offer private study facilities and public internet access (you can usually use the internet for an hour at a time but you may have to book). Some public libraries on the Costa del Sol stock a limited selection of foreign-language books, but this is the exception rather than the rule.

Public libraries make no charge for borrowing books; you simply register at your local library (you need two passport photos and some identification) and with your library card you can take out two or three books for around two weeks from any library in Andalusia.

Public libraries can be found at the following places:

Area One – The West

Estepona	Plaza de las Flores 9 Open morning and afternoon.	☎ 952-750 900
Istán	C/ Calvario Mondays to Fridays 4pm to 8pm.	
Manilva	C/ Duquesa s/n Open morning and afternoon.	
Marbella	Avda del Mercado s/n Open 10.15am to 1.15pm and from 4.45 to 7.45pm.	☎ 952-828 839

Urb Las Chapas   ☎ 952-838 410
Open 10.15am to 1.15pm and 4.45 to 7.45pm.

C/ Nueva s/n, San Pedro   ☎ 952-783 097
Open morning and afternoon.

Ojén   C/ Colegio 2   ☎ 952-881 003
Open afternoons only.

Sotogrande   Avda Tierno Galván s/n, Guadiaro ☎ 956-614 067
Open 4.30 to 8.30pm.

Area Two – Central Costa Del Sol

Alhaurín De   C/ Jabalcuzar s/n   ☎ 952-490 143
La Torre   Open Mondays to Fridays 4 to 8pm.

Alhaurín   Plaza del Mercado s/n   ☎ 952-490 143
El Grande   Open afternoons only.

Alora   Avda Cervantes s/n.
Open Mondays to Fridays 7 to 9pm.

Benalmadena   Parque de la Paloma s/n   ☎ 952-444 689
Open mornings and afternoons.

Coín   C/ Manuel García s/n   ☎ 952-450 179
Open mornings and afternoons.

Fuengirola   C/ Victoria s/n   ☎ 952-474 800
Open mornings and afternoons.

Avda Jesús Cautivo s/n, Los Boliches   ☎ 952-460 750
Open Mondays to Fridays 10.30am to 2pm and 5 to 8pm.

Mijas   Avda Virgen de la Peña s/n   ☎ 952-485 544
Open Mondays to Fridays 10am to 2pm and 5 to 8pm.

C/ San Valentín s/n, Las Lagunas   ☎ 952-586 926
Open Mondays to Fridays 9am to 1pm and 5 to 8pm.

La Cala   C/ Marbella s/n   ☎ 952-494 016
Open Mondays to Fridays 10am to 2pm and 4 to 7pm.

Torremolinos Avda Manantiales s/n   ☎ 952-374 131
Open afternoons only.

Area Three – Malaga

The city of Malaga has numerous libraries, including specialist libraries and archives. A complete list of libraries, with addresses and phone numbers, can be found at the following website: 💻 *www.malagavirtual. com/cultura/biblio.*

Area Four – The East

Frigiliana	C/ Franco 140 Open afternoons only.	
Nerja	C/ Diputación 2 Open Mondays to Fridays 5 to 8pm.	☎ 952-528 252
Rincón De La Victoria	C/ Mediterráneo 140 Open afternoons only.	
Torre Del Mar	Paseo Marítimo s/n Open Mondays to Fridays 10.30am to 2pm and 5 to 8pm.	☎ 952-544 399
Vélez-Málaga	Avda de Andalucía 92 Open Mondays to Fridays 10.30am to 2pm and 5 to 8pm.	☎ 952-500 784

Library times may be restricted in the summer months, when many are open in the morning only.

English-Language Books

There are other ways of finding and borrowing English-language books, including the following:

● Some expatriate clubs and associations have lending library facilities, usually small (but better than nothing!) and there may be a small charge or lending facilities may be limited to members only.

● Most international schools have good libraries and parents of pupils may be allowed to borrow books.

● Get together with friends and start your own library or reading circle!

PETS

If you plan to bring your pet to the Costa del Sol (and many people do), you should check the latest regulations, particularly if you're bringing a pet from the UK or another country with strict quarantine regulations. Bear in mind that you may have to return to the UK at short notice and need to take your pet with you.

Spanish Regulations

Travellers to Spain may bring a maximum of two pets with them, and a rabies vaccination is usually compulsory, although accompanied pets entering Spain directly from the UK (i.e. by air or sea) and pets under three months old are exempt. If a rabies vaccination is given, it must be administered not more than a month and no more than 12 months before the pet enters Spain. **If you come to Spain via France (e.g. if you drive to Spain) a rabies vaccination is compulsory.**

You also need two official certificates: one signed and stamped by a registered vet declaring that the animal has been vaccinated against rabies, and the other signed by the owner declaring that the animal has been under his supervision for at least three months before entering Spain. Both certificates are in Spanish and English and are valid for 15 days **only** after signing. You can obtain the certificates from Spanish consulates abroad (they're downloadable from some consulate websites).

Pets other than dogs, cats, hamsters and rabbits may require a special import licence and the importation of 'exotic' animals is generally prohibited. All international airports and sea ports in Spain accept imported animals, but you should inform the carrier beforehand.

British Regulations

In 2000, the UK introduced a pilot Pet Travel Scheme (PETS), which replaced quarantine for qualifying cats and dogs. Under the scheme, pets must be micro-chipped (they have a microchip inserted in their neck), vaccinated against rabies, undergo a blood test and be issued with a health certificate ('passport'). **Note that the PETS certificate isn't issued until six months** *after* **the above have been carried out!** Pets must also be checked for ticks and tapeworm 24 to 48 hours before embarkation on a plane or ship.

The scheme is restricted to animals imported from rabies-free countries and countries where rabies is under control, including France, Spain and Gibraltar. The new regulations cost pet owners around €300/GB£200 (for a microchip, rabies vaccination and blood test), plus €90/GB£60 per year for annual booster vaccinations and around €30/GB£20 for a border check. Shop around and compare fees among a number of veterinary surgeons.

To qualify, pets must travel by sea via Dover or Portsmouth, by train via the Channel Tunnel or via Gatwick or Heathrow airport (only certain carriers are licensed to carry animals and they can usually take only one animal per flight). Additional information is available from Department for Environment, Food and Rural Affairs (DEFRA), Animal Health (International Trade) Area Two, 1A Page Street, London SW1P 4PQ, UK (☎ 0870-241 1710, 💻 *www.defra.gov.uk/animalh/quarantine*).

British owners must complete an Application for a Ministry Export Certificate for dogs, cats and rabies-susceptible animals (form EXA1), available from DEFRA at the above address. DEFRA will contact a vet you've named on the form and he will perform a health inspection. You will then receive an export health certificate, which must be issued no more than 30 days before your entry into another EU country with your pet.

Further information is available from DEFRA (☎ UK 020-7904 6000 or 020-7238 6951, ✉ *pets.helpline@defra.gsi.gov.uk*).

Dogs

When you arrive on the Costa del Sol, you must register your dog and have a microchip fitted – most vets provide this service, which costs from €30. The microchip contains the owner's name and address so don't forget to change it if you move. Dogs should be kept on a lead at all times and are generally not allowed in public parks, on beaches (some permit dogs from October to April) or in restaurants, cafés or shops. Bear in mind that the Spanish aren't generally enthusiastic about dogs in public places and it's probably best to leave them at home.

If you bring your dog to the Costa del Sol, the following information may be useful:

● **Cleaning Up!** – Many streets on the Costa del Sol are a minefield of dog excrement. **Always clean up after your dog**. It's illegal not to and you can be fined in many towns.

● **Leishmaniasis** – Leishmaniasis (also called Mediterranean or sandfly disease), which is carried by mosquitoes and is almost always fatal, is common on the Costa del Sol. There are collars on the market which are claimed to provide protection, but the only sure way of preventing this disease in your dog is to keep him inside from dusk to dawn and fit windows and doors with fly screens. For most dog owners, this isn't practical, particularly during the summer when everyone's outside. However, according to experts, this is the only way to effectively protect your dog.

- **Poison** – If you walk your dog in rural areas, beware of poisoned bait (usually meat laced with strychnine) left by hunters and poachers to control predators such as foxes. Although the practice is illegal, many dogs have died as a result. Fit your dog with a muzzle to prevent it eating while out in a rural area.

- **Processionary Caterpillars** – Certain pine trees in many areas on the Costa del Sol are favoured by the processionary caterpillar moth, which lays its eggs in the branches. The caterpillars hatch in the early spring and descend to the ground, where they bury themselves. Their hairs are extremely toxic to animals (fatal in many cases) and cause intense irritation in humans. The caterpillars are easy to identify from their striped, hairy bodies (about 6cm/2.5in long) and by the fact that they attach themselves to each other in a kind of conga (hence their name). If you have these caterpillars in trees on your property, you can have the trees treated. Pine trees in many public areas are also treated and it's hoped that the caterpillar will eventually be exterminated. However, many tree owners don't treat their pines, so you should be vigilant.

- **Summer Temperatures** – Bear in mind that the Costa del Sol can be very hot in summer (from June to September) and dogs need plenty of fresh water and shade. **Never leave your dog in the car in the summer, even in the shade.**

- **Ticks & Leeches** – Ticks infest rural areas on the Costa del Sol (mainly from sheep and goat herds) and are particularly virulent in early spring. You can buy effective tick collars or capsules to prevent these. Treatment takes around a week to become effective and needs repeating every three to six months. Leeches are common in water (fresh or stagnant) – the best prevention is to not allow your dog to go in water and especially not to drink from it. Leeches can be removed only by vets.

- **Vaccinations** – **Vaccinate your dog against rabies (preferably before arrival), leptospirosis, parvovirus, hepatitis, distemper and kennel cough.** Vaccinations must be renewed every year.

Dangerous Dogs

Spain has strict regulations on ownership of certain breeds of dog regarded as dangerous, namely Akita, American Staffordshire Terrier, Dogo Argentino, Fila Brasileirso, Japanese Tosa, Pit Bull, Rottweiler and Staffordshire Bull Terrier. 'Dangerous' breeds also include dogs that have all or most of the following characteristics: a strong and powerful appearance; a strong character; short hair; shoulder height between 50 and 70cm and weight over 20kg (44lb); a square and robust head with large jaws; a wide, short neck; a broad, deep chest; robust forelegs and muscular hind legs. If you aren't sure whether your dog has the 'required' number of these characteristics, you should consult your vet. Dangerous dog owners must be over 18, have no criminal record, undergo psychological and physical tests, have third party insurance for €120,000 and have a special licence (available only from local councils). Dangerous dogs must be muzzled and kept on a lead no longer than 2m (6ft 6in) in public places.

Cats

Cats should be vaccinated against feline gastro-enteritis, typhus, feline leukaemia virus and feline enteritis. Cats also need regular treatment against fleas – powder or collars are effective.

You should have your cat neutered, unless you plan to breed from it, as there's a plague of stray and unwanted cats on the Costa del Sol, and there's little point in adding to the already overlarge population.

Pet thieves operate on the Costa del Sol and often steal to order. If you have an unusual and/or expensive breed of dog or cat, look after it and don't let it roam free.

Kennels & Catteries

There's a good choice of kennels and catteries on the Costa del Sol, most of which are located on the outskirts of towns or in the country. Services and facilities vary greatly and you may wish to check these before you leave your dog or cat there. Check also that the establishment is registered with the local authorities – ask to see a current opening licence (*licencia de apertura*). Fees start at around €4 per day for a small cat and from €6 per day for a small dog, more for larger animals. Many kennels offer discounts for long stays. Pets must be vaccinated in order to stay at kennels. Kennels and catteries advertise in the English-language press and at veterinary clinics.

If you cannot bear the thought of your dog or cat being 'imprisoned', alternatives are a house-sitter (this service is quite common on the Costa del Sol, but check the sitter's references) or a private residence – some people look after dogs or cats (again, you should ask for references). These services are considerably more expensive than kennels, but your pet should receive better care and attention.

Vets

There are plenty of vets on the Costa del Sol – most large urbanisations have one and there are several in towns – and most of them speak English. Vets are generally highly trained and offer an excellent (if expensive) service as well as invaluable advice about looking after your pet. Clinics usually have a 24-hour emergency service. Ask around for recommendations or look in the English-language press, where many advertise, or the yellow pages. Vets also sell animal food and accessories, although cheaper dog and cat food is sold at supermarkets and hypermarkets.

RESIDENCE PERMITS

EU & EEA Nationals

In theory, if you're an EU national and are an employee or self-employed in Spain **and** paying Spanish taxes (income tax and social security), you don't need a residence card. However, for some transactions (e.g. to open a resident's bank account or take out a resident's mortgage) you **do** need a residence card. which can be obtained from a national police station (see below), usually quite quickly. You must present proof of identity, three photographs and evidence that you're working in Spain (e.g. work contract, salary slip or evidence of being self-employed).

Retirees & Students

If you're an EU retiree or student, you must apply for official resident status. Once you've arrived in Spain, you should go to your nearest national police station within 15 days of arrival and apply for a residence card – see **National Police Stations** below. At the police station (see below) you should go to the foreigners' department where there may be someone who speaks English, French or German, although at locations inland this is less likely.

Information about what's required is available online (in Spanish only) from the Ministry of the Interior, who should but may not have the definitive information! (⌨ *www.mir.es*). The site includes downloadable forms. The Ministry runs a free telephone helpline (☎ 900-150 000), open during office hours.

You will need to fill in the required form and take along the following:

● Your passport and one photocopy of the pages showing your particulars;

● Three photographs (passport size);

Retirees

In addition to the above you will need evidence that you have sufficient funds to support yourself (e.g. bank statements) and proof of medical insurance or that you're entitled to medical treatment under the Spanish public health system.

Students

In addition to the above you will need evidence that you've been accepted on a course and that you have sufficient funds to support yourself and pay for your studies, plus proof of medical insurance.

Family Members

The applicant's family members, including spouse and children under 21, may also apply for residence with the main application. Children are included on one of their parents' residence card. Each family member needs to fill in the required form and take along the following documents:

- Passport and one photocopy of the pages showing the particulars;

- Three photographs (passport size);

- A certificate of good health (this may not be required);

- A document proving the family link (e.g. marriage certificate, birth certificate, family book);

If the family member doesn't plan to work, the main applicant must prove that sufficient funds are available to support the whole family and that each family member has medical insurance.

Documents which aren't in Spanish (e.g. marriage certificate, birth certificate) will need to be translated by an official translator.

Once you've presented the correct documentation, your application is processed and the authorities contact you when your card is ready (this takes from one to six months). In the meantime you're given a receipt for your application and this serves as proof that you've applied for residence. Once you've been notified, you return to the police station to collect your card and have your fingerprints taken for police records.

Non-EU Nationals

Obtaining permission to reside in Spain if you aren't an EU or EEA national is considerably more difficult and the documentation required more complicated. You must usually obtain a current residence visa from a Spanish consulate in your home country **before** you arrive in Spain. Regulations often change and before applying you should check the latest requirements with a Spanish consulate or embassy in your home country. **Don't be tempted to come to Spain for a tourist visit and stay on; if you're caught, you will be deported and possibly not allowed back.**

National Police Stations

National police stations (Comisaría de Policía Nacional) on the Costa del Sol can be found at the following locations:

Area One – The West

Estepona	C/ Valle Inclán Open 9am to 2pm Mondays to Fridays.	☎ 952-798 300
Marbella	Avda Arias de Velasco 25 Open 9am to 2pm Mondays to Fridays.	☎ 952-762 600

Area Two – Central Costa Del Sol

Fuengirola	Avda Conde de San Isidro 98 (west side of the town) Open 9am to 2pm Mondays to Fridays.	☎ 952-473 200
Torremolinos	C/ Skal 12 Open 9am to 2pm Mondays to Fridays.	☎ 952-378 720

Area Three – Malaga

Malaga	Pl Manual Azaña 3 (central Malaga) Open 9am to 5.30pm Mondays to Thursdays and 9am to 2pm Fridays.	☎ 952-046 200
	Avda Juan Sebastián Elcano 44 (Malaga east) Open 9am to 2pm Mondays to Fridays.	☎ 952-299 300
	Avda de la Palmilla 20 (Malaga north) Open 9am to 2pm Mondays to Fridays.	☎ 952-615 500

Area Four – The East

Torre Del Mar	Avda de Andalucía 55 Open 9am to 2pm Mondays to Fridays.	☎ 952-965 100

LOCAL COUNCIL REGISTRATION

Many foreign residents live on the Costa del Sol without registering with their local council. In most cases, registration (*empadronamiento*) – a process similar to registering on the electoral roll in the UK – isn't compulsory, but it provides benefits for both you and the council. Local councils in Spain receive money (from €60 per person) from central and regional governments to pay for education, police and health services. If residents don't register, the amount of money paid to the local council is less than it should be and local services are therefore underfunded and over-stretched, and additional services (e.g. extra classrooms or police) aren't provided.

Benefits of registering include the following:

● Access to local sports facilities and leisure activities – subsidies are often available for registered residents and local residents are given priority;

● Inclusion on the electoral roll, which allows EU nationals to vote in local elections.

Note that registration is a different process from obtaining a residence permit and doesn't necessarily make you liable for Spanish taxes, although if you're resident you may have to pay income tax and all property owners are liable for property taxes. Note also that in some cases you must register, e.g. if you want to enrol your child at a local state school.

Registration is a straightforward process: you simply go to your local council office, fill in a form and show some identification and proof that you're living in a property in the area (e.g. title deeds, rental contract, electricity bill in your name). **Many councils claim that, if all foreign residents were registered on the Costa del Sol, provisions and facilities would improve markedly.**

SERVICES

A full range of services is available on the Costa del Sol, including building, carpentry, electrical installation and maintenance, and plumbing, and numerous companies, both Spanish and foreign, offer just about everything in the way of goods and services. Many companies provide services throughout the coast, although those located in Malaga may be reluctant to travel very far along the coast, those concentrated on the east or west side may only serve areas on their side of the coast, and some companies may not travel to inland locations.

Most companies and businesses on the coast offer bona fide services and have a good reputation (and wish to keep it). They should offer a full guarantee for both goods and services and provide an official bill. Some companies and individuals, however, are little more than 'cowboy' outfits working illegally before they do a vanishing act. Be very wary of these – they're usually foreign-owned (mostly British): if they do a bad job or provide faulty goods, you have no means of tracing them to complain. Be wary of companies or individuals with the following characteristics:

● Their **only** means of contact is a mobile phone (mobiles with cards aren't registered with a name and their owners cannot be traced);

● They cannot provide evidence of a fiscal number (CIF in the case of a company, NIF in the case of an individual), e.g. a printed bill or receipt.

● They will accept cash payment only. It's tempting to pay cash without a bill, as you save 16 per cent VAT, but without a bill you have no guarantee, no means of complaining and no proof that you've paid!

Finding A Company

● Word of mouth and recommendation are the best ways of finding a reputable company. Ask neighbours and friends, and ask to see examples of goods and/or services.

● Telephone directories:

  – A comprehensive list of companies in Malaga province is provided in the yellow pages (⌨ *www.paginasamarillas.es*). An index of listings is provided in Spanish and English at the front of the directory.

  – *Tu Distrito* (⌨ *www.tudistrito.com*) is a local directory specialising in listings in specific areas within Malaga province. An index of listings is provided in Spanish and English at the front of the directory.

● Local newspapers and magazines, both Spanish and English, include advertisements for goods and services. *Sur in English* has a particularly comprehensive selection.

● Visit local warehouses and factories. Most towns have several warehouses and factories on the outskirts or in industrial areas (*polígonos industriales*) where you can inspect and purchase goods.

With the current boom in construction and related industries on the coast, it's difficult to obtain many goods and services quickly. Practically all builders, carpenters, electricians and plumbers are snowed under with work and you must therefore book their services several weeks in advance and many often don't turn up when arranged simply because they don't have time. If you need any work doing at home, arm yourself with patience!

TELEPHONE

Telephone technology on the Costa del Sol is as good as anywhere in Western Europe and phone lines are available just about anywhere in all but the most remote country areas. At present telephone lines are provided only by Telefónica (the monopoly holder), but calls are provided by numerous companies and there are some good deals available.

Line Installation & Registration

If you require a phone line, you must go to a Telefónica office, phone 1004 or fill in a form online (🖳 *www.telefonica.net*). You must provide proof of identity and a copy of your title deeds or rental contract. Installation of a new line costs €77.53 plus VAT and, if the infrastructure is already in place, takes around a week. Installation in remote areas (if possible) takes considerably longer and costs are far higher. If you live in a house, you're responsible for the laying of the phone line from the house to the road if a line isn't already installed.

If you move into a house with a phone line already installed you can arrange with the previous owner or occupant to have the account transferred to your name when you move in. Don't forget to check that previous bills have been paid.

Costs

Line rental costs around €13 per month plus VAT. Call charges depend on your service provider and there are numerous companies offering good deals. You should shop around for the best price and consider registering with several companies. Registration usually costs nothing and many companies don't make a monthly charge and only charge per call.

The main companies operating on the Costa del Sol are:

● **Auna** – ☎ 015, 🖳 *www.auna.es*;

● **Spantel** – ☎ 900-181 718, 🖳 *www.span-tel.com*;

● **Tele2** – ☎ 900-760 772, 🖳 *www.tele2.es*;

● **TeleConnet** – ☎ 900-902 122, 🖳 *www.teleconnect.es*;

● **Telefónica** – ☎ 1004, 🖳 *www.telefonica.es*.

Mobile Phones

You can buy mobile phones from numerous outlets on the Costa del Sol, including supermarkets, hypermarkets, department stores and specialist shops. Prices vary tremendously according to the type and make of phone, the cheapest model costing around €80 (including €30 in calls). There are three mobile phone companies:

- **Amena** – ☎ 1474, 💻 *www.amena.es*;

- **Movistar** – ☎ 1485 from a fixed line, ☎ 609 from a mobile, 💻 *www.movistar.net*;

- **Vodafone** – ☎ 1444 from a fixed line, ☎ 123 from a mobile, 💻 *www.vodafone.es*.

There are two options when it comes to choosing a mobile phone, and it's wise to weigh up the advantages and disadvantages before you make a purchase:

- **Card Phone** – New phones usually come with a fixed amount in calls already in the card (e.g. €30) and you top up the card when it runs out. Cards can be topped up for €5, €10, €20, €30 and €50 in numerous establishments including supermarkets, petrol stations, newsagents and specialist shops.

- **Contract Phone** – Similar to a fixed phone line and you must usually provide proof of accommodation and a bank account, as payment must be made by direct debit. If you plan to use the mobile phone a lot, experts agree that it's worth having a contract phone rather than a card.

Rates for calls depend on where and when you're calling, and it's worth shopping around for the best deal, as prices can vary more than 100 per cent between companies. However, it's almost always more expensive to phone anywhere by mobile phone than by fixed phone.

> Mobile phone theft is rife on the Costa del Sol. Don't leave your phone unattended anywhere, even for a second. If you have an expensive phone, don't flash it around.

Internet

Internet connection is widely available on the Costa del Sol from many companies, including most telephone companies (see **Telephone** above). Rates and deals vary greatly according to when you use the internet and how often. Most companies offer deals, and it's worth shopping around to get the best rates for your usage.

Broadband

Broadband (ADSL) technology is available on the Costa del Sol, but not yet in all areas. It's generally available in the main towns (e.g. Fuengirola, Malaga and Marbella) and some large urbanisations (e.g. Calahonda), but cables haven't been laid everywhere yet. To find out whether ADSL is available in your home you must phone Telefónica (☎ 1004) and provide your telephone number. If you haven't bought or rented a property and need to find out before you commit yourself, ask a neighbour for his number and give this to Telefónica. Make sure it's an immediate neighbour though, because a connection may be available in one street but not in an adjacent one. ADSL isn't available in most rural areas.

There are numerous ADSL providers and competition is intense. Shop around because prices and conditions vary considerably. Bear in mind that all providers rent lines from Telefónica and it's best to get your service from a large operator (and preferably one that invests in the service) with good customer service. Complaints about ADSL services are common among users – usually because the speed of the connection is slow or because it's difficult to terminate the contract.

There are around 50 ADSL providers in Spain, but the main ones are:

- **Telefónica** – The largest, with over 1 million clients (☎ 1004, 🖳 *www.telefonica.net*);

- **Terra** – An affiliate of Telefónica with around 160,000 clients (☎ 902-152 025, 🖳 *www.terra.es*);

- **Tiscali** – The smallest but fastest-growing, with 65,000 clients (☎ 902-765 657 and 🖳 *www.tiscali.es*);

- **Wanadoo** – The second-largest, with 180,000 clients (☎ 902-011 902, 🖳 *www.wanadoo.es*);

- **Ya.Com** – Has over 100,000 clients (🖳 *www.ya.com*).

Internet Cafés

All towns on the Costa del Sol have internet cafés (*cibercafés*) or premises where you can surf the internet and check your emails. Some (but by no means all) offer broadband connection. Prices are around €3 an hour. You can also use the internet at public libraries, although use is usually limited to an hour and you may have to wait for a terminal to become available. Telephone kiosks (*locutorios telefónicos*) may also provide internet services.

Some of the many internet cafés can be found at the following venues:

Area One – The West

Estepona	Bourger Bar Comp, Avda España 168	☎ 952-808 386
	MT NT 21, Avda Andalucía s/n	☎ 952-798 324
Marbella	CiberCafe, C/ Buitrago 24	☎ 952-858 262
	LocuWeb, C/ Virgen del Amparo 5 bajo	☎ 952-823 514
San Pedro	Big Orange Video-Ciber, Dr Eusebio Ramírez, s/n, Edif Triana	☎ 952-799 060

Area Two – Central Costa Del Sol

Alhaurín De La Torre	Ciber Bone, C/ Mediterráneo 24	☎ 952-415 623
Benalmadena	Costa Business Bureau, Avda Gamonal 12, Arroyo de la Miel	☎ 952-444 048
	Juan Murillo, Puerto Marina (Dársena de Levante A5)	☎ 952-576 583
Fuengirola	Wine Internet Bar, C/ La Pandereta 10	☎ 952-663 604
	Zip Internet Café, C/ Marconi 11	☎ 952-586 638
Torremolinos	Ciber Café Torremolinos, Avda Manantiales 4	☎ 952-053 291
	CiberMaster, Avda Manantiales 18	☎ 952-371 796

Area Three – Malaga

| Malaga | Ciber-Alameda, Avda Andalucía 13 | ☎ 952-354 222 |

Area Four – The East

| Nerja | Medweb Cafe, C/ Castilla Pérez 21 | ☎ 952-520 735 |
| | Web 4U, Avda Mediterraneo 3 (opposite Hotel Mónica) | |

Torre Del Mar	Ciber Espacio, C/ Santa Margarita 8	☎ 952-542 492
Vélez-Málaga	Ciberzona, C/ Van Dulken 21-A	☎ 952-558 420
	Internate, C/ Dr Casquero 15	☎ 952-505 516

REFUSE

Refuse is collected daily in most areas on the Costa del Sol and usually at night (don't be surprised to hear the clang of bins at 2am), although the service in some urbanisations, villages and less inhabited areas may be less frequent. There may be large bins at different points on streets or complexes may have a refuse point or small shed where bins are kept. For hygiene reasons you're supposed to put rubbish out after a certain time (usually 9pm) and some areas impose a fine for not respecting this. If a bin is full, put your rubbish in another – don't be tempted to leave your rubbish outside a bin, as the local dogs and cats will shred them and scatter the contents everywhere, and the refuse collectors won't clear it up.

There are no rubbish bins in Fuengirola centre, where the council has installed innovative 'ecological islands' instead. These consist of silver funnels on the pavement which lead to underground containers, emptied daily. These improve the appearance of the area and don't smell!

Household Goods

All councils and many urbanisations provide a household goods collection service, which is usually made once a week. The service will generally take anything (furniture, appliances), but it's best to check beforehand. The usual procedure is to phone and enquire which day collections will be made in your area and arrange where to leave your unwanted goods. Regular refuse collectors don't usually take household goods.

When you buy a new household appliance, many large shops include the removal of the old appliance in their price. Smaller shops may offer this service but at extra cost.

Recycling

Recycling has improved a lot on the coast in recent years and you can now recycle a substantial part of household waste reasonably easily. It's worth getting into the habit of recycling, as it will be compulsory by 2007 when Spain is obliged to comply with the EU directive of separating household rubbish for recycling. Recycling containers can be found all over the coast, often next to general rubbish bins and are colour-coded as follows:

- **Dark Blue** – Paper (including newspapers and cardboard);

- **Green** – Glass (any colour) but no corks or bottle tops;

- **Yellow** – Plastic (such as water bottles, margarine, yoghurt and egg cartons, cellophane, string bags from fruit), tins (drink and food) and cartons (the sort that juice and UHT milk come in);

- **Yellow Metal** – Clothes, shoes and household fabrics. You should put items in bags before putting them into the bin and only recycle items that are clean and in reasonable condition, as many clothes are passed on to people who need them.

Other Waste

Batteries

There used to be numerous battery collection points, but they're now few and far between after it was discovered that the collectors emptying the points were disposing of the batteries in normal rubbish bins. Nevertheless, it's worth looking for a point – ask at your council – and making the effort, as batteries are one of the most contaminating objects in household rubbish.

Car Waste

Just about any sort of waste (e.g. oil, batteries, tyres) from a car can be disposed of safely at a reputable garage, many of which have 'green points' where you can leave potentially contaminating material.

Garden Waste

Many areas have disposal points for garden rubbish (e.g. grass cuttings). If you cannot find a point, ask at your local council or community office. **Under no circumstances should you leave garden rubbish anywhere else, as it's a serious fire hazard and also attracts rats and other vermin.**

TELEVISION & RADIO

The Costa del Sol has no local English-language television channels, although Canal Malaga in association with *Sur In English* newspaper broadcasts a weekly round-up of news and events in English on

Saturdays at 2pm (repeated on Sundays at 9pm). Tuning on UHF for most areas is 53 – except in Alhaurín de la Torre and Torremolinos (49) and Malaga (57). Some areas of the coast (mainly those west of Marbella) can receive broadcasts from Gibraltar television (GBC), a mixture of 'home-grown' and BBC programmes. Spanish television broadcasts in Spanish with occasional original version films shown on La 2 channel, but to watch English-language television you need to install satellite TV. Reception is excellent in most areas of the coast. Note that there's no TV or radio licence.

TV Standards

TVs and video recorders operating on the British (PAL-I), French (SECAM) or North American (NTSC) systems don't work in Spain, which, along with most other continental European countries, uses the PAL B/G standard. You can buy a multi-standard European TV (and VCR) containing automatic circuitry that switches between different systems. Some multi-standard TVs also include the North American NTSC standard and have an NTSC-in jack plug connection allowing you to play back American videos. A standard British, French or US TV can be modified. The same applies to 'foreign' video recorders, which won't operate with a Spanish TV unless they're dual-standard.

Satellite TV

There are generally two options for English-language satellite TV and both are widely available on the Costa del Sol: a basic satellite package with BBC and ITV channels (no Sky) plus many European channels costing from around €500; or a Sky satellite package with Sky, BBC and ITV channels costing from around €550. Installation is usually straightforward and numerous specialist companies operate on the coast, where competition is keen. Many advertise in the expatriate press (e.g. *Sur In English*), but shop around and compare prices (which vary greatly), and ask friends and neighbours for recommendations. Be wary of companies offering cut-price offers and check a company's credentials – satellite companies are notorious for 'disappearing', leaving customers with systems that don't work.

Before installing a satellite dish, you must check whether you need permission from your landlord or the local authorities. Some towns and buildings (such as apartment blocks) have strict laws regarding the positioning of antennae, although generally owners can mount a dish almost anywhere without receiving complaints. Dishes can be usually be mounted in a variety of unobtrusive positions and can also be painted.

Radio

There are now several English-language radio stations broadcasting on the Costa del Sol. Most offer a similar pattern of chat shows and music with news, sports and traffic bulletins. Some offer coverage of local sporting events.

- **Central FM** – Broadcasts on 98.6FM and 103.8FM (☎ 952-566 256, 💻 *www.centralfm.com*);

- **Coastline Radio** – Broadcasts on 97.6FM (☎ 952-531 691, 💻 *www.coastlinefm.net*);

- **Global Radio** – Broadcasts on 96.5FM (☎ 952-930 088, 💻 *www.global.fm*);

- **Octopus FM** – Broadcasts on 98.3FM on most of the coast – 92FM in Marbella (☎ 952-667 896, 💻 *www.octopusfm.com*);

- **Onda Cero International (OCI)** – Broadcasts from Gibraltar to Motril on 101.6FM (☎ 952-821 818);

- **REM** – A new station broadcasting from Nerja to Gibraltar and possibly the Costa de la Luz on 104.8FM;

- **Spectrum FM** – Broadcasts on 105.5FM (☎ 902-105 551, 💻 *www.spectrumfm.net*);

- **Sunshine Radio** – Broadcasts to the Nerja area on 99.1FM (☎ 952-526 319, 💻 *www.sunshinecomm.com*).

UTILITIES

Electricity

The electricity supply in Spain has been liberalised and, in theory, you can now choose who supplies your electricity, but in practice on the Costa del Sol there's only one supplier, SevillanaEndesa (known by most people as Sevillana, ☎ 902-509 509, 💻 *www.endesaonline.com* – for general enquiries and information; ☎ 902-516 516 – for faults or problems with the supply) and no other companies currently show any interest in providing an alternative. The service is generally good, although power cuts are common during storms and some areas are prone to occasional power surges.

Most communications to do with electricity (except paying the bill) can be done by telephone or online and you shouldn't have to go to an office in person. **Note that when you contact SevillanaEndesa you need to provide your supply number (*contrato de suministro*) found at the top left of your bill.** Staff who answer the phone don't usually speak English.

SevillanaEndesa has offices in the main towns on the coast (take plenty to read – queues are **very** long). There may be staff who speak English, but don't count on it. Offices, generally open from 9am to 2pm and from 4 or 5pm to 7 or 8pm Mondays to Fridays, are situated at the following locations:

Area One – The West

Estepona	Avda San Lorenzo 41	☎ 952-800 792
Marbella	C/ Castillo 1	☎ 952-766 320

Area Two – Central Costa Del Sol

Alhaurín De La Torre	Avda Juan Carlos I, 43	☎ 952-416 160
Alhaurín El Grande	Virgen de la Paz 9	☎ 952-490 408
Arroyo De La Miel	C/ Moscatel 35	☎ 952-444 146
Coín	Plaza Escamilla 11	☎ 952-450 045
Fuengirola	Pl de la Hispanidad	☎ 952-474 039
Mijas Costa	CC Cala del Sol, La Cala	☎ 952-493 153
Torremolinos	Plaza Goya 1	☎ 952-380 093

Area Three – Malaga

Malaga	Avda Juan XXIII 29	☎ 952-324 192
	C/ Cuarteles 47	☎ 952-327 588
	Fdo Camino 10	☎ 952-608 960
	Maestranza 4	☎ 952-211 400
	Obispo Oria 22	☎ 952-308 212

Area Four – The East

Nerja	C/ Cristo 12-14	☎ 952-520 442
Rincón De La Victoria	C/ Córdoba 11	☎ 952-401 775
Torre Del Mar	Ctra de las Angustias	☎ 952-540 662

Bills

Bills can be paid by direct debit (by far the most convenient method), at most banks or at electricity offices. Bills are issued every two months and if you pay by direct debit there's usually a week between the bill being sent and the bank paying for it. Electricity currently costs €0.08 per kwh and you also pay a monthly standing charge, for the hire of equipment, electricity tax at 4.864 per cent (!) and VAT at 16 per cent.

Moving Into A Property

When you move into a property, you should immediately make sure that the electricity supply hasn't been cut off and that bills will be sent to you. The procedure to follow depends on the type of property.

Resale Properties

If you're taking over the electricity supply from the previous owner, there are two possible procedures, described below.

1. Telephone SevillanaEndesa with the electricity supply number and give them the new details and a bank account number. The next bill should then be sent to you and paid by your bank. **Although this method is simpler, the electricity contract remains in the previous owner's name and he might cancel the contract in the future, with the result that your supply is cut off without warning!**

2. Arrange with the previous owner to change the electricity contract into your name as soon as you move in. This is done by means of a simple document signed by the previous owner giving his authorisation. This document is sent together with copies of identity documents (e.g. passport, residence card) of both previous and new owners to SevillanaEndesa, and costs around €30. Any *gestoría* can do the paperwork for you for a small charge.

New Properties

In order to obtain a contract for an electricity supply in a newly built property, you will need an electricity certificate (*boletín de electricidad*) from the developer. This certificate must be sent to SevillanaEndesa, who will send an electrician to the property to connect the supply at a cost of €90 to €110 depending on the power of the supply. It takes at least ten days to get connected and in some areas new owners are currently having to wait much longer, simply because SevillanaEndesa cannot keep up with the demand for new contracts in new properties.

Rental Properties

Under most rental contracts you're responsible for the electricity charges. You can either pay electricity bills at a bank or telephone SevillanaEndesa with your bank details and arrange the bills to be paid by direct debit.

Gas

Mains Gas

Mains gas is currently available only in some parts of Malaga city and is provided by Gas Natural Andalucía (☎ 900-760 760 for customer services; ☎ 900-750 750 for repairs and emergencies). There are advanced plans for mains gas to be piped along the entire Costa del Sol once the gas duct is laid between Algeria and Spain.

Bottled Gas

Bottled gas (*butano*) provides a popular and economical means of heating and cooking, and is widely available. Bottles are available in 12.5kg and 20kg sizes and can be delivered to your home or collected from an authorised point. Small (camping) gas bottles can be bought at Repsol service stations. On the Costa del Sol, Repsol Butano is the official distributor and has representatives in all main towns, listed below:

Area One – The West

Estepona	Costa Gas	☎ 952-800 299
Marbella	Gas Costa del Sol	☎ 952-772 952
Monda	GuadalGas SL	☎ 902-222 112
San Pedro	Gas Costa del Sol	☎ 952-772 952

Area Two – Central Costa Del Sol

Alhaurín De La Torre	Gas Alhaurín	☎ 952-410 180
	GuadalGas SL	☎ 902-222 112

Alhaurín El Grande	GuadalGas SL	☎ 902-222 112
Benalmadena	Butasol SL	☎ 952-214 152
Coin	GuadalGas SL	☎ 902-222 112
Fuengirola	Moreno Rivera Gas	☎ 952-587 100
Mijas	Moreno Rivera Gas	☎ 952-587 100
Torremolinos	Butasol SL	☎ 952-214 152

Area Three – Malaga

Malaga	Butasol SL	☎ 952-211 521
	GuadalGas SL, Cártama	☎ 902-222 112
	Solgas SL	☎ 952-071 213

Area Four – The East

Nerja	Fco Macías Cervan	☎ 952-500 894
Rincón De La Victoria	Gas Ruiz Claros SL	☎ 952-401 641
Vélez-Málaga	José Luis García Chica	☎ 952-500 740

Water

Water is provided by numerous private companies on the Costa del Sol, which contract the water supply from the central Acosol. For information on the water supplier in your area contact the local council or your community of owners' office.

The main water supplies are the Istán reservoir (supplying most of the west side of the coast and the best tasting), wells (mainly in Fuengirola, Mijas and Benalmadena), the Malaga reservoirs (Malaga water has the worst taste, but it has improved recently) and the Viñuela reservoir on the east side.

Tap water is safe to drink everywhere on the coast and it isn't necessary to buy bottled water unless you prefer the taste. Some residents fill water bottles and containers from springs along the coast (those in Istán, Mijas and on the way to Ronda are particularly popular). Water from drinking fountains and springs is safe to drink unless there's sign saying '*Agua No Potable*'. Water is generally inexpensive in most areas, although prices have risen in recent years.

In spite of the abundance of green areas and extensive irrigation, water is in short supply on the Costa del Sol, where rainfall is erratic – it may not rain a drop for months at a time and then pour for several weeks – and droughts aren't uncommon. Many residents remember the 1991 to 1995 drought, when the water supply was restricted to a few hours a day and the water quality was dreadful. There's a large desalination plant at Marbella (built at huge public cost and as yet unused), but no further water infrastructure has been built to provide water for the vastly increased population. There are government plans to expand the Istán reservoir, but funds have not been released – in winter 2003/04 the equivalent of a year's supply of water was let out of the reservoir into the sea! It's only a matter of time before it stops raining and the water supplies dry up again. **Use every drop of water carefully!**

VIDEO & DVD RENTAL

English-language videos and DVDs are available for rent in most locations on the coast, e.g. 'Video Club 2000' in Estepona, '21st Century Video' in Calahonda, Estepona and Puerto Banús, and 'Princess Video Club' in Fuengirola. Some shops renting Spanish videos and DVDs also have a (limited) selection of English-language films. You must usually be a member of the club in order to take films out, although some allow one-off rental if you pay a deposit. Films cost from €3 to €6 a night. Some shops also hire out computer games.

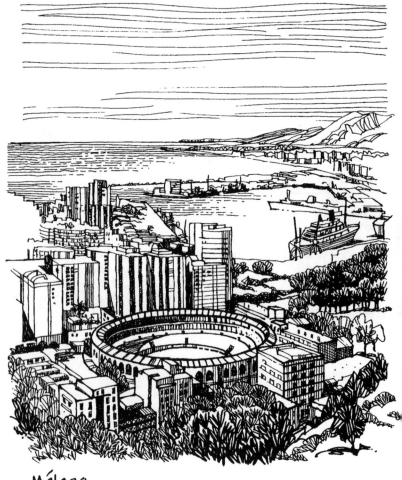

Málaga

Appendices

Appendix A: PUBLICATIONS

English-Language Newspapers & Magazines

Absolute Marbella (also published under the name **Absolute Sotogrande**), Office 21, Edif Tembo, C/ Rotary International, 29660 Puerto Banús (☎ 902-301 130, 🖳 www.absolutemagazine.com). Free monthly glossy with news of events on the Costa del Sol.

The Broadsheet (☎ 915-237 480, 🖳 www.thebroadsheet.com, ✉ frontdesk@bear-publishing.com). Free monthly magazine about Spain in general with listings and articles relating to the Costa del Sol.

Costa del Sol News, CC Las Moriscas Local 10, Avda Juan Luís Peralta, 29629 Benalmadena Pueblo (☎ 952-448 730, 🖳 www.costadelsolnews.es). Weekly newspaper containing news, event details and small ads, published on Fridays.

Euro Weekly, Avda de la Constitución, Edif Fiesta, Locales 32 & 33, Arroyo de la Miel (☎ 952-561 245, 🖳 http://euroweeklynews.com). Free weekly newspaper published on Thursdays.

Estepona Magazine, Avda de Andalucía 42, Edif Espiga 1ºB, Estepona (☎ 902-310 313, 🖳 www.esteponamagazine.com). Free monthly magazine with news and event details for the Estepona and Sotogrande areas.

Everything Spain, Medway House, Lower Road, Forest Row, East Sussex RH18 5HE, UK (☎ 01342-828 700, 🖳 www.everythingSpainmag.co.uk). Bi-monthly lifestyle and property magazine.

INland Magazine, Buzón 111, Avda de la Constitución 3, Alhaurín el Grande (☎ 952-596 346, 🖳 www.inlandmagazine.com). Monthly magazine for localities in the Guadalhorce Valley (including Alhaurín de la Torre, Alhaurín el Grande, Alora, Cártama, Monda and Pizarra).

Insight Magazine, C/ Pintada 105, 29780 Nerja (☎ 952-529 746, 🖳 www.insightmagazine.eu.com). Free monthly magazine with news and event details for the Nerja area.

Key to Mijas Costa, Apdo Correos 496, La Cala, Mijas Costa (☎ 952-939 536, 🖳 www.keytomijascosta.com). Free guide to Mijas Costa.

La Chispa/The Spark, Apdo Correos 281, 29100 Coín (☎ 659-537 525, 🖳 www.lachispa.net). Free bi-monthly magazine in both English and Spanish on alternative living in Andalusia.

Living Spain, Albany Publishing, 9 High Street, Olney, Bucks MK46 4EB, UK (☎ 01234-710 992, 🖳 www.livingspain.co.uk). Bi-monthly lifestyle and property magazine.

Marbella Paso a Paso (☎ 952-902 603, 🖳 www.marbellapasoapaso.com). Free bi-monthly guide to restaurants and services in the Marbella and San Pedro areas with comprehensive street map.

El Periódico de Sotogrande (🖳 www.elperiodicodesotogrande.com). Fortnightly free newspaper about the area in both English and Spanish.

La Revista de Sotogrande (🖳 www.larevistadesotogrande.com). Monthly free magazine about the area in both English and Spanish.

The Reporter, Avda Alcade Clement Díaz Ruiz 37, Pueblo López, Fuengirola (☎ 952-666 234, 🖳 www.spanishreporter.com). Free monthly news and comment magazine.

Spanish Magazine, Cambridge House South, Henry Street, Bath BA1 1JT, UK (☎ 01225-786 844). Bi-monthly lifestyle and property magazine.

Sur in English, Diario Sur, Avda Dr Marañón 48, Malaga (☎ 952-649 600, 🖳 www.surinenglish.com). Free weekly newspaper published on Fridays with extensive small ad sections.

Town Crier, Edif Alfares 2, Oficina 1, Plaza de la Villa, Coín (☎ 952-455 185, ✉ info@towncrier.es). Free weekly magazine.

Views, Centro Nórdico 12/13, Ctra de Mijas km 1.5, Mijas (☎ 952-588 758, 🖳 www.viewsonline.net). Free monthly lifestyle magazine.

Spanish Newspapers

The newspapers below are published daily and are also available online. All offer daily events listings, small ads and useful local information. *Diario Sur* is the most widely read.

Diario Malaga (🖳 http://nuevo.diariomalaga.com).

Diario Sur (🖳 www.diariosur.es).

La Opinión de Málaga (🖳 www.laopiniondemalaga.es).

Property Publications

There are numerous property magazines and newspapers on the Costa del Sol, some of which are listed below. Some estate agents also publish magazines.

123 Property News, Unit 36, Harbour's Deck, Rosia Rd, Gibraltar (☎ 9567-47123, 🖳 www.123propertynews.com). Free bi-monthly magazine for Gibraltar and the Costa del Sol.

Llave en Mano (🖳 www.llaveenmano.com). Free weekly magazine in Spanish with resale and new property.

Primera Mano (🖳 www.deprimeramano.net). Monthly magazine in English and Spanish with details of new developments on the coast.

Property News, Jarales de Alhamar, Calahonda, Mijas Costa (☎ 952-931 603, 🖳 www.property-spain.com). Free monthly newspaper.

Property World, C/ España 1, Edif Buendía 1°A, Fuengirola (☎ 952-666 234, 🖳 www.propertyworldmagazine.com). Free monthly magazine.

Villas &..., SKR Española, Apdo Correos 453, San Pedro de Alcántara (☎ 952-884 994, 🖳 www.villas.com). Monthly property magazine with articles in English, French, German and Spanish.

Books

The books listed below are just a selection of the hundreds written about Spain and the Costa del Sol. The publication title is followed by the author's name and the publisher's name (in brackets). Note that some titles may be out of print but may still be obtainable from book shops or libraries. Books prefixed with an asterisk are recommended by the author.

Food & Wine

*AA Essential Food and Drink Spain (AA)

*The Best of Spanish Cooking, Janet Mendel (Santana)

The Complete Spanish Cookbook, Jacki Passmore (Little Brown)

*Cooking in Spain, Janet Mendel (Santana)

Delicioso: The Regional Cooking of Spain, Penelope Casas (Knoff)

A Flavour of Andalucía, Pepita Aris (Chartwell)

*Floyd on Spain, Keith Floyd (Penguin)

The Food and Wine of Spain, Penelope Casas

404 Spanish Wines, Frank Snell (Santana)

Great Dishes of Spain, Robert Carrier (Boxtree)

*The 'La Ina' Book of Tapas, Elisabeth Luard (Schuster)

Mediterranean Seafood, Alan Davidson (Penguin)

**Rioja and its Wines, Ron Scarborough (Survival Books)

Shopping for Food and Wine in Spain (Santana)

*Spanish Cooking, Pepita Aris (Apple Press)

*The Spanish Kitchen, Pepita Aris (Wardlock)

The Spanish Table, Marimar Torres (Ebury Press)

*Spanish Wines, Jan Read (Mitchell Beazley)

The Spanishwoman's Kitchen, Pepita Aris (Cassell)

The Tapas Book, Adrian Linssen & Sara Cleary (Apple Press)

Tapas, Silvano Franco (Lorenz)

*The Wine and Food of Spain, Jan Read & Maite Manjón (Wedenfeld & Nicolson)

The Wine Roads of Spain, M&K Millon (Santana)

**The Wines of Spain, Graeme Chesters (Survival Books)

Living & Working In Spain

**The Best Places to Buy a Home in Spain, Joanna Styles (Survival Books)

Choose Spain, John Howells & Bettie Magee (Gateway)

Introducing Spain, B.A. McCullagh & S. Wood (Harrap)

Life in a Spanish Town, M. Newton (Harrap)

**Living and Working in Spain, David Hampshire (Survival Books)

Simple Etiquette in Spain, Victoria Miranda McGuiness (Simple Books)

Spain: Business & Finance (Euromoney Books)

Tourist Guides

AA Essential Explorer Spain (AA)

Andalucía Handbook, Rowland Mead (Footprint)

***Andalucía: The Rough Guide** (Rough Guides)

***Baedeker's Spain** (Baedeker)

Berlitz Blueprint: Spain (Berlitz)

Berlitz Discover Spain, Ken Bernstein & Paul Murphy (Berlitz)

***Blue Guide to Spain: The Mainland**, Ian Robertson (Ernest Benn)

***Cadogan Guides: Spain**, Dana Facaros & Michael Pauls (Cadogan)

Collins Independent Travellers Guide Spain, Harry Debelius (Collins)

Daytrips Spain & Portugal, Norman Renouf (Hastings House Pub)

Excursions in Southern Spain, David Baird (Santana)

***Eyewitness Travel Guide: Spain**, Deni Bown (Dorling Kindersly)

Fielding's Paradors in Spain & Portugal, A. Hobbs (Fielding Worldwide)

***Fodor's Spain** (Fodor's)

***Fodor's Exploring Spain** (Fodor's Travel Publications)

***Frommer's Spain's Best-Loved Driving Tours**, Mona King (IDG Books)

Guide to the Best of Spain (Turespaña)

***Inside Andalusia**, David Baird (Santana)

The Insider's Guide to Spain, John de St. Jorre (Moorland)

***Insight Guides: Spain** (APA Publications)

Lazy Days Out in Andalucía, Jeremy Wayne (Cadogan)

*Let's Go Spain & Portugal (Macmillan)

*Lonely Planet Spain (Lonely Planet)

*Michelin Green Guide Spain (Michelin)

*Michelin Red Guide to Spain and Portugal (Michelin)

Off the Beaten Track: Spain, Barbara Mandell & Roger Penn (Moorland)

Rick Steves' Spain & Portugal, Rick Steves (John Muir Pubns)

*Rough Guide to Andalucía, Mark Ellingham & John Fisher (Rough Guides)

The Shell Guide to Spain, David Mitchell (Simon & Schuster)

Spain: A Phaidon Cultural Guide (Phaidon)

Spain at its Best, Robert Kane (Passport)

Spain: Everything Under the Sun, Tom Burns (Harrap Columbus)

Spain on Backroads (Duncan Petersen)

*Spain: The Rough Guide, Mark Ellingham & John Fisher (Rough Guides)

Special Places to Stay in Spain, Alistair Sawday (ASP)

Time Off in Spain and Portugal, Teresa Tinsley (Horizon)

Travellers in Spain: An Illustrated Anthology, David Mitchell (Cassell)

Welcome to Spain, RAN Dixon (Collins)

*Which? Guide to Spain (Consumers' Association and Hodder & Stoughton)

Travel Literature

*As I Walked Out One Midsummer Morning, Laurie Lee (Penguin)

*Between Hopes and Memories: A Spanish Journey, Michael Jacobs (Picador)

*The Bible in Spain, George Borrow (Century Travellers Series)

*Cider With Rosie, Laurie Lee (Penguin)

Gatherings in Spain, Richard Ford (Dent Everyman)

*Handbook for Travellers in Spain, Richard Ford (Centaur Press)

Iberia, James A. Michener (Fawcett)

In Search of Andalucía, Christopher Wawn & David Wood (Pentland Press)

*In Spain, Ted Walker (Corgi)

*A Rose for Winter, Laurie Lee (Penguin)

*Spanish Journeys: A Portrait of Spain, Adam Hopkins (Penguin)

*South from Granada, Gerald Brenan (Penguin)

*A Stranger in Spain, H.V. Morton (Methuen)

Two Middle-Aged Ladies in Andalusia, Penelope Chetwode (Murray)

Miscellaneous

The Art of Flamenco, DE Pohren (Musical News Services Ltd.)

*Blood Sport: A History of Spanish Bullfighting, Timothy Mitchell

**Buying a Home in Spain, David Hampshire (Survival Books)

Cities of Spain, David Gilmour (Pimlico)

Dali: A Biography, Meredith Etheringon-Smith (Sinclair-Stevenson)

*A Day in the Life of Spain (Collins)

*Death in the Afternoon, Ernest Hemingway (Grafton)

Gardening in Spain, Marcelle Pitt (Santana)

The Gardens of Spain, Consuela M. Correcher (Abrams)

*In Search of the Firedance, James Woodall (Sinclair-Stevenson)

The King, Jose Luis de Vilallonga (Weidenfeld)

*Nord Riley's Spain, Nord Riley (Santana)

On Foot Through Europe: A Trail Guide to Spain and Portugal, Craig Evans (Quill)

Or I'll Dress You in Mourning, Larry Collins & Dominique Lapierre (Simon & Schuster)

La Pasionaria, Robert Low (Hutchinson)

Spain: A Literary Companion, Jimmy Burns (John Murray)

Spain's Wildlife, Eric Robins (Santana)

Trekking in Spain, Marc S. Dubin (Lonely Planet)

Walking Through Spain, Robin Nellands

Wild Spain, Frederic Grunfeld & Teresa Farino (Ebury)

Xenophobe's Guide to the Spanish (Ravette)

Appendix B: Property Exhibitions

Property exhibitions are commonplace in the UK and Ireland and are popular with prospective property buyers, who can get a good idea of what's available in Spain and make contact with estate agents and developers. The Costa del Sol is usually well-represented at property exhibitions and most large estate agents on the coast exhibit there. Below is a list of the main exhibitions organisers in the UK and Ireland. Note that you may be charged a small admission fee.

Homes Overseas (UK ☎ 020-7939 9852, 🖳 www.blendoncommunications. co.uk). Homes Overseas is the largest organiser of international property exhibitions and hold several exhibitions annually at various venues in both the UK and Ireland.

Incredible Homes (UK ☎ 0800-652 2992, Spain ☎ 952-924 645, 🖳 www. incredible-homes.com). Incredible Homes is based on the Costa del Sol and organises several large exhibitions a year in both the UK and Ireland.

International Property Show (UK ☎ 01962-736712, 🖳 www.international propertyshow.com). The International Property Show is held several times a year in London and Manchester.

Spain on Show (UK ☎ 0500-780878, 🖳 www.spainonshow.com). Spain on Show organises several annual property exhibitions at venues around the UK.

Town & Country (UK ☎ 0845-230 6000, 🖳 www.spanishproperty.uk.com). This large estate agency organises small Spanish property exhibitions at venues around the UK twice a month.

World Class Homes (UK ☎ 0800-731 4713, 🖳 www.worldclass homes. co.uk). Exhibitions organised by World Class Homes, in small venues around the UK, feature mainly British property developers.

World of Property (UK ☎ 01323-726040, 🖳 www.outboundpublishing. com). The publisher of *World of Property* also organises three large property exhibitions a year, two in the south of Britain and one in the north.

Appendix c: USEFUL WEBSITES

The following list contains some of the many websites dedicated to the Costa del Sol and Spain in general. Websites about particular aspects of the Costa del Sol and town council and tourist sites are included in the relevant chapters of this book.

Costa del Sol

Costa del Sol (🖥 www.visitacostadelsol.com): the official tourist website for the area.

The Costa Guide (🖥 www.costaguide.com): general information.

Maps Costa del Sol (🖥 www.mapscostadelsol.com): maps of many areas of the coast.

Webmalaga.com (🖥 www.webmalaga.com): comprehensive information about Malaga province.

Spain

About Spain (🖥 www.aboutspain.net): information about specific regions of Spain.

All About Spain (🖥 www.red2000.com): general tourist information about Spain.

Andalucía (🖥 www.andalucia.com): comprehensive information about the region of Andalusia in English.

Escape to Spain (🖥 www.escapetospain.co.uk): general information and a property guide to the Costa del Sol.

Ideal Spain (🖥 www.idealspain.com): information about many aspects of living in Spain.

Spain Alive (🖥 www.spainalive.com): information about specific areas of Spain as well as general information.

Spain Expat (🖥 www.spainexpat.com): information about living in Spain, including an 'ask the legal expert' facility. The site has particularly good links.

Spain For Visitors (⌨ http://spainforvisitors.com): good general information about visiting Spain.

Spanish Forum (⌨ www.spanishforum.org): a wealth of useful and continually updated information about all aspects of living and working in Spain, including a free monthly 'e-newsletter'.

Survival Books (⌨ www.survivalbooks.net): Survival Books are the publishers of this book and *Buying a Home in Spain, Living & Working in Spain, The Best Places to Buy a Home in Spain,* and *The Wines of Spain.* The website includes useful tips for anyone planning to buy a home, live, work, retire or do business in Spain.

Travelling in Spain (⌨ http://travelinginspain.com): information about Spanish cities.

TurEspaña (Spanish National Tourist Office) (⌨ www.tourspain.co.uk or ⌨ www.spain.info).

TuSpain (⌨ www.tuspain.com): general information about Spain with the emphasis on buying property and residential matters.

Typically Spanish (⌨ www.typicallyspanish.com): information about a wide range of Spanish topics and a listing of services.

INDEX

D

E

U

V

W

Z

ORDER FORM 1

Qty.	Title	Price (incl. p&p)*			Total
		UK	Europe	World	
	The Alien's Guide to Britain	£6.95	£8.95	£12.45	
	The Alien's Guide to France	£6.95	£8.95	£12.45	
	The Best Places to Buy a Home in France	£13.95	£15.95	£19.45	
	The Best Places to Buy a Home in Spain	£13.95	£15.95	£19.45	
	Buying a Home Abroad	£13.95	£15.95	£19.45	
	Buying a Home in Florida	£13.95	£15.95	£19.45	
	Buying a Home in France	£13.95	£15.95	£19.45	
	Buying a Home in Greece & Cyprus	£13.95	£15.95	£19.45	
	Buying a Home in Ireland	£11.95	£13.95	£17.45	
	Buying a Home in Italy	£13.95	£15.95	£19.45	
	Buying a Home in Portugal	£13.95	£15.95	£19.45	
	Buying a Home in Spain	£13.95	£15.95	£19.45	
	Buying, Letting & Selling Property	£11.95	£13.95	£17.45	
	Foreigners in France: Triumphs & Disasters	£11.95	£13.95	£17.45	
	Foreigners in Spain: Triumphs & Disasters	£11.95	£13.95	£17.45	
	How to Avoid Holiday & Travel Disasters	£13.95	£15.95	£19.45	
	Costa del Sol Lifeline	£11.95	£13.95	£17.45	
	Dordogne/Lot Lifeline	£11.95	£13.95	£17.45	
	Poitou-Charentes Lifeline	£11.95	£13.95	£17.45	
				Total	

Order your copies today by phone, fax, mail or e-mail from: Survival Books, PO Box 146, Wetherby, West Yorks. LS23 6XZ, UK (☎/🖷 +44 (0)1937-843523, ✉ orders@ survivalbooks.net, 🖳 www.survivalbooks.net). If you aren't entirely satisfied, simply return them to us within 14 days for a full and unconditional refund.

Cheque enclosed/please charge my Amex/Delta/MasterCard/Switch/Visa* card

Card No. _ _ _ _   _ _ _ _   _ _ _ _   _ _ _ _

Expiry date _____ Issue number (Switch only) _____

Signature _____ Tel. No. _____

NAME _____

ADDRESS _____

_____

_____

* Delete as applicable (price includes postage – airmail for Europe/world).

ORDER FORM 2

Qty.	Title	Price (incl. p&p)*			Total
		UK	**Europe**	**World**	
	Living & Working Abroad	£14.95	£16.95	£20.45	
	Living & Working in America	£14.95	£16.95	£20.45	
	Living & Working in Australia	£14.95	£16.95	£20.45	
	Living & Working in Britain	£14.95	£16.95	£20.45	
	Living & Working in Canada	£16.95	£18.95	£22.45	
	Living & Working in the European Union	£16.95	£18.95	£22.45	
	Living & Working in the Far East	£16.95	£18.95	£22.45	
	Living & Working in France	£14.95	£16.95	£20.45	
	Living & Working in Germany	£16.95	£18.95	£22.45	
	L&W in the Gulf States & Saudi Arabia	£16.95	£18.95	£22.45	
	L&W in Holland, Belgium & Luxembourg	£14.95	£16.95	£20.45	
	Living & Working in Ireland	£14.95	£16.95	£20.45	
	Living & Working in Italy	£16.95	£18.95	£22.45	
	Living & Working in London	£13.95	£15.95	£19.45	
	Living & Working in New Zealand	£14.95	£16.95	£20.45	
	Living & Working in Spain	£14.95	£16.95	£20.45	
	Living & Working in Switzerland	£16.95	£18.95	£22.45	
	Renovating & Maintaining Your French Home	£13.95	£15.95	£19.45	
	Retiring Abroad	£14.95	£16.95	£20.45	
	Rioja and its Wines	£11.95	£13.95	£17.45	
	The Wines of Spain	£13.95	£15.95	£19.45	
					Total

Order your copies today by phone, fax, mail or e-mail from: Survival Books, PO Box 146, Wetherby, West Yorks. LS23 6XZ, UK (☎/🖥 +44 (0)1937-843523, ✉ orders@survivalbooks.net, 🖳 www.survivalbooks.net). If you aren't entirely satisfied, simply return them to us within 14 days for a full and unconditional refund.

Cheque enclosed/please charge my Amex/Delta/MasterCard/Switch/Visa* card

Card No. __ __ __ __   __ __ __ __   __ __ __ __   __ __ __ __

Expiry date _____   Issue number (Switch only) _____

Signature _____   Tel. No. _____

NAME   _____

ADDRESS   _____

_____

_____

* Delete as applicable (price includes postage – airmail for Europe/world).

SURVIVAL BOOKS ON SPAIN

Buying a Home in Spain is essential reading for anyone planning to purchase property in Spain and is designed to guide you through the property jungle and make it a pleasant and enjoyable experience. Most importantly, it's packed with vital information to help you **avoid the sort of disasters that can turn your dream home into a nightmare!**

Living and Working in Spain is essential reading for anyone planning to live or work in Spain, including retirees, visitors, business people, migrants and students. It's packed with important and useful information designed to help you **avoid costly mistakes and save both time and money.**

The Best Places to Buy a Home in Spain is the most comprehensive and up-to-date homebuying guide to Spain, containing detailed regional guides to help you choose the ideal location for your home.

Costa del Sol Lifeline is the essential guide to the most popular region of Spain, containing everything you need to know about local life. Other titles in the series include Dordogne/Lot, and Poitou-Charentes.

Foreigners in Spain: Triumphs & Disasters is a collection of real-life experiences of people who have emigrated to Spain, providing a 'warts and all' picture of everyday life in the country.

Order your copies today by phone, fax, mail or e-mail from: Survival Books, PO Box 146, Wetherby, West Yorks. LS23 6XZ, United Kingdom (☎/▤ +44 (0)1937-843523, ✉ orders@ survivalbooks.net, 💻 www.survivalbooks.net).

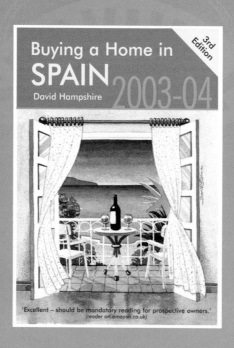